Success Through the Stars

Success Through the Stars

An Astrological Guide to Defining

and Living a Satisfying Life

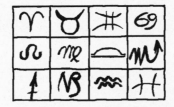

CAROLE GOLDER

AN OWL BOOK

HENRY HOLT AND COMPANY

Henry Holt and Company, Inc.
Publishers since 1866
115 West 18th Street
New York, New York 10011

Henry Holt® is a registered
trademark of Henry Holt and Company, Inc.

Published in Canada by Fitzhenry & Whiteside Ltd.,
195 Allstate Parkway, Markham, Ontario L3R 4T8.

Library of Congress Cataloging-in-Publication Data

Golder, Carole.
Success through the stars : an astrological guide to defining
and living a satisfying life / Carole Golder. 1st ed.
p.   cm.
"An Owl book."
1. Astrology.   2. Success—Miscellanea.   I. Title.
BF1729.S88G65   1996
133.5—dc20   95-4472
                              CIP

ISBN 0-8050-3977-5

First Edition—1996

Designed by Ann Gold

Printed in the United States of America ∞
All first editions are printed on acid-free paper.

1   3   5   7   9   10   8   6   4   2

This book is dedicated to a true Leo success,
my wonderful artist soulmate Peter Prins,
whose paintings are an inspiration.

Contents

ACKNOWLEDGMENTS

I want to thank Lee Johnson for being such a special creatively supportive friend; Silvia and Jose for the splendid times spent at the Casabela Hotel in the Algarve, Portugal; everyone at Air India who made my New York trips so great; the Gracie Inn, a real home away from home while I was editing in New York; and my other friends all over the world who have always been such an important part of my life and will continue to be so.

Thank you to my editor, Tracy Sherrod, and everyone at Henry Holt; this will be my fifth book published by them. And a special thank you to Robert Currey and Barry Street of Equinox, who compiled the Ascendant table.

Introduction

What Is Success?

When I wrote my last book, *Star Signs: An Astrological Guide to the Inner You,* I wanted to show you how to delve beneath the surface of your personality, to get in touch with your inner self and to grow spiritually. My earlier books, *The Seductive Art of Astrology, Love Lives,* and *Moon Signs for Lovers,* dealt with the different aspects of your emotions, while helping you to relate better in love relationships, leading to greater understanding of yourself and your partner.

Now, with *Success Through the Stars,* I would like to help you make more of a success of your life in *every* possible way. Success will always mean different things to different people. Some people may equate success with having a million dollars in the bank, and others may define it as reaching a stage where you can fulfill your heart's desires without having to worry about anything at all. Success could also mean fulfilling a long cherished work ambition, having a solid, passionate relationship with a partner or a strong emotional bond with family members, or simply feeling better about yourself overall.

Over the past few years I have wondered why I continue to come across more and more people who appear successful on the outside, only to find they are frustrated with their lives and are searching for emotional and or material satisfaction. Beauty is often in the eye of the beholder, and other people may sometimes perceive you as successful when your own opinion of yourself is very different. My long experience as an astrologer has convinced me that almost everyone who consults me is searching for *some* kind of self-fulfillment, whether emotional or material. I decided to write this book to show you that no matter what success means to you, it involves making the best possible use of your star sign characteristics—using the tools provided you by way of your birth date.

Naturally, in any astrology book it is necessary to generalize, because in order to make an in-depth analysis of your personality, a chart needs to be prepared for your particular date, time, and place of birth. But knowing even just a little about the personality traits of your star sign enables you to learn and understand a great deal about yourself and the people around you. Think how wonderful it will be to find out more about making the most of *YOU*. This insightful book explains there is more to you than simply, for example, a laid-back and indecisive Libran, a sensitive Cancerian, or an overly anxious and self-critical Virgo.

Success Through the Stars will show you how to maximize your potential by capitalizing on your special strengths and conquering your weaknesses. It will also tell you how to harness your special personality traits to achieve material and emotional satisfaction.

I remember thinking, many years ago while vacationing on a wonderful little Italian island called Pantelleria, between Sicily and Tunisia, how marvelous it would be to live in a tiny village, growing grapes, with no television, telephone, and perhaps even no electricity! I felt people without these things could be much happier, shielded from what was happening in the world. Perhaps this is true. (Ironically, Pantelleria has now become a trendy playground for the rich.) But, of course, others may find this life-style boring and prefer to take advantage of the resources advanced technology has produced—cellular phones, laptop computers, and the like. Whatever your chosen life-style, though, it is important to maximize your success potential through greater self-understanding, and this book will help you to do so.

It is very important to feel successful as a human being, for an aura of success will invariably bring greater success your way, in the same way that a positive approach to life is far more likely to bring positive results than a negative one. By utilizing the strengths your star sign bequeaths you, and working through your weaknesses, you will discover you can live a far more satisfying life and you will not be dependent on affirmations of your success from other people. This unique astrological guide will enable you to believe in yourself on a deeper level, because you will feel more confident in knowing and understanding yourself.

I have found that the most successful people are those who have balanced their lives, emotionally and materially, who appreciate themselves for their achievements in reaching well-defined goals. Such people accept a degree of vulnerability as a natural part of one's emotional character. They are also receptive to learning more about themselves and the world around them. These qualities go a long way on the path to self-contentment.

This book starts with a quiz that will assist you in determining your success potential. It will reveal how you currently see yourself and enable you to determine your strengths and weaknesses. *Success Through the Stars* will show you how you can benefit from the power of your sign's particular element— Fire, Earth, Air, or Water—and from the influence of your ruling planet. I give short examples of how your Ascendant, or rising sign, can modify your personality. On pages 278–79 you will find a table of Ascendants, which will enable you figure out your rising sign.

Success Through the Stars will show you how to make distinctions among the various traits of men and women, which will help you get along better with other signs and achieve your emotional goals. It will help you to turn some of your dreams into reality, whether they be of an emotional or material nature. You will learn how to achieve your material goals, how to become more successful at finding the right job, and how to strengthen family ties. You will also find various do's and don'ts throughout the book, pointers that will add to your success potential.

In the introduction to *Love Lives,* I wrote that the trouble is we don't always know who we are and what we're capable of. With one person, we may feel insignificant, while with another who loves us, our spirit may shine like the sun. In *Star Signs* I stressed the importance of learning to balance mind, body, and soul. My purpose in *Success Through The Stars* is to emphasize that we all have the potential to achieve a satisfying life, when we put to use and take advantage of our star sign personality traits. With *Success Through The Stars,* I want to show you how to make more of a success of your life and, more important, how to keep it that way.

Determining Your Star Potential—A Quiz

Each star sign is governed by one of the four elements: Fire, Earth, Air, Water.

The element that relates to your star sign provides you with certain qualities, which is why I have structured the quiz by element. The purpose of this quiz is to enable you to determine your maximum potential, so make sure you answer it honestly. Everyone has an equal chance at making his or her life a success, whether the person is a Fire, Earth, Air, or Water sign. When you read the chapter on your sign you will learn more about not only your element, but everything in your personality that will help you to achieve a happier and more successful life.

Answer *yes, sometimes,* or *no* to the questions under your element. Score 3 for *yes,* 2 for *sometimes,* and 1 for *no.* The answers will give you your rating in the success stakes.

THE FIRE SIGNS: ARIES, LEO, SAGITTARIUS

Are you good at acting on your own initiative?	Yes	Sometimes	No
Do you enjoy taking on challenging tasks?	Yes	Sometimes	No
Do you think patience is a virtue?	Yes	Sometimes	No
Do you think carefully before starting something new?	Yes	Sometimes	No

Do you see yourself as a leader?	Yes	Sometimes	No
Are you good at taking time out for yourself?	Yes	Sometimes	No
Would you say you often feel under a great deal of stress?	Yes	Sometimes	No
Do you rush into love relationships?	Yes	Sometimes	No
Do you put sex before romance?	Yes	Sometimes	No
Are you basically optimistic?	Yes	Sometimes	No
Do you have many insecurities?	Yes	Sometimes	No
Are you a risk taker?	Yes	Sometimes	No
Do you often feel lonely?	Yes	Sometimes	No
Are you close to your family?	Yes	Sometimes	No
Are you good at taking orders?	Yes	Sometimes	No

WHAT YOUR SCORE REVEALS

If your score is below 25, more than likely you have a tendency to undervalue yourself, and to sit back and let other people ride roughshod over you, which is not what a Fire sign should do. In the chapter for your sign, you will discover ways to enhance your true potential.

If your score is 25–35, you have the potential to be more successful, but sometimes negate it by somewhat selfish or lazy behavior.

If your score is above 35, you definitely have star potential, but don't let it go to your head. You can't *always* be in charge of everyone and everything.

THE EARTH SIGNS: TAURUS, VIRGO, CAPRICORN

Score 3 for *yes*, 2 for *sometimes*, 1 for *no*

Are you always very practical?	Yes	Sometimes	No
Do you seize opportunities when they arise?	Yes	Sometimes	No
Do you invariably fulfill your basic needs?	Yes	Sometimes	No

Is your home life important to you?	Yes	Sometimes	No
Are you in tune with your physical senses?	Yes	Sometimes	No
Are you assertive?	Yes	Sometimes	No
Do you think before you act?	Yes	Sometimes	No
Are you usually dependable?	Yes	Sometimes	No
Are you a really hard worker?	Yes	Sometimes	No
Are you ever narrow-minded?	Yes	Sometimes	No
Is your outlook traditional?	Yes	Sometimes	No
Do you find it easy to relax and have fun?	Yes	Sometimes	No
Does any idea of change worry you?	Yes	Sometimes	No
Are you always efficient?	Yes	Sometimes	No
Do you worry about the future?	Yes	Sometimes	No

WHAT YOUR SCORE REVEALS

If your score is below 25, you are more likely to wait for things to happen of their own accord, rather than to initiate them. If you do this *too* often, don't be surprised if success eludes you; you must definitely read the chapter for your sign to discover ways to enhance your true potential!

If your score is 25–35, you have potential, but you are still not doing enough on your own initiative.

If your score is above 35 you definitely have star potential—but don't get *too* complacent about it or stay *too* long rooted to the same spot!

THE AIR SIGNS: GEMINI, LIBRA, AQUARIUS

Score 3 for *yes*, 2 for *sometimes*, 1 for *no*

Do you consider yourself adaptable?	Yes	Sometimes	No
Are you logical in the way you think?	Yes	Sometimes	No
Are you usually reasonable?	Yes	Sometimes	No
Do you keep up with intellectual pursuits?	Yes	Sometimes	No

xx / *Success Through the Stars*

Do you always evaluate your thoughts?	Yes	Sometimes	No
Can you make quick decisions?	Yes	Sometimes	No
Do you become restless after a short while?	Yes	Sometimes	No
Are you a good communicator?	Yes	Sometimes	No
Do you talk over your ideas with others?	Yes	Sometimes	No
Can you sell yourself well?	Yes	Sometimes	No
Do you express your emotions easily?	Yes	Sometimes	No
Is commitment easy for you?	Yes	Sometimes	No
Is your social life important to you?	Yes	Sometimes	No
Is mental stimulation more important than the physical kind for you?	Yes	Sometimes	No
Do you think you're easy to understand?	Yes	Sometimes	No

WHAT YOUR SCORE REVEALS

If your score is below 25, you tend to be too scattered in your thoughts and ideas to be truly successful. By reading the chapter for your sign you will discover ways to maximize your potential.

If your score is 25–35, you have potential, but sometimes you don't stay focused enough.

If your score is above 35, you have star potential, but you may need to show your real feelings a little more to the people closest to you.

THE WATER SIGNS: CANCER, SCORPIO, PISCES

Score 3 for *yes*, 2 for *sometimes*, and 1 for *no*

Do you listen to your intuition?	Yes	Sometimes	No
Do you consider yourself to have strong emotions?	Yes	Sometimes	No
Are you very idealistic?	Yes	Sometimes	No

Do you allow for the intangible in your life?	*Yes*	*Sometimes*	*No*
Are you good at channeling your talents?	*Yes*	*Sometimes*	*No*
Do you often feel vulnerable?	*Yes*	*Sometimes*	*No*
Are you very self-protective?	*Yes*	*Sometimes*	*No*
Do you usually feel protective toward other people?	*Yes*	*Sometimes*	*No*
Do you have a retentive memory?	*Yes*	*Sometimes*	*No*
Are your surroundings important to you?	*Yes*	*Sometimes*	*No*
Do you relate well to others?	*Yes*	*Sometimes*	*No*
Do you think you need a soulmate?	*Yes*	*Sometimes*	*No*
Are you scared deep down of success?	*Yes*	*Sometimes*	*No*
Do you always admit what you feel?	*Yes*	*Sometimes*	*No*
Are you loyal to your family?	*Yes*	*Sometimes*	*No*

WHAT YOUR SCORE REVEALS

If your score is below 25, you don't trust your intuition nearly enough and tend to think you are more vulnerable than you are. By reading the chapter for your sign, you will discover ways to increase your true potential.

If your score is 25–35, you have potential, but you are still not maximizing it by believing wholeheartedly in who you are.

If your score is above 35, you definitely have star potential, but you may sometimes cling to other people a bit too much!

Success Through the Stars

Becoming a
More Successful
Aries

If you came into this world between March 21 and April 20, you were born under the sign of Aries, the first sign of the zodiac. Aries is a masculine, cardinal, positive, Fire sign ruled by Mars, the god of war. Your planetary symbol is the Ram.

The first day of Aries coincides with the first day of spring, and just as those green shoots can't wait to start bursting from the ground to greet the sunlight, the typical Aries can't wait to get on with life. You race forward to meet its challenges with enthusiasm and exuberance.

If the description "go-getter" could be confidently applied to any sign, it would have to be the designation for you. For Aries no challenge is too great, no task too difficult, and no danger too frightening. It's also true, however, that while your fiery personality can be exhilarating, it can also be exhausting. It is extremely difficult for you to wait for anything. There is an old maxim that if someone wants something done quickly, they should always ask a busy person to do it. To take that a little further, if that person also happens to be an Aries, they can be pretty sure they won't have to think about it further—it will be done.

For a typical Aries to become more successful, it is wise to keep in mind that not everyone else is such a whirlwind of action as you.

Each sign of the zodiac relates to a different area of the body, starting with Aries at the head and ending with Pisces at the feet. So it's no coincidence that all those words and phrases starting with "head" such as "headstrong," "headfirst," "head over heels" fit you so well. Your head is also the most notice-able part of your body. Think of the Ariens Gloria Swanson, Bette Davis, Marlon Brando, Peter Ustinov, Warren Beatty, Emma Thompson, and David Letterman—something about their heads stands out. Ariens tend to be healthy people, thriving on exercise and leading a busy life. But when you feel under the weather, it can almost turn into a full-scale drama, for you hate to be sick.

Since Aries rules the head, your weak areas generally revolve around this part of the body, such as headaches, migraines, and dental or eye problems. If you're up against a major traumatic illness or have to recover from a serious accident, your inimitable Aries courage comes up trumps.

In many ways you're extremely fortunate to have Mars, the god of war, as the ruler of your sign. Mars's influence gives you the courage to deal with the difficult aspects of life in an enterprising and fearless way. You have an amazingly positive and heroically idealistic determination to beat any problem. This is when the challenges of life can be a fantastic experience for a determined Aries who refuses to give up without a fight. Your Martian characteristics will work for you in the best possible way in these situations. I think one of the reasons you are so successful in getting so much done is again due to the influence of Mars, which is responsible for your physical stamina and energy.

However, your tendency to be headstrong can lead you into all sorts of scrapes you could well do without. Rushing headlong into emotional situations often involves you in a whole lot of trouble. When your Martian energy is not harnessed correctly, you are sometimes too inclined to face daily life as though it were a battlefield, with you mounted on a white charger brandishing your sword.

The successful Aries is one who can appreciate the value of balancing your life, so that you're not in a continual battle against time. You don't always have to rush for planes; it isn't essential that you finish reading that new novel before you go to sleep; the world won't come to an end if you don't wake up at the crack of dawn. If you're married or living with someone your partner will appreciate you a whole lot more if you don't insist that he or she try to keep up with your pace.

Defining Your Goals

Not everyone reading this book aspires to be a millionaire or the president of a company, to own half a dozen race horses, to achieve some kind of stardom, to own a luxury home in Palm Beach or the South of France, or to find a wonderful new husband, wife, or lover. Whatever your goals are, however, as an Arien you are more than keen to overtake anyone else who may have similar ambitions because of your "me-first" attitude.

How to Achieve Your Emotional Goals

On the surface you appear to be bright, brash, confident, and full of exuberance, but you aren't as self-confident as you appear. Emotional security can go a long way in helping you define and achieve your material desires. If you are typical of your birth sign, regardless of your life accomplishments, deep within you beats the heart of a child, and that child wants to be appreciated and loved by the people you care about.

The trouble is, you sometimes rate extremely low in patience. Unless you learn to have greater patience you will find yourself in unnecessarily difficult predicaments as you try to achieve emotional and material success. Remember, what is worth having is definitely worth waiting for.

Emotionally, you often seem to enjoy being a child, and a rather spoiled one at that. Whatever the Aries eye lights upon in glee, the Aries must have. There is nothing more exciting for you than an emotional challenge. And charging into battle on that white steed is never more stimulating than where love is concerned. Passion personified is an ideal description for an Arien in the first flush of love. You thrive on the idea of being in love, and you positively glow with exuberance and perhaps a little too much self-esteem when the object of your affections seems prepared to return your feelings.

To become more successful emotionally, it's about time you realized that more often than not it's the thrill of the chase and not the capture that appeals to your Aries character. Try a little harder to work at things when you get down to day-to-day living within a relationship, for you can become bored much too quickly. You need just as much mental stimulation as a Gemini, despite your conviction that the physical side of love is what you desire most. Sex and sensuality are definitely high on your list, but even a passionate Fire sign can lose interest if you and your partner have few mutual interests outside of the bedroom.

EMOTIONS AND THE ARIES WOMAN

It's often amazing to see how someone who can be such a successful firebrand in other areas of your life can so easily come unstuck when love comes along. Stop fooling yourself into thinking you're so tough and invincible. Underneath your aggressive stance is a heart every bit as romantic as that of a Piscean woman, and often a whole lot more. You don't really see yourself going off to battle on a white charger searching for your knight, no matter how much you might fool yourself into thinking so. Deep down you visualize yourself as the fair maiden locked in the dungeon, for whom a knight is prepared to give his life. But because you're so determined to hide the emotional vulnerability we all possess, you tend to go to the other extreme, anxious to show your independence and love of freedom. You may also have an all-consuming need to be the winner in any power conflict.

Pay attention to two words that should never be underestimated in your vocabulary: *patience* and *balance*. You could argue that with Mars as your ruler, it's unfair to expect you to be the most patient person in the world. However, if you are prepared to reflect upon some of the emotional disasters that have occurred in the past, you will probably admit that half of them wouldn't have happened if you had been a little less inclined to rush headlong into something.

More than most people, you need someone who can help to balance your fiery personality. Aries, the first sign of the zodiac, relates to the ego; Libra, your opposite sign, is the seventh sign and represents marriages and partnerships. Our opposite signs always have something to teach us that is lacking within our own personalities. Since Libra is the sign of the Scales—balance, peace, and harmony—it's important for an Aries to take a leaf out of the Libran book and incorporate some of these qualities into your own nature. You could not ask for a better sign as your opposite, and if you go through the birthdays of your friends and colleagues, don't be surprised to discover that a great many of them are Librans. Your subconscious mind knows what you need.

Once you have realized that balance is what is required for you to achieve greater emotional success, stability, and serendipity, your path will be a much easier and a more enjoyable one. You will accept and appreciate the importance of understanding your partner better, and will learn to work a little harder at turning an initial attraction into a lasting relationship. Accept your partner's needs and desires along with your own!

EMOTIONS AND THE ARIES MAN

It always used to be a joke of mine that the Aries man could probably make love and conduct a telephone conversation at the same time. Later, I read in a gossip magazine that Arien Warren Beatty had done just that! Maybe that was only gossip, but the truth is that just like your female counterpart, the most exciting part of a love affair for an Aries is the chase. Once you know you have got her, it's quite possible for your emotions to cut off from her to deal with something else—yes, at the same time!

The emotions of an Aries man can be hard to fathom. You often come across as extremely macho and egotistical, convinced no woman can do without you. But just like the female of the species, you have an amazing amount of vulnerability, which creates a real-life "little boy lost." If you would learn to accept your vulnerability and understand it is not simply a weakness confined to Ariens, it would be much easier for you to feel secure with yourself, and you would not have to prove your manhood by having every woman you desire.

I once sat at a dinner table with Jill Bennett, a wonderful actress who sadly died a few years back. At one time she had been married to an Aries man, and was convinced that both male and female Ariens were very weak individuals. I was determined to put her right, telling her that even as a generalization this was very wide of the mark. What is true is that some male Ariens do appear to be weaker than their female counterparts, and nowhere is this more apparent than in love. Aside from Warren Beatty, who now seems happy and content with his ideal partner, at various times the papers were often full of the emotional dramas of Ariens Dudley Moore, and a married Spencer Tracy who was also involved in a long-term love relationship with Katharine Hepburn.

Some of you inwardly yearn for a perfect long-term relationship, yet fear having to change your life in too many ways. If you're a typical Aries man—extremely masculine, virile, and passionate—you sometimes don't bother to think enough about tomorrow when you're off on one of your chases after a new conquest. But how many times have you woken up beside someone and wondered just why you're there? Do you sometimes in the heat of excitement forget we're living in an age when it's not merely unwise to take these kind of sexual risks, it's downright crazy? Don't you sometimes yearn for a single partner who can be desirable, sexy, mentally stimulating, and understanding? The sort of woman who accepts that one minute you can be unbearably immature, yet adorably sweet and generous the next? Wouldn't you like to have a go at committing yourself to just one person, to try being a little more Libran in your efforts to balance out your life? You never seem to have time to discover whether your current flame could turn out to be the love of your life, because you're too busy moving on to the next. Warren Beatty was very often described as a type of playboy of the Western world, but now he certainly seems to enjoy being a husband and father.

Emotional maturity suits you, Aries, and it also paves the way to greater success in the other areas of your life. Don't be afraid to commit yourself to the right person when she does turn up.

How to Achieve Your Material Goals

Your material goals will involve being right up there at the top. Accept that not every single Aries can be at the top, and that perhaps your own particular horoscope gives you an Ascendant, Moon sign, and planetary aspects that allow you to be perfectly happy *not* being there.

Success for you may often involve a challenge, for there is nothing you like better to get you going. However, there is no denying you are a born leader, and since Aries rules the head it presumably endows you with a good brain, too. Your enthusiasm, energy, vitality, courage, drive, and determination cannot be disputed, and no one can fail to be bowled over by your confident approach to everything you undertake. Take for example the Ariens John Major, who was determined to become the British Prime Minister, the actress Emma Thompson with her Oscar achievement; designer Vivienne Westwood with her flamboyant designs; or Andrew Lloyd Webber with his musicals. These Ariens were unlikely to let any setbacks, disappointments, conflicts, or disapproval put them off their tracks to success!

Nevertheless, just as in your emotional life, you do need to balance things out. Maybe almost more important is your need to be fulfilled in whatever you do. The one thing your Aries brain cannot cope with is boredom—not even for a few minutes! Your boredom threshold is horrendously low. Unfortunately, boredom can all too easily become your pet excuse for not finishing something you started enthusiastically. Or is it simply that you expect everything you start to be finished quickly—not today, tomorrow or, heaven forbid, a long while from now, but yesterday.

Your idea of material success doesn't always involve making a great deal of money, as your prestige and standing in the world can be of major importance to you. There is often an extremely idealistic side of your personality that makes you work hard at something challenging. I was privileged to spend some time with Gloria Swanson a few years before she died. We used to drink herbal teas together on my regular visits to New York, discussing her interest in health foods and the bad effects of white sugar. Her Aries challenge at that time was trying to convince people of the negative effects of much of the food we eat.

The greater the challenge, the sweeter the victory for anyone born under the sign of Aries. By taking up the challenge of learning to understand the way other people work, you will perhaps discover facets in their characters that in turn help to fill in missing pieces in your own personality.

The Powerful Assets at Your Disposal to Become More Successful

The Power of Your Element . . . Fire

The Fire element in your sign makes Ariens fiery individuals. You are intensely motivated and are excellent at getting new projects off the ground.

At times it's almost as though you radiate heat through your personality. An Aries in a bad mood is definitely not someone to be near. Aggressive and self-assertive, argumentative and volatile, your Aries face can become as red as the astrological color bequeathed to you.

The positive side of the Fire element gives you the courage to face adversity and all its challenges, the ability to accept a great deal of pain and suffering without flinching, and the will to dauntlessly fight your own battles without running crying to someone else. Even as small children, Ariens are not simply tomboys, they are natural fighters, not only standing up for themselves, but standing up for anyone who is smaller and weaker than themselves.

Your Fire element also emphasizes your enterprising, enthusiastic, impulsive, and often aggressive approach to just about everything you undertake—which can be both a plus and minus. Sometimes you need to sit back and remember that fire, while being a beneficial provider of warmth and heat, can also lead to danger, especially when you are provoked. Try at times to use your Fire power in a gentler way to achieve your maximum success potential.

Your Fire power enables you to be a fearless and assertive initiator, a true pioneer. Challenges are the ideal fuel for your Arien fire, but you don't need to prove your case by showing us a firework explosion of Arien expletives if someone tries to beat you at your own game. You love any kind of competition, especially if you end up the winner. However, you might try to retain your initial enthusiasm and exuberance and not give up on something halfway through. Take a tip from the Earth signs, Taurus, Virgo, and Capricorn, and become more organized and businesslike.

The Power of Your Ruling Planet . . . Mars

It's all up to you, Aries. Your ruling planet, Mars, was renowned as the god of war in Roman days, and it will be hard to stop you if you're determined to charge your way through life like an ancient warrior. I honestly don't believe that any of us changes unless we decide to change ourselves. Other people can try or help to influence us to rid ourselves of our bad habits, but unless we truly want to behave differently we will go on in the same old way, for better or worse throughout our lives.

With Mars as your ruling planet you are prepared to take risks for anything you believe. You will fearlessly take the lead, create action, and use your seemingly endless energy and innovative powers to take you higher up the ladder to success and to achieve your heart's desires.

But do remember that those attributes are the positive side of Mars; perhaps we can also blame this planet for your unbelievable inability to rest and relax when you need it, your impulse to drop something almost as soon as you have started it, and that determination to charge ahead even if deep down you know you may be wrong. At times it's almost as though Mars forces you to have a battle with yourself—a battle that started when you were still a child. You had temper tantrums not only when it was time to sleep and you still wanted to play but also when you were determined to get up at the crack of dawn and thus prevented your hard-working parents from enjoying the sleep they deserved—and needed with you around!

The Power of Your Rising Sign

Your Ascendant, or rising sign, is the sign that was rising on the eastern horizon at the time of your birth. In many ways it is as important as your sun and moon signs because the way you live out your life is very much influenced by this rising sign.

In the table on pages 278–79 you will be able to determine your ascendant sign. In the meantime I will describe how each ascendant influences your sign.

ARIES WITH ARIES RISING
Think of everything you know about your sign, and magnify it!

You truly do consider yourself a born leader, and heaven help anyone who stops you in your quest for success. With this combination you learn to appreciate the importance of good timing and a little patience.

ARIES WITH TAURUS RISING

An Aries with the patience to see beyond yesterday and today, that's you. You're prepared to spend the time and effort on some of the necessary spadework to fulfill your heart's desires. Just make sure you're not stubborn about getting your way.

ARIES WITH GEMINI RISING

No one can fault your ability to communicate on many levels, but your level of success depends on your determination to stick at what you start and not lose interest before you're even halfway done. Try to stick to a workable schedule.

ARIES WITH CANCER RISING

There is a gentler and more sensitive touch in the way you race through life. You'd never neglect your home or family in your desire to be successful. Try not to give in to sulks and bad moods if things don't always go your way.

ARIES WITH LEO RISING

Your delight in getting good results is invariably well deserved, but just make sure you don't overdo it and become too convinced of your own self-importance. Being the star of the show isn't always necessary and pride can come before a fall!

ARIES WITH VIRGO RISING

A leader with real powers of analysis and discrimination can be powerful indeed. You should certainly know the way to get ahead, but don't let the Virgo side of your personality make you become too much of a nit-picking critic.

ARIES WITH LIBRA RISING

Libra gives Aries an ability to see both sides of any situation and to judge accordingly before rushing ahead, as well as the vision to accept that sometimes you work better in a partnership than alone. Watch out you don't become too indecisive.

ARIES WITH SCORPIO RISING

Hopefully no one will attempt to get the better of you, for this combination is usually invincible in just about anything. Don't let your steely determination make you a tyrant. Watch out that you don't become overly jealous or possessive, too.

ARIES WITH SAGITTARIUS RISING

Your confidence and optimism cannot be faulted, but you may take too many risks in your determination to reap the rewards of success. Don't let the Sagittarian side of your personality mean that you always think you know all the answers.

ARIES WITH CAPRICORN RISING

Material security is more important than is usual with Ariens, and you don't care how hard you have to work to achieve it. This combination helps you persevere to the end. Don't lose sight of your childlike innocence, which is a refreshing part of you.

ARIES WITH AQUARIUS RISING

Watch out you're not too unpredictable, headstrong, and impulsive, which could make you lose out when you're playing for high stakes in the success game. There is a nice humanitarian side to your Aries ego, which helps to tone down your "me-first" attitude.

ARIES WITH PISCES RISING

The recognizable Aries firebrand is given a soft, more sentimental touch. Your ideals often have a romantic flavor, but your sensitivity can lead you on to even greater success, too. Make sure you're not carried away by impractical schemes.

How to Create Greater Success

Creating Greater Success . . . in Your Everyday Life

To the typical Aries the idea of structure and organization can seem like a nightmare. I have an extremely neat and tidy Virgo friend who thinks you're the sort of person who lives in a beautiful room where nothing appears to be out of place, but if you bothered to look under the cushions or behind the couch you would find everything that had been strewn all over the place just minutes before.

It's also quite likely, though, that you know just where everything you need can be found at a moment's notice. That is your own particular way of organizing things. Even so, don't you think it would be worth trying a different way of doing things? Perhaps you could try to be a little more organized, and structure your days so that you don't always wake up in a mad panic thinking of everything you have to do, and wondering if you really can remember where you put those important papers, which must be dealt with before lunchtime?

One of your assets is that you thrive on being busy, but your Arien nature sometimes makes it impossible for you to delegate jobs without trying to force others to work at your fast pace, even when there is no need for hurry. So often Aries the Ram charges full steam ahead without looking left or right, and this is not always the best nor the fastest way to do things. Tasks begun enthusiastically are often left unfinished because something more interesting has come your way.

If you feel you've reached a point in your life where it seems as though you are running on full batteries yet somehow losing out in the success stakes, the following checklist will give you some pointers on creating a better regime for yourself.

DO . . .
- learn to appreciate the value of patience.
- take a few deep breaths before you argue your point.
- stay enthusiastic, enterprising, and eager.
- use your courage, energy, and vitality in a positive way.
- look for challenges that stimulate your mind, body, and your soul.
- remember that you're the pioneer of the zodiac—but finish what you start.

DON'T . . .
- make being "me first" the be-all and end-all of your life.
- let arrogance and aggression turn you into a bully.
- insist on other people keeping up with your fast pace.
- let greed and selfishness control you in your search for success.
- forget the little details when you're planning big things.
- try to do every single thing yourself when often a partner can help.

Creating Greater Success . . . in Love

The Aries personality has a need for good relationships. You don't have to fear you are losing control by placing greater importance on them, but you will have to minimize your "me-first" approach. As strong as you are, there is definitely more strength in a united front, and Aries isn't meant to walk alone. It isn't only the chase and challenge that are exciting, and the best love affair needs to be worked on by both partners if it's going to last. Playing the field might once have been fun, but promiscuity can be very dangerous these days. And the expense of divorce settlements can be financially and emotionally draining. Ask yourself what you really need in a partner, and believe in your own power to create the right relationship.

In your sex life, you sometimes are too concerned, again, with the initial excitement and might even be called a selfish lover. Once you are fulfilled you can quickly and easily be ready to move on to something else. No one can dispute your ability to be passionate, but all too often your passion ties in with your own needs and desires and excludes the needs of your bedmate! It's not that you don't want to please someone else, only that it's difficult for you to get past your "me-first" focus.

Do be open, enthusiastic, and carefree, but don't be too assertive, demanding, and unreasonable.

Creating Greater Success . . . in Dating

When you first start dating as a youngster, it is often a wonderfully exciting challenge. You probably have no fears of rejection. You set your cap for someone and bowl them over with the sheer strength of your vibrant Aries personality.

But if you decide to start dating again after a breakup, divorce, or the passing away of a partner, you may be more vulnerable and less independent in your ways. You may fear the thought of too much competition in your search for an ideal relationship.

Never lose faith in yourself, Aries. You will always retain the power to achieve the success you crave. No matter what has transpired so far, when you decide to get out there and shine— that's when your power will shine forth, too.

ARIES DATING TIPS
- Be friendly and sociable and let your Aries charisma shine through.
- Don't be too pushy and attention-grabbing, especially on a first date.

- Vow to be more patient when waiting for the phone to ring.

Creating Greater Success . . . in Family Ties

It's often very important for you to forget about that Aries ego, making you a lot less understanding to the needs and desires of others. Sometimes you are so absorbed in your own fast lane that you simply don't take the time to stop and think about other people. This is sad, because despite your "me first" attitude, you can also be extremely unselfish and generous. You want to be loved by everyone who knows you. It all comes down to the acting-before-you-think part of your personality, which leads you off into your own little self-involved world.

You are probably much better at keeping in touch via the telephone than in any other way. But to create truly successful family ties that usually is not enough. Because you are basically such an honest and truthful person, misunderstandings arise when you let fly with some of your ideas. Happily, a fiery Arien does not typically bear grudges, so that when an argument does flare up, your anger is usually short-lived and easily forgotten. But you need to put a little more effort into understanding how other members of your family might feel when this happens.

Try to avoid conflicts between your professional and domestic life. Even if you want to be a star outside your home environment, you want your home and family life to be successful too.

TIPS FOR SUCCESSFUL FAMILY TIES
- Try to think about how family members will react before you say something you may regret later.
- Adjust your busy schedule to make sure no one feels neglected.
- Don't behave like a spoiled child when you don't get your way.

Creating Greater Success . . . at Work

Come on now, Aries, not *all* of you can end up as the boss! And I'm afraid that when you do become the leader of the pack, it is all too easy for you turn into a real megalomaniac. It's fine to be ambitious, but make sure you don't become too greedy along the way, climbing over other people as you search for new and better opportunities. This is the negative side of Aries in the workplace—which also relates to your low tolerance for boredom. Or is it simply that you expect everything you start to be finished almost immediately?

The positive side of your leadership qualities is that you tend to have a fresh and invigorating approach to projects. This combined with your mental and physical energy, boundless enthusiasm, and initiative inspires a great many people to follow you. They may prefer to work at a slightly slower pace, but if this does not create any problems, why not learn to accept it.

To become more successful at work, pay attention to the following do's and don'ts.

DO . . .
- remember that something you start enthusiastically needs to be completed.
- try to be more diplomatic with peers and colleagues.
- remember you can be a leader in your chosen field when you work at it.

DON'T . . .
- be a trouble-maker by arguing too much about too many issues.
- insist on creating changes before you've discussed them with others who may be involved.
- let your Aries ego take over the whole show so that you become a dictatorial slave driver.

Creating Greater Success . . . in Finding the Right Job

Even though you may be convinced that you're a natural-born leader, you will still benefit from some advice on finding the right job.

The trouble with a typical Aries is that your renowned impatience can sometimes let you down when you're job-hunting. Often so keen to start at something, you rush headlong into a job that sounds fine, only to discover that it may not lead anywhere. The best way to overcome this problem is to give yourself a little more time in looking for the right occupation and finding out as much as possible about what the position entails. If finding a job is imperative for financial or other reasons, take a part-time job until the right opportunity comes along.

Ariens make excellent explorers and pioneers of just about anything. In the professional realm you are drawn to advertising, public relations, journalism, politics, and broadcasting.

Creating Greater Success . . . in All Your Relationships

One extremely important factor of success in life is relating well to other people. The following guide will show how to maintain the best relationships with all the signs.

ARIES AND ARIES

This combination is a challenge! Since you should know each other inside out—the good bits as well as the not so good—your mirror image will help you to understand yourself a little better too.

ARIES AND TAURUS

Taurus the Bull can teach you a whole lot about patience, and the need to build something slowly, so a relationship with steady, sensual, and dependable Taurus can be of real value.

ARIES AND GEMINI

Gemini can be flighty and fickle if mental stimulation flies out the window. Temper tantrums won't work with this sign, nor will an overly inflated ego. If you argue, don't be a bad loser when Gemini wins.

ARIES AND CANCER

Respect and appreciate the sensitivity of Cancer, and enjoy the domesticity this sign loves so much. Accept that Cancerians are affected by the cycles of the moon, and when feeling moody need the comfort of their shell.

ARIES AND LEO

Two Fire signs vying for attention and the limelight can be a powerful duo. Both of you need admiration and affection, and you're both little children at heart, so you will each need to give and take.

ARIES AND VIRGO

You will often learn something from Virgo's critical and analytical advice, so don't criticize them too much if they worry about things you consider unimportant. Don't let yourself be put down unfairly by them.

ARIES AND LIBRA

Libra is the sign of partnership and both of you can give so much to each other in so many different ways. Just calm down and admit that peace, harmony, and fair play can add security to your life and make it a whole lot more pleasurable too.

ARIES AND SCORPIO

You've met your match here, Aries! Invincible Scorpio is also ruled by Mars, god of war. Relating better means respecting Scorpio's space, and not giving any cause for jealousy, or sparks will definitely fly.

ARIES AND SAGITTARIUS

Show that you're just as positive and outgoing as the Archer, but don't be upset if his or her outspoken remarks are not always what you want to hear. Honesty is the name of the game here. Don't try to pin down this free and easy sign too much.

ARIES AND CAPRICORN

Always understand that Capricorn's ambitious streak is based on the need for material security and prestige, and is not usually of a selfish nature. Never try to force the Mountain Goat off his chosen path or you will encounter a ruthless streak.

ARIES AND AQUARIUS

Don't expect Aquarius to continually tell you how wonderful you are for this sign's actions speak louder than their emotional words. Be adaptable in your ways, for the Water Carrier is an unconventional sign and hates to feel hemmed in.

ARIES AND PISCES

Hopefully your idealistic view of the world will be tempered with more reality than that of romantic Pisces, otherwise any kind of relationship with the sign of the Fishes could be your bank manager's or accountant's worst nightmare.

Becoming a
More Successful
Taurus

If you came into this world between April 21 and May 20, you were born under the sign of Taurus, the second sign of the zodiac. Taurus is a feminine, negative, fixed, Earth sign ruled by Venus, the goddess of love. Your planetary symbol is the Bull.

Aries, the sign that precedes yours, is the go-getter of the zodiac, rushing full steam ahead. You, by contrast, are far more cautious, and are inclined to sit back and weigh the pros and cons of every situation. You tend to confront issues in a pragmatic, materialistic way. Feeling grounded is a necessity for you, which is no surprise, considering you are an Earth sign.

People who harbor a grudge against you might rather sarcastically call you a plodder. Your feet are so firmly planted on the ground it takes you forever to move on. If you're honest, you will admit that you prefer sticking to safe ground, rather than having to take any risks. Consequently, you may lose out on something you hoped for and end up feeling dejected and disappointed.

Since you are one of the most loyal, steadfast, caring, and responsible signs, anyone who needs your help can be assured you will endeavor never to let them down. You take your responsibilities very seriously, even when you are slow to start. Sometimes you can be more than a little power crazy too, especially when you stubbornly insist on going your way—even when deep down you know you are wrong.

Each sign of the zodiac relates to a different area of the body, starting with the head and ending with the feet, from Aries to Pisces. Taurus relates to the neck and throat. The neck is often fairly thick in people born under your sign. "Stubborn" and "bull-headed" are two of the adjectives most frequently used to describe you. This can be seen in the Taurean Jack Nicholson's reluctance to make his way to the altar (at the time of writing), even though he obviously cares deeply about his on/off love Rebecca Broussard and their two children. Of course, not every

Taurean is going to be thick-necked and chunky-looking, but there is often something very special about the Taurus throat. Singer Barbra Streisand has proved this a million times over with her powerful voice. There is also a very special Taurean sensuality shown by actresses like Uma Thurman, Michelle Pfeiffer, Debra Winger, Cher, and "Absolutely Fabulous" star Joanna Lumley.

It's wonderful to have Venus, the goddess of love, as the ruler of your sign (a privilege you share with Libra), for Venus endows you with your love of art and beauty, your sensuality, seductive wiles, and need for peace and harmony in your life. That's the plus side! But Venus can also create laziness and inertia. In addition, the influence of Venus may at times make you vain and selfish, so that you put your sensual needs before all others. However, there is no doubt that Venus brings you a special kind of charisma, with the ability to understand and appreciate pleasure in all its many forms.

Successful Taureans are people who can see the beauty in life, and do not simply sit back and moan about problems or injustices around them or become locked into the same old routine day in and day out. They harness their energies, take a deep breath, and try to change the things they can. Charm is one of your greatest assets, but laid-back charm is productive only if used in the right way.

Everyone's definition of success is different. For you to feel successful, you need to feel good about yourself, and look good. Looking good is not a waste of time, but you mustn't concentrate on your appearance alone.

Defining Your Goals

Not every Taurean reading this book wants to be a millionaire, own a luxury hotel, open a successful restaurant (where you can indulge your gourmet tastes from morning to night), marry a movie star, or become a top model. Whatever your goals are, when you have set them you go about achieving them with steely-eyed determination. You may be slow to start on something, but you don't intend to be a nonachiever and be overtaken at the finish line by a rank outsider!

How to Achieve Your Emotional Goals

Your emotional goals generally seem to run parallel to your material ones. It's hard for you to feel emotionally secure if the material side of your life gives you cause for concern. Taurus is the builder of the zodiac. Bricks and mortar are like your lifeblood. The smallest apartment, house, or piece of land to call your own makes you feel like a millionaire in material terms. But don't neglect your emotional needs. To achieve your emotional goals you may sometimes have to set your material priorities a little lower. In my years of astrological counseling I've come across many successful Taureans who, perhaps wanting for nothing in the material sphere, have found that the right relationship has always eluded them. This seems to be particularly true for Taurean women who have been determined to rise to the top of their chosen profession—working long hours every day and into the weekends to the exclusion of almost everything else. When they reached their late thirties and early forties and had become very successful, they realized that many of their friends were married with kids, and they could not even find a date for a Saturday night. Of course, this doesn't only apply to Taureans. But if you're totally honest with yourself, you will admit that while many of your wants and needs revolve around your material life, you suffer if your emotional needs aren't met.

Being successful in a material sense is only one part of the Taurean personality. Emotionally, there is a side of your personality that can make you as possessive and jealous as any Scorpio—a sign noted for jealousy. Since you are a fixed sign, there is no doubt that you are set in your opinions, thoughts, ideals, and ideas. "Stubborn, what me?"—I've heard this many times from a Taurean client. As tactfully as possible, I've had to explain to her that the Taurean emotional need to put a dollar worth on a partner instead of following her feelings could put a lover off. Remember, to become more successful emotionally, it is important to define your truest and deepest emotional needs. Your earthy sexuality mean love and passion are extremely important to such a sensual sign as yours. This can be love without either any power play or the need to impose impossibly high standards on a partner. Class differences need not make any difference to you when you fall in love. Love can break down all barriers.

EMOTIONS AND THE TAURUS WOMAN

I'm always fascinated by the Taurus woman. You seem so complete in many ways, capable of handling your own life in a perfectly adequate manner, and appearing to be cool, controlled, and competent. Dare I say that a calculating side of your nature also reveals itself in your search for a lasting relationship, be it with a husband or a live-in partner? The controlling aspect can unfortunately be a little too much for the one on whom you set your sights!

On the other hand, you may meet someone who seems perfect for you in every way. Unlike an Aries, who rushes straight in impulsively, you go the other way. You find every possible practical reason this prospective partner couldn't fit into your life. At the same time, some women of your sign are inordinately jealous and possessive, even with platonic friends.

To grow past these issues of intimacy and possessiveness, it is important for you to feel grounded and secure. If you are one who desperately longs for the perfect relationship, remember that you are your own powerhouse of emotional security. You don't actually need someone else to bring this out in you. Once you have learned to accept this, you will find it much easier to sustain good, productive, and long-lasting relationships.

EMOTIONS AND THE TAURUS MAN

The Taurus man has deep emotions, but it can take quite a while to plumb them. On the surface he may appear slow to move, although it is obvious he has a roving eye. Underneath the surface, it is sex and security he's looking for—I'm not quite sure in which order, though! You might say that surely this is what most men are looking for; the Taurus man, though, is quite manipulative in his efforts to fulfill his emotional needs. As a Taurus man, you will have to admit that when you fall for someone, you use every seductive wile in the book to get her interested in you. You're capable of planning a definite and controlled campaign. As far as you're concerned, you have time on your side. You don't like to rush or be rushed. It's taking no for an answer that you don't like!

Being a fixed Earth sign ruled by the goddess of love endows you with certain attributes. To be ruled by Venus is to appreciate beauty in all its shapes and forms. In fact, I'm sorry to have to say that you sometimes place a little too much emphasis on how someone looks and not enough on what they have to say.

If you're a typical Taurus man, you don't really want to play the field for your entire life. Having the right person by your side is very important to you, as is feeling secure. But you also can be stubborn, refusing to change the habits of a lifetime, even for the perfect partner.

The Taurus man is an earthy and sensual mate and, like the Taurean woman, can be as jealous and possessive as a Scorpio. When you settle into a relationship, you expect it to last— maybe forever—and you're quite prepared to provide your partner with all the creature comforts it's in your power to confer. Since you're often extremely ambitious and hard-working, you're often simply not aware you are neglecting your partner.

Try to be more concerned about what she feels, wants, or needs from your relationship.

Don't limit your communications to the physical. It's wonderful to achieve sexual compatibility, but for a relationship to survive, there needs to be more than sex to keep you by each other's side. You need to relate emotionally on all levels.

How to Achieve Your Material Goals

When you Taureans focus on your chosen material goals, you often have a steely glint in your eye. That glint is your determination to get what you want—no matter how long it might take. In case you never realized it before, power is all-important to Taurus. One of the ways you feel powerful is by becoming financially secure. Taurus is the builder of the zodiac. You want to build security in your life, so you don't have to worry in your old age.

In addition, it's important for you to have a sense of purpose in your undertakings. The trouble with some Taureans is that you often stick to something that has become purely routine. This is in part because you lack the energy, initiative, or perhaps, a dare-devil attitude necessary to bring about change.

It is exceedingly important to ensure that a power complex doesn't turn you into a megalomaniac. Hitler was a Taurus!

Taurean careers often involve "big business." You tend to prefer working in a "safe" profession: one unlikely to leave you worse off than when you started. However, building empires and improving your financial position are Taurean characteristics. Surely it is no coincidence that the publishing magnate William Randolph Hearst was born under your sign.

Try not to let power and money rule your life; don't deny yourself sufficient time for personal and emotional happiness. Imitate the successful young Taurean New Yorker I know who is vice president of her thriving company. She works extremely hard, even sometimes traveling overseas for her job, but she is delighted to spend time at the end of the day with her husband and baby daughter. She is achieving her material goals, but not at the cost of something equally valuable.

The Powerful Assets at Your Disposal to Become More Successful

The Power of Your Element . . . Earth

Taurus is the first of the Earth signs—possibly the most earth-bound and grounded sign of the entire zodiac. This is not necessarily bad. Often the people who have no Earth anywhere in their charts are those who find it impossible to settle down, or even establish any routines in their lives. The Earth is the provider of so much, but its presence in our lives needs to be nurtured.

For you, a Taurean, the earth itself brings solace and inspiration. I think it's so important to communicate with your element. Feel yourself on firm ground. Sit beneath a tree and think. Sometimes you are so busy concentrating on external issues that you almost lose sight of who you are.

Just like your fellow Earth signs, Virgo and Capricorn, you are restrained and practical in your way of dealing with everyday issues. Unlike these two signs, however, you can be very stubborn and persistent when it would be better to try being understanding and receptive when dealing with others. An interesting fact about bulls is that when they are totally cornered in the bullring, they retreat to a special area of the ring hoping to avoid further danger. There are times when retreating, rather than pushing, can also be beneficial for human Bulls.

Your Earth power emphasizes your ability to keep both feet on the ground when people around you are losing their heads over one hare-brained scheme or another. Your earthiness helps you avoid taking risks on the stock exchange or investing in fly-by-night enterprises. On the negative side this can still mean you dig those feet in too deeply, so that when it comes time to move, you're stuck!

The Power of Your Ruling Planet . . . Venus

Throughout the centuries, Venus has been revered as the goddess of love. Some modern interpretations of classical mythology have also thought of her as the goddess of sex. There is certainly no doubt that sexuality and sensuality are all-important to your sign. Indeed, they can be your undoing if you let them dominate your life at the wrong time or take precedence over some other important areas in your life.

Venus bestows upon you a sense of refinement; a love of beautiful people, places, and things; a calm, peaceful, and uncluttered life; and a delight in art and music.

Another aspect of Venus's influence is the importance you place on your attachment to people and objects that fit snugly into your own little world. Furthermore, you can become lazy, expecting your sensuality to allow you conquest after conquest. A sort of inertia overcomes you if you're too content. You become reluctant to take steps that may take you away from what you're used to—steps that are necessary for the achievement of a further goal. Try not to be a stubborn Bull, refusing to take the right moves to advance yourself.

Venus enables you to look on the brighter side of life. It encourages you to see the positive aspects of the most dire situations. It also helps you to sparkle in the face of the strongest competition.

The Power of Your Rising Sign

Your Ascendant, or rising sign, is the sign that was rising on the eastern horizon at the time of your birth. In many ways it is as

important as your sun and Moon signs. Using the table on pages 278–79 you will be able to determine your ascendant sign.

Here are examples of how your rising sign will affect your Taurean personality.

TAURUS WITH ARIES RISING

With an Aries Ascendant there should be no stopping you from achieving success in all areas of your life. You don't stubbornly stick to the tried and true for fear of what tomorrow could bring. Your enthusiasm for trying out new ideas is a powerful asset.

TAURUS WITH TAURUS RISING

A double Taurus! Loyal, dependable, and patient—that's you. Unfortunately, these traits could make you far too set in your routine, and far too stubborn to change—even when you know it's for the best.

TAURUS WITH GEMINI RISING

A Taurus with the ability to create new ideas at the drop of a hat and to follow through on them is in a powerful position to achieve success. Your Gemini Ascendant helps you to become more flexible and free-thinking.

TAURUS WITH CANCER RISING

This combination offers more emotional security and domestic bliss. Try not to let coziness get in the way of your long-term aims and ambitions. It's far too easy for you to stay happily ensconced in a rut.

TAURUS WITH LEO RISING

This is a Taurean definitely determined to be a star! You don't want to sit back when the limelight beckons. But try to be less fixed in so many of your opinions.

TAURUS WITH VIRGO RISING

This combination is great if you want to work ninety percent of the time, for you enjoy being amazingly disciplined and organized. Don't forget the more sensual pleasures of life as well, or you could end up being accused of being a bore.

TAURUS WITH LIBRA RISING

Charm and diplomacy personified—that's you! Your love of beauty, peace, and harmony is enhanced by this other Venus-ruled sign. But you may be lacking in initiative. Don't sit back and simply wait for all the good things in life to come your way. Get out there and look for what you want!

TAURUS WITH SCORPIO RISING

Your opposite sign, Scorpio, as your Ascendant intensifies your somewhat possessive ways, possibly some manipulative ones, too. You must try harder to respect the space needed by others for *their* way of life.

TAURUS WITH SAGITTARIUS RISING

Far more outgoing and outspoken than the average Taurus, you have an optimistic and adventurous streak that enables you to achieve a great deal in life. You will happily move on, when you are mentally stimulated or challenged by someone or something.

TAURUS WITH CAPRICORN RISING

Double Earth again! Unless you're careful, this combination can make you almost too materialistic—in both your emotional and your professional life. Being ambitious is fine, but watch out that you don't become too ruthless.

TAURUS WITH AQUARIUS RISING

The Builder and the Humanitarian—an interesting duo. You may be far more idealistic and unconventional than the average Taurus. Your idea of success involves a life that could never be described as humdrum.

TAURUS WITH PISCES RISING

Practical Taurus combined with those impractical Pisces Fishes swimming in two different directions: sensuality combined with sensitivity. You are kind, loving, and loyal. Try not to become too sympathetic or emotional when dealing with business and material issues.

How to Create Greater Success

Creating Greater Success . . . in Your Everyday Life

If you're a typical Taurus, structure and organization aren't likely to faze you. Likewise, discipline and routine are not difficult to master. Though your patience and persistence make you a brilliant empire builder, your home and family life tend to take second place. Priding yourself on your organizational skills, you rarely stop working to sit back, enjoy life, and spend time with those you care about.

Don't give way to unnecessary inner fears over your material security. Deep down you should know that the hard work you have invested in your career will pay off. Learn to be more philosophical: There are several great Taurean philosophers, including Bertrand Russell and Pierre Teilhard de Chardin.

Don't become so inflexible that you alienate people who are important to you. Resolve not to let your slow burning anger turn into a temper tantrum.

If you yearn for success, yet feel that it eludes you, the following checklist will give you some pointers on how to create a better daily regime, without having to completely change your life.

DO . . .
- try to be a little more flexible in your day-to-day life.
- be quicker off the mark when something grabs your attention.

- make the most of your creative and artistic skills.
- become more aware of other people's needs and feelings.
- be prepared to let go of any deadwood—for example, set ideas that hold you back.
- believe in your own inner security to gain greater power over your life.

DON'T . . .

- put your material needs before *everything* else.
- wait *too* patiently for things to happen, without going after them yourself.
- upset others by being too stubborn, status-conscious, and unyielding.
- let the pleasures of the flesh rule your life.
- ever forget your wonderful sense of humor—a definite asset in today's world.
- equate success only with money; you need the power to be happy, too.

Creating Greater Success . . . in Love

Because you are ruled by the goddess of love, you hate to live without this emotion. Avoid being too pushy and demanding when you don't gain someone's love. If you do want to set those Taurean roots firmly in the ground, you cannot afford to make this desire too obvious—certainly not at the start—unless you happen to fall for another Taurus who feels the same way.

You're nowhere near as impulsive as Aries, nor as convinced that you are wonderful as a Leo. But you're a master of plotting strategies that make for a more successful romantic relationship. Strangely enough, while plodding along in so many areas of your life can become almost second nature, when your sexual urges are aroused, it's almost impossible for you to practice the art of self-restraint. Watch out that you don't concentrate on self-gratification to the exclusion of all else. It can work against you in the long run. *Do* be seductive and sensible, and *don't* be obstinate and overly subjective.

Creating Greater Success . . . in Dating

No matter at what age a Taurean starts dating, it is probably serious business right from the start. And, since there is an earthy sexuality about your sign, you are determined to enjoy yourself (and to go on enjoying yourself)—with the perfect partner, of course.

If you've been hurt by the breakup of a relationship, a divorce, or the death of a partner, it becomes serious in a different way. You fear making a mistake or you fear being alone. Security and sensuality will be important to you all your life, but when you are dating make sure you don't concentrate too much on the material or the physical assets of your date, to the exclusion of other good qualities.

Your Taurean personality gives you great power to create successful partnerships. Use it in a positive way. Don't be afraid to let things build up slowly in the beginning of a relationship. This is one area of your life where it is often a good idea to hold back and let events take their course.

TAURUS DATING TIPS
- Be a good listener as well as a good lover.
- You status-conscious Taureans, don't always insist on going to the latest "in" place to eat.
- Avoid placing too much importance on appearance and first impressions. Get to know what's behind that pretty face or sexy body.

Creating Greater Success . . . in Family Ties

Home and family are extremely important to most Taureans. It's all part of the security you crave and wish to provide. At times you can be as domesticated as a Cancerian, or as proud of your loved ones and possessions as a Leo. You are kind, generous, and extremely hospitable and excel in cooking wonderful gourmet meals for family and friends.

However, to be more successful in this area of your life, you do need to overcome your preoccupation, even obsession, with the material side of family ties. Providing and being provided for on a material level are necessary, but they are not the be-all and end-all of creating the right balance in family ties. Money cannot buy love. Sometimes you are just a little too enthusiastic about providing everything you can, and consequently miss out on having the right emotional and intellectual communication with your nearest and dearest.

All too often, when divorce cases get messy, you drive a hard bargain over some particular asset, even when there is plenty to go around. The most successful way for you to establish happy family ties is to pay more attention to the emotional needs of your family than to the material ones.

TIPS FOR SUCCESSFUL FAMILY TIES
- Keep in touch with elderly relatives, preferably by visiting them.
- Let your kids grow up with the gift of feeling emotionally secure with you, and don't let them place too much importance on presents.
- Don't be too hard on other family members who don't fit in with your idea of what they *should* be like.

Creating Greater Success . . . at Work

To maximize success at work, be as determined, motivated, and ambitious as you naturally are. There is no doubt that you can be extremely successful if you're a typical Taurus. You are prepared to put in long, hard hours working at something you strongly believe in.

Because you are a fixed Earth sign, your attitude can be fairly uncompromising, and it is important not to be stubborn and obstinate all the time. You want to be paid well for your efforts. You want to feel secure and not be laid off during an economically difficult period. It is important that you show you are indispensable through thorough and methodical work—and your willingness to compromise.

You hope to feel you have accomplished something worthwhile in your working life, and to be recognized for it. You already know the value of persistence in trying to achieve your objectives, especially if it takes a long time. It took many years for the Taurean Barbra Streisand to be praised by the rest of Hollywood for her talents as a singer, actress, and director. Her determination made it happen in the end.

Not all working Taureans can become the heads of multi-million-dollar companies, but they can be perfectly happy and fulfilled with work to which they are committed. Fortunately, not every frustrated Taurean ends up like Hitler, Machiavelli, Saddam Hussein, or Eva Peron.

If you really want to become more successful at work, the following do's and don'ts will be a guide for you:

DO . . .
- remember that a step-by-step process is often the best way for you.
- be open to advice and feedback from those you respect.
- make sure you have a well-organized working environment—you feel more secure that way.

DON'T . . .
- get into a flap if your routine has to be altered.
- spend too many hours at your favorite lunchtime restaurant, even if it is a business appointment.
- dig your heels in and refuse to budge if you know deep down you're on the wrong track.

Creating Greater Success . . . in Finding the Right Job

Before an interview, make sure you know as much as possible about the position. Look for an opening in a profession that gives you financial security and a chance to build a solid future.

Many Taureans turn to real estate, banking, stock-broking, economics, hotel management, and, of course, building and construction. You also have a great love for the arts. Often you have inborn managerial capabilities, so look for a position that will give you the opportunity to develop these skills.

One of the most important things a Taurus must remember in looking for the right job is that you need to feel comfortable with the goals you set, and with the means you decide on to achieve your goals.

Create Greater Success . . . in All Your Relationships

Relating well to other people is always important in order to be successful in life.

TAURUS AND ARIES

The fiery enthusiasm of Aries may sometimes exhaust you, but it may spur you on to achieve more than you dared hope for. Aries is the initiator of great things; you Taureans sometimes hold back too long.

TAURUS AND TAURUS

Two set-in-their-way Bulls! You are a patient, dependable, methodical pair who won't set the world on fire, but will certainly achieve considerable success by sticking to tried and true methods and adding a little extra flair.

TAURUS AND GEMINI

The air-ruled Gemini thrives on mental stimulation, so don't take forever going over ideas and plans. You need to be faster off the ground to keep up with Geminis, as they lose interest very quickly.

TAURUS AND CANCER

Aims common to you both are attaining financial security and sustaining a good home life. Both of you can be stubborn. A bull-headed Taurus won't get very far pushing an ultraemotional Crab on any sensitive issues.

TAURUS AND LEO

You are both fixed signs—steadfast in ideas and opinions. Since Leo likes to be the star of the show, and since you don't mind taking second place as long as you feel good about yourself, relationships between you two can work out fine.

TAURUS AND VIRGO

Virgo is known as the "sign of service," and you're pretty used to taking care of people yourself, which gives this relationship the potential for good teamwork. Make sure you don't throw a temper tantrum, though, if Virgo is one hundred percent accurate about your faults.

TAURUS AND LIBRA

Basically this should be a harmonious relationship, whether the parties are family members, colleagues, or love partners. Both ruled by Venus, you both enjoy the beautiful things of life. Make sure you don't encourage each other to be too lazy and laid-back.

TAURUS AND SCORPIO

Since opposite signs generally have something to learn from each other, this combination can be interesting. Both of you are passionate about the sybaritic side of life. Both of you are determined to fulfill your ambitions. But remember that you can both also be manipulative and jealous.

TAURUS AND SAGITTARIUS

Don't be too set in your ways or carry on about being depressed over world issues if you are to have any kind of relationship with an optimistic and outgoing Sagittarian. Never be too possessive with this adventurous Fire sign.

TAURUS AND CAPRICORN

Since you both often have similar material aims and an interest in being empire builders, you can expect to have a lot in common with the Mountain Goat. But both of you will have to put some effort into saying what you really feel and revealing some of your emotional needs to make this relationship work.

TAURUS AND AQUARIUS

Taurus loves routine, Aquarius adores the unpredictable. As both work mates and lovers you could have problems dealing with each other's time schedules. Learning to adjust is the name of the game here.

TAURUS AND PISCES

It's great to be a successful romantic duo, but in more material matters you will need to pass on some of your practical organizational skills to the sign of the Fishes. Pisces will teach you to be more sensitive to other people's feelings.

Becoming a
More Successful
Gemini

GEMINI

If you entered this world between May 21 and June 20, you were born under the sign of Gemini. This is the third sign of the zodiac—a masculine, mutable, positive Air sign ruled by Mercury, the winged messenger of the gods. Your planetary symbol is the Twins.

Mercury, the planet of communication, is your ruler, and you are the communicator of the zodiac. The ability to create ideas and translate them into viable projects is an integral part of your personality. Mercury's influence makes you brilliantly communicative on most subjects. You make your points succinctly and clearly; Gemini hates to sit still, and when the rest of your body is still, your hands express your feelings.

Since you were born under the sign of the Twins, there is a certain duality about your nature. Some people may even describe you as having a Dr. Jekyll and Mr. Hyde personality. This may be extreme, but you do have a tendency to flit from subject to subject without a second's pause, to cram a million and one things into each and every day, and to leave out important tasks because you are not well organized. To create a more successful life for yourself, you need to establish some sort of pattern to your existence. I'm not suggesting that you make routine your mainstay, though, for if I did, you would probably stop reading this chapter right now!

Each sign of the zodiac relates to a different area of the body, starting with the head and ending with the feet, from Aries to Pisces. You probably won't be surprised to know that the hands, the nervous system, and thus the brain are closely related to Gemini, as is the power of speech. It's no coincidence that using your hands to emphasize a point is second nature to you. A Gemini's mind is always active, so going to sleep isn't always easy. Marilyn Monroe, George Bush, Joan Collins, Barry Manilow, Brooke Shields, and Donald Trump are an interesting group of people born under your sign.

You Geminis have far too great a tendency to go off at a tangent, not bothering to complete one sentence before you move on to the next. It's no wonder that at the end of the day, you can't fathom where the time has gone, and why you still have a myriad of tasks to complete. It is important to channel your energy and your mind to concentrate on one thing at a time. Successful Geminis learn to harness their energy and minds to become more effective communicators. Otherwise you could become neurotic and begin waving your hands in the air when setbacks occur.

Everyone's definition of success is likely to be different. A typical Gemini's definition is sure to change frequently, according to his or her frame of mind at the time. The truly successful Gemini is one who knows how to focus. This is one of the most important abilities for you to cultivate. It's not always easy, but it can be done. I know a very successful Gemini TV producer and director who is extremely disciplined about locking himself away—not literally, of course— to finish his work. He even goes so far as to instruct his wife not to accept any social invitations for him until his current work is done. Once he has completed his tasks, he will return to his social and gregarious self. You have nothing to lose and everything to gain when you concentrate on what is important.

Defining Your Goals

*T*hough communications-adept Geminis would probably be wonderful talk-show hosts, not every Gemini longs to be a media star, best-selling author, or salesperson of the year. But you are loaded with ideas. This section will show you how to turn ideas into achievements.

How to Achieve Your Emotional Goals

It is often difficult to pin down Gemini men and women and get them to define their emotional goals. Hearing this question is one of the few occasions when Geminis stop talking and think seriously about what they do want. For you as a Gemini, being in a mentally stimulating environment is essential. Watch out, though, because although you are brilliant at communicating your thoughts and ideas, listening is quite another thing. Sometimes you may *think* you are listening but in reality let the words go in one ear and out the other. That is no way to be successful in building relationships.

You are certainly a "thinker" rather than a "doer." You are convinced you are a master of reasoning, and that you behave appropriately even in the most awkward situations. Emotionally, however, life is sometimes complicated for you because it is difficult for you to understand your own feelings, so it's hard for you to see why other people may fail to grasp what you're really about and find you difficult to "read." If you're not careful, you come across as too flip and superficial.

Some of you are inherently fearful of losing control, and are concerned that your actions will lead to later regrets. To avoid dealing with these issues you tend to rely on your puzzling persona to remain an enigma to those potentially nearest and dearest to you. To become more successful emotionally, discover and define yourself by your innermost emotional needs. No matter how mentally stimulated and successful you are by your work or financial accomplishments, it's unlikely that you will feel totally fulfilled without some equally stimulating love interest in your life. I have never yet met a Gemini who did not want emotional fulfillment, even if you do not always admit it right away.

Anyone who has ever been involved with a Gemini will already be well aware that deep down you are often terrified of a long-term romantic commitment. If the mental stimulation flies out the window, the relationship can falter.

Though many Geminis marry, some more than once, you seem to be on a continual search for someone who will truly understand your Peter Pan personality.

EMOTIONS AND THE GEMINI WOMAN

You may like to pretend you don't have particularly deep emotions, but you do; it's just that you don't like to reveal them. You cover up your difficulty in showing your feelings by pretending that you don't have them.

You are easily carried away by first appearances. There is also a childlike quality in your attitude toward love. You search for someone who stimulates your mind, who sets your heart ablaze and brings excitement into your life. You don't necessarily think of the practical issues. As a result, you may become involved too easily with people who are already committed to other relationships, and your own life becomes complicated. You may put your own marriage at stake, allowing flirtations to get out of hand because of a need for extra excitement in your life. Astrologers always bring up Marilyn Monroe as a prime example of a Gemini woman who lost herself in romantic entanglements.

I have known Gemini women who have suffered desperately from a love relationship gone wrong. This is because when they become involved with a fascinating man, they use their Mercurial minds to talk themselves (and their friends) into focusing on the most interesting part of the relationship. They somehow manage to ignore that he is married, living with someone else, or perhaps just playing games.

To be successful in love, face the realities. Avoid giving the impression you are an incorrigible flirt, or that the idea of a steady relationship conjures up images for you of a life filled with nothing but housework. Try to accept the duality in your personality—this thirst for excitement and stimulation combined with your need for someone to love and cherish you forever. It's not necessarily easy to find everything you want in life. As the the social butterfly of the zodiac, make sure you don't spend too much time flitting from one likely partner to another, playing mind-games with every one of them, then deciding far too late that none of them is perfect enough for you on a long-term basis.

EMOTIONS AND THE GEMINI MAN

A social butterfly, that's you. You always have an eye for a pretty face and a personality that challenges your mind. The best way to get you interested is to keep you guessing, for once you become totally sure of someone you have a tendency to become bored and want to move on to a new conquest.

If you're prepared to be totally honest, you will admit that the idea of a total commitment is often extremely daunting to you. Corresponding with your Peter Pan image—the little boy who didn't want to grow up—you tend to keep a youthful appearance and personality throughout your life: John F. Kennedy and Barry Manilow are examples of this. Not only do you look youthful, you often play childish games too.

It is important to choose a partner who can keep pace intellectually with your alert and active mind, who has a similar sense of humor, and who will be prepared to put up with your need to feel inwardly free.

To become more successful, you need to make an effort to show that you *do* possess deep emotions, even though they may be hidden away. It's strange that someone who is brilliant at discussing and debating issues can also find it hard to express heartfelt feelings. But it's never too late to let love empower you to say what you feel.

Like Aquarius, another Air sign, you appear to think that falling in love should be hidden away, or is easier for men born under the more passionate Fire signs of Aries and Leo to demonstrate.

You are a wonderful man to have a flirtatious dalliance with, for it is almost impossible to become bored with you. I've often thought you'd make an ideal long-distance lover, provided you were faithful. In such a relationship, you would thrive on the renewed mental and sexual excitement when reunited. You would be very good at calling and writing during the time apart, too—the fax machine could have been invented just for you!

However, there is no reason you can't make any relationship mentally and emotionally exciting all the time. For the typical Gemini, virtually everything in your life is a product of your own mind—a mind that tends to be at war with your emotions. Why not start to lighten up by letting love into your life.

How to Achieve Your Material Goals

When you are serious about achieving your material goals, you will stop at nothing to ensure success. You are not necessarily motivated purely by financial desire, although you certainly expect to receive what you deserve. And you are not discouraged by failure. An example of this phenomenon is the Gemini Donald Trump: He received unbelievably adverse publicity for his major financial problems, but this spurred him to fight to come out on top once again.

You are the sign of communication and the master of the fast line. You are perceptive, inquisitive, and highly observant. This allows you to keep up with the latest business news. You probably also use the latest software, and keep all the technological advantages at your fingertips to help you achieve your material goals.

You consider yourself rational and reasonable in virtually everything you say and do, and you sometimes find it hard to believe that not everyone else sees you the same way. Although you are a brilliant "ideas" person, you often have too many ideas whirling through your head at the same time. This may lead you to waste a great deal of time going round in circles, rather than in taking concrete steps toward your goals. You must learn to harness that restless Gemini mind. Take a tip from Taurus, the sign that precedes yours, and establish some routine in your life. It could be amazingly beneficial for someone as restless and scattered as you.

To become more successful, plan a sensible daily schedule and resolve to follow it. Start by organizing your thoughts. Divide a blank sheet of paper into three columns (or put it on your computer screen). In the first column jot down your aims and ambitions; in the second, your current involvements; and in the third, your priorities. You are often prevented from fulfilling some of your aims and ambitions by leaving yourself with insufficient hours in a day to do everything. Take another sheet of paper, and write down the priorities from the first paper. Try not to spend quite so much time on other "current" involvements until these priorities have been dealt with successfully. Make at least three copies of this second page; keep one at home, put one in a prominent position on your desk, and give one to an assistant or secretary, if you have one. You will find you can achieve a whole lot more when your energies are less scattered. Careful planning also means you will still have time enough to rest your active Gemini mind and enjoy a social life, too.

The Powerful Assets at Your Disposal to Become More Successful

The Power of Your Element . . . Air

Gemini is the first of the three Air signs, Libra and Aquarius being the others. Gemini is also a mutable sign (mutable is defined as "subject to change" and "inconstant"). The key-words for the Air signs are "mentally active" and "communica-tive." You have these qualities in abundance. It is up to you to use them in the right way to achieve success. You like to con-sider yourself "free as air," but be sure that you do not become a jack of all trades and master of none.

Influenced by Air, you can be very hard to pin down, which is frustrating for those who have to conduct any kind of business with you. You may see yourself as logical, but in fact you can be very unreasonable and even superficial in the way you deal with people and issues. As the sign of the Twins, it seems your Air element is blowing one side of you one way, and the other side another way. Organizing yourself better will eliminate this effect, and allow you to achieve greater success.

It is beneficial for you that Gemini is also a positive sign. This makes you spontaneous and expressive, with the ability to project enthusiasm in the way you deal with daily issues.

The Power of Your Ruling Planet . . . Mercury

Mercury, winged messenger of the Gods, is the planet repre-senting speech, communication, and commerce. Mercury in Gemini empowers you to be talented in all three of these.

Mercury moves faster than all the other planets, and its planetary power helps you to move through life in your own speedy fashion—all mental agility and nervous energy!

Your ability to speak at least one foreign language; your determination to keep up with the latest on-line computer technology, enabling you to communicate with the world at large in the fastest possible way; and your innovative ways of dealing with daily plans and projects are all given a big boost by Mercury. As a Mercury-ruled Air sign, you are a mentally alert human being. This all sounds wonderfully positive, but sometimes you tend to think far more than you feel. We all know you can also be brilliantly intuitive, but revealing your deepest feelings to others is often difficult for you. It can also be hard for you to empathize with other people's ways of thinking and feeling.

Since Mercury is the planet of communication, don't you think you could make more of an effort to communicate on all levels? Sometimes you come across as superficial, interested only in the light, frothy, and amusing side of life. Or you give evidence that your Jekyll and Hyde aspect is no figment of someone else's imagination, but in fact is near the truth.

Mercury brings a big bonus to your life. It adds a twinkle to your eyes, and a sparkle to your voice. It will also help you to move like greased lightning when time is of the essence. Mercury helps you invent new ideas and projects with flair, and reinvent others with a fresh approach. But don't sit back and let ideas flow through you. Be prepared to get out there and prove you can be successful in all the areas of your life, not just as an idea person.

The Power of Your Rising Sign

Your Ascendant, or rising sign, is the sign that was rising on the eastern horizon at the time of your birth. In many ways it is as important as your Sun and Moon signs.

The table on pages 278–79 will help you determine your Ascendant sign. Here are some short examples of how different rising signs influence your Gemini personality and enable you to be more successful.

GEMINI WITH ARIES RISING

The headstrong Arien influence makes you a real go-getter with the ability to talk anyone into just about anything. To achieve maximum success in life, it's vital to follow through on your ideas, rather than let Arien impatience influence you.

GEMINI WITH TAURUS RISING

A Taurus Ascendant gives you the ability to stay focused on all your projects—an admirable asset! It could make you somewhat stubborn, too. But you usually have no problem getting your ideas across to others.

GEMINI WITH GEMINI RISING

Help! Does double Gemini ever stay still? Your alert and agile mind and ability to communicate with almost anyone on almost any subject makes you an intellectual powerhouse. However, you need to devise an organized schedule to stay on target.

GEMINI WITH CANCER RISING

Cancer rising gives you a gentleness and love of home and family. A need for domestic security means you pursue relationships on a deeper emotional level than many Gemini people. But you can be moody if you don't get your way.

GEMINI WITH LEO RISING

There is something regal about you. Your determination to become more successful is combined with an inner knowledge that you have the ability to be so. With a Leo rising you are quite brilliant at publicizing yourself and your talents.

GEMINI WITH VIRGO RISING

Heaven help anyone who tries to criticize or analyze you. You are brilliant at summing people up, assessing every situation, and getting straight to the point during arguments. But don't be too abrasive with your comments.

GEMINI WITH LIBRA RISING

A double ration of the Air element here, this is a powerful combination of cool appraisal and calculated assessment. The only source of problems is that you may become doubly disorganized and indecisive when quick decisions are called for.

GEMINI WITH SCORPIO RISING

A massive dose of intensity of purpose and deep, deep emotions summarize a Gemini with Scorpio Ascendant. Your personal magnetism will go a long way to show other people that you will not give up on your beliefs. But don't be too possessive of anyone or anything.

GEMINI WITH SAGITTARIUS RISING

You should be a brilliant opponent when mind-games are played, with your opposite sign of the zodiac as your Ascendant. Make sure you don't become careless or too judgmental in your appraisal of others. You could have a tendency to think you know all the answers.

GEMINI WITH CAPRICORN RISING

Capricorn Ascendant enables you to become totally focused on your ideals and ambitions, once you have defined their importance in your life. You have to work hard on showing your deepest emotions to those you truly care for.

GEMINI WITH AQUARIUS RISING

The Air combination again. You could be an intellectual dynamo, but your interesting plans and projects must be turned into reality once you have thought them up. Endless discussion of all the finer points could mean you never get down to work.

GEMINI WITH PISCES RISING

The Pisces influence is humane and compassionate. It's wonderful to have humanitarian ideals and to want to make the world a better place, but don't be too much of a dreamer. Avoid spending too much time on impractical ventures and keep your spending under control.

How to Create Greater Success

Creating Greater Success . . . in Your Everyday Life

If you're a typical Gemini, the thought of structure and organization in your daily life is likely to bring raised eyebrows and a look of disdain to your face. In spite of your lack of interest in these qualities, cultivating them will allow you to achieve greater success in life. It is a great asset to be a brilliant conversationalist, to be a master of the fast line, and to be perceptive of and receptive to what takes place in the world around you. But be prepared to accept commitment when necessary, and don't give other people the chance to accuse you of being a flighty butterfly of the zodiac just because you are a Gemini! You must shed some superficiality and become a better listener.

The following checklist will give you some pointers on how to create a more successful regime without completely altering your Gemini life.

DO . . .
- try to give yourself a workable daily schedule.
- resolve to concentrate on one issue at a time.
- make a vow to finish what you start.
- be scintillating and challenging, but a little more sensual and seductive too!
- show more awareness of and interest in other people's needs and desires.
- try to delve deeper into life's mysteries, not simply skim the surface.

DON'T . . .
- take an overly superficial view of people and things.
- Be *too* much of a social butterfly.
- Be fickle, flirtatious, and fun-loving when it's time for serious work.

- refuse to stick to routine when you know routine is necessary.
- take shortcuts to success when there is hard work to be done.
- let your mind continually battle with your emotions!

Creating Greater Success . . . in Love

Since you are ruled by that little winged messenger of the gods, Mercury, planet of communication, love is often an interesting challenge for the typical Gemini. It is difficult for your relationships to survive if you do not find them mentally stimulating. The flush of first love with a childhood sweetheart can lose its sparkle if the two of you do not share similar interests and aspirations. Sex alone is rarely enough to keep the typical Gemini involved in a relationship. You need compatibility of minds and a shared direction. But I'm afraid I have to lecture you at this point: You sometimes do not appear to be sufficiently concerned about your partner's needs in your relationship.

I've often heard from my Gemini clients that relationships make them feel claustrophobic. However, many of you also tell me how much you *do* appreciate and enjoy a good relationship in your life. The more effort you put into making something work, the better it will turn out. Be kind, caring, and loving, not superficial and emotionally cool.

Creating Greater Success . . . in Dating

If there is any activity most suited to a typical Gemini it has to be dating! You have no hang-ups when it comes to chatting up someone you fancy, and no insecurities about your ability to charm the birds off the trees, so you are rarely turned down.

This is all very well, but if you want that first date to become the first of many, you must address some of your shortcomings and not simply bask in the glory of your communication successes. You tend not to take sufficient time to get to know your companion. All too often you become bored fifteen minutes after meeting someone new. Your eyes wander around the room, possibly looking for someone even more fascinating and interesting. Physical attraction can be immediate, but it takes longer to get to understand another person's mind.

GEMINI DATING TIPS . . . IN CASE YOU NEED ANY!
- Concentrate on one person at a time.
- Take the necessary time to get to know your date.
- Don't continue to play the field if you've met someone you feel is a soulmate, mentally *and* emotionally.

Creating Greater Success . . . in Family Ties

To maintain a good relationship with any member of your family it is important for you to understand each other. You have to admit that you are not always the easiest person in the world to get along with. You tend to insist on a fair amount of freedom in your life, which makes you hard to pin down. If intellectual communication is lacking, you do not have a great deal of patience or tolerance. For example, you may be responsible for something going wrong, and still want family members to go along with your idea of how things should be. You must fight your intolerance, which leads you to discount others' opinions.

It may be hard for you to come out with loving words and actions, almost as though you feel it is a weakness to show too much emotion. You may consequently come across as excessively cool and aloof. You cannot deny you have emotional needs, and by the same token you know that other members of your family also have their own needs. Even if your family is scattered over the country, and even if you do lead a very busy life, try to keep in contact. The art of communication *is* your forte, so endeavor to start communicating on all levels.

TIPS FOR SUCCESSFUL FAMILY TIES
- A kiss or a hug can work wonders after misunderstandings.
- Aim for a total understanding with your kids, so they don't hold anything back from you.
- Don't be ashamed to show that your emotions are just as deep and strong as those of any other sign.

Creating Greater Success . . . at Work

A maxim Geminis often use is "I think, therefore I am." To be more successful at work, it is important to say "I think, therefore I do." All too often you have brilliant ideas whirling around in your mind, but find that putting them into action is a challenge.

Your primary motive isn't necessarily to make big bucks from your work. You consider yourself an idealist, but your coworkers may think of you more as a highly talented, restless jack-of-all-trades who doesn't always succeed in your objectives. Don't downplay the need to earn a good living wage, for you invariably like to spend money when you have it.

Becoming more successful requires becoming more steadfast in your determination to conquer your chosen field. Don't put off till tomorrow what you should be doing today.

You are often very serious about what you want to achieve, even if you are not highly ambitious or power-hungry. You are brilliant at putting across your ideas and inventions, but are inclined to put your creative energies and talents into too many different endeavors. You often do not focus on one particular idea long enough for it to bear fruit.

Always try to work in an environment you find mentally stimulating, with as many like-minded peers and colleagues as possible. Also, choose a field in which you are strongly interested. I have a friend who found it hard to settle down for a long time. One of his many projects was even climbing Mount Everest! Now he is not only contented but also successful, combining his love of the outdoors with his Gemini ability to make people feel extremely at ease in his company, organizing walking tours in Le Marche, a beautiful part of Italy.

The following do's and don'ts provide a guide for you to become more successful at work.

DO . . .
- appreciate the value of a daily schedule.
- resolve to concentrate more on the matters at hand.
- take heed of other people's ideas, not just your own.

DON'T . . .
- be a Dr. Jekyll and Mr. Hyde in your business dealings.
- have too many occupations or projects in the pipeline at once.
- be too changeable and unreliable in your daily life.

Creating Greater Success . . . in Finding the Right Job

Perhaps the most obvious thing to say at this point to any Gemini is, never take a dead-end job involving something you find unutterably boring. It really would be hard for you to stick to it. Look for something that offers you variety, where your ability to communicate and project yourself is valued.

Many Gemini men and women are attracted to working in the media. You make wonderful journalists, advertising executives, copy writers, and publicists. You may also be brilliant at dealing with stocks and bonds, if your powers of concentration do not slip!

There truly is no one to surpass you as a salesperson, whether you are selling your own talents and abilities to a prospective employer or selling a company's product to others. If you focus on the job in hand, greater success will be on the way.

Creating Greater Success . . .
in All Your Relationships

One of the most important factors in a successful life is relating well to other people. Even though you are an adaptable, free and easy Gemini, you can still benefit from a few tips on how to relate to those around you.

GEMINI AND ARIES

While there is no doubt you will stimulate each other mentally, and perhaps physically, at times the Arien sense of urgency may be a little too much for the more laid-back and commitment-shy Gemini.

GEMINI AND TAURUS

Sensible, practical, and patient Taurus. You have plenty to learn from the Bull, but whether you're prepared to stick around long enough to do so depends on you. Just remember that even Taurean patience runs out when the duality of your sign becomes too irritating.

GEMINI AND GEMINI

Gemini talks, talks, talks about everything under the sun, but whether either of you can truly listen to the other is probably more to the point. This can be a successful relationship if you bother to find out just what makes your counterpart Gemini tick.

GEMINI AND CANCER

Because Cancer is a far more sensitive and emotional sign than you, it's important for you to become more in touch with your own feelings and instincts for any relationship to work between you. Cancer probably thinks you're much too erratic in your restless, frenetic way of life.

GEMINI AND LEO

On a social level this can be a successful team. However, you may not appreciate Leo's somewhat bossy behavior. You will need to make this clear if you work together. Remember, Leos can be vulnerable—that's why they need lots of praise.

GEMINI AND VIRGO

To be successfully compatible with this sign, you will need to organize yourself better at home and at work. Virgo is the sign of the critic and analyst and finds it hard to put up with anything less than perfection. You both have good minds.

GEMINI AND LIBRA

Astrologers often say that you two Air signs make an ideal team. To be really successful, make sure you understand each other's aims and aspirations. Geminis need to be less scattered in their objectives and Librans less indecisive in theirs.

GEMINI AND SCORPIO

Scorpio brings an air of mystery into your life, but it will be difficult for you to handle the Scorpio intensity and powerful emotions. Creating a successful relationship will involve your being far more passionate about people and projects than you tend to be.

GEMINI AND SAGITTARIUS

They say opposite signs attract, so perhaps here you have met your perfect match on every level. You will both need to commit yourselves more deeply to the things you believe in, and to stop trying to change the world before working on your own faults.

GEMINI AND CAPRICORN

If you listen to Capricorn's good advice on practical matters, you could be well on the way to greater success. Maybe you can even persuade the Mountain Goat to take a little time off from work to have some fun. That way you offer each other something positive and complementary.

GEMINI AND AQUARIUS

Aquarians invariably make for very good friends of Geminis. You will have plenty to talk about with this extroverted and unpredictable sign. To sustain a successful relationship, you will both need to structure your lives better.

GEMINI AND PISCES

Since both of you tend to go off in too many different directions at once, it may be hard for you to relate. However, you have a lot to learn about sensitivity and empathy from the Fishes—and this will help you get on better with all the other signs.

Becoming a
More Successful
Cancer

If you were born between June 21 and July 21, you were born under the sign of Cancer, the fourth sign of the zodiac. Cancer is a feminine, cardinal, negative Water sign. You are ruled by the Moon, and your planetary symbol is the Crab.

Like the Crab, you are hard-shelled and soft-centered. Under your surface, you are sensitive and vulnerable, sometime carrying your wounds within you while you comfort others. But there is definitely a toughness about you that helps you to overcome problems and satisfy your need for material security and success.

You are often accused of moodiness, and it is true that your moods can be somewhat like the ebb and flow of the ocean tides, which is perhaps not surprising, for your ruler, the Moon, rules those same tides. The wise Cancerian knows that when those moods start to take you over, you are best left alone. You get over them so much better that way, like the crab scuttling into its shell to hide away, coming out when it knows the time is right.

Whereas Gemini, the sign that precedes yours, is a thinker, you are a feeler. This is why you are usually soft, sympathetic, and ultrasensitive. You strongly feel emotional pain, for yourself and others. You are also quick to empathize with others, and you care about what goes on in the world around you.

To capitalize on your Cancerian personality in the most successful way, be aware that your caring attitude, one of your most positive traits, can also make you possessive. Also, the thought of separation, from a person or job or even from a house, can be extremely hard for you. But you must let go. The successful Cancerian knows that hanging on too long can be detrimental in certain situations.

Each sign of the zodiac relates to a different area of the body, starting with the head and ending with the feet, from Aries to Pisces. Cancer rules the breasts, stomach, and digestive system. If you find that your stomach is sensitive, it is very important for you to maintain a proper diet. Note also that inches can increase far too quickly around this area of your body—a problem for all you Cancerians who are very fond of food and love to show off your culinary skills. Equally important, though, is not becoming overly sensitive about this, so that you do not go to any extremes such as bulimia and anorexia.

The caring and compassionate aspect of your sign, together with your ability to psychically attune yourself to the atmosphere around you, increases your chances for living a successful life. Elisabeth Kübler-Ross, the Dalai Lama, and Princess Diana were all born under the sign of Cancer. Creatively, you are able to see others with a deep poetic vision. The subtlety and genius of the Cancerian painters Rembrandt, Modigliani, and Chagall prove this point.

You are fortunate in having the Moon as your ruler, as she helps to make you receptive to your deepest feelings, adding to your feminine, maternal, and nurturing instincts as well as your inborn ability to heal others. You also benefit from a wonderfully retentive memory: you remember details from the past that many other people have forgotten long ago. To be successful, avoid being distracted by daydreams or by cluttering up your mind with memories that you should let go.

Every person has a different definition of success, but if you are a typical Cancerian, your ideal way of life will combine the perfect domestic setup with an ideal job situation. You like to be involved in a very close-knit unit, whether it is at home or within a company. However, your habit of clinging to the past can hold you back in both your domestic and professional aspirations, unless you are firm with yourself.

Avoid your tendency to become too smothering of other people by not allowing them to think for themselves. Try not to sink into a depression if things are not going the way you would like. The successful Cancerian recognizes the importance of accepting that everyone has up and down moods and difficult days. You yourself will benefit from taking a positive view of life, especially since in your heart of hearts you know you have the ability to make your mark on the world.

Defining Your Goals

Not all Cancerians can be a princess like Diana, own an airline like Richard Branson, or paint masterpieces like Chagall and Modigliani. But I'm sure you have some goals of your own that you would like to fulfill! As long as you are grounded in reality, there is no reason why you will not achieve them. Your Cancerian personality with its powerful imagination and strong instincts will be an extremely important influence in your path to achieving your goals. Of course, I won't promise you that by developing your intuitive nature you are going to pick the right numbers for Lotto, or win a world cruise from a raffle ticket. Once you have defined your personal goals, however, this book will guide you in the right direction to achieve greater success, whether your aims are of an emotional or material nature.

How to Achieve Your Emotional Goals

Emotional goals are of paramount importance to a typical Cancerian. Your goal may be to have a perfect one-on-one relationship with someone special, or simply to refuse to allow yourself to be ruled by your moods. But whatever it is, if you do not feel emotionally secure within yourself, it is often hard for you to be totally fulfilled in the other areas of your life, no matter how successful you appear on the surface. Your sensitivity will be a great bonus provided you do not allow it take over to such an extent that you wallow in self-pity or creep into your shell if someone upsets you.

However, knowing what your emotional goals are can be a stumbling block for you. Because you are so motivated by your feelings, and because you sometimes find it hard to be objective about life, you are occasionally extremely unclear about what you are searching for. By tuning more deeply in to your heartfelt emotions, you will understand yourself a whole lot more and start to change your behavior patterns. You are brilliant at caring for others, but you do not necessarily know the best way to care for yourself.

You have an incredible depth of emotional feelings, which can be a great asset too. There are times, however, when you become amazingly self-centered, your attention directed far too strongly toward yourself. Keep the balance between illusion and delusion so you don't lose sight of what is going on around you. It is good to be able to nurture others in your caring and protective way, but don't try to control them.

To achieve emotional success, try to overcome your possessiveness. Attempting to gain a tight hold on others can easily turn them against you.

No matter what your emotional goals may be, resolve that you will not become so overly dependent on other people that you cannot perceive the relationship clearly. Don't create a self-imposed prison for yourself or try to rule others because of your own emotional needs. Resolve that you will break any negative or overly possessive habits. This will allow you a greater sense of freedom, which will make you an even stronger person emotionally.

Your emotions are powerful, and no one can deny that your maternal and paternal instincts are amazingly strong. Your character is also strong, for just like Aries and Capricorn you are a cardinal sign, which carries the attributes of being ambitious and having great drive and initiative. Once you truly accept your strength you will find it unnecessary to be so self-protective and cautious.

I have noticed that many Cancerians are fearful of commitment in the initial stages of a relationship. Conversely, they may fear the loss of someone or something even when it is no longer right for them. Listen to your intuition when it tells you it's time to move on.

Direct confrontations are not always easy for you, but you may need to have one with yourself to establish your emotional goals. Don't keep crawling back into your shell, Cancer; turn those daydreams into realities.

EMOTIONS AND THE CANCER WOMAN

If you're a typical Cancer woman, how you deal with your emotions will often depend on how you spent your formative years. If you were a loved and cherished daughter it will be much easier for you to allow your own sensitive feelings to flower in relationships. But if you had a tough time when you were growing up, you learned to hide your feelings at an early age, and now it is harder for you to open up and trust another human being. Learn to think of tomorrow as another day, and not to feel so controlled by those past experiences.

In many ways, you are one of the most feminine of all women, and very adept at marshaling your feminine wiles to captivate someone who appeals to you. This may be why so many people are surprised to discover that inside you may feel inadequate and unsure of yourself. While you want all the good things a loving relationship can offer, your Cancerian personality can make you overly fearful of rejection. You usually try to compensate for this fear by coming across as cold and moody. To be successful in love you must remember that sulky moods and possessiveness are big turn offs to most people. You often don't realize you are doing it, and since deep down you are soft and sympathetic, it would probably mortify you to know you could be guilty of such behavior.

You adore being in love and are one of the most loving people around. But greater love comes to those who don't wear their hearts on their sleeves. Once you learn to appreciate yourself more for who you are, it will become much easier for you to sparkle and shine without feeling inadequate. Be tender without being tenacious; this will lead to more successful emotional relationships.

As a Cancerian woman you need someone to cherish and adore, and you expect others to want the same. You also need someone who appreciates your wonderful domesticity and natural ability to be a fantastic mother to your children. Your natural mothering instincts may, however, be overwhelming to prospective partners looking for an equal and not a parent.

You are skilled at handling money because of your need for financial security. Thus, it may be difficult for you to fall for someone who is not particularly well off. You are more than willing to do your share of hard work, though, when you know you have met the right person.

Because you are so concerned about other people's problems, you sometimes make them your own. Be compassionate, but remember there is only so much you can do. While being overly protective about others, don't neglect your own vulnerability and emotional needs.

Your feelings may be fragile, but you are fabulously intuitive. Don't be clinging when circumstances require you to present a cool exterior, or moody when your partner has something important to do. Forget about past hurts. Resolve not to make someone feel guilty if a relationship comes to an end. Concentrate on the good things in your life.

EMOTIONS AND THE CANCER MAN

I have sometimes gone so far as to say that what the true Cancerian man needs in his emotional life is a second mother. It has certainly been interesting to discover that the wives or lovers of certain Cancerian men I know had a great deal in common with their mothers, and sometimes have almost been younger look-alikes.

The Cancer man likes to be nurtured and protected from the problems of life by the perfect partner. Your mother is usually a great influence on your life from babyhood onward. Many Cancerian men have strong mothers, or mothers who do insist on mothering their sons considerably after they are adult men. Think of Cancerian Sylvester Stallone, whose mother makes it very clear what she thinks the woman in his life should be like. Stallone's ex-wife, Brigitte Nielson, is also a Cancerian. Two Cancerians together are not likely to make for an easy relationship unless they truly understand and accept each other's needs.

Regardless of whether or not your relationship with your mother has been difficult, try not to allow this motherly influence, which may lead to insecurities, to affect your own emotional relationships. I have always felt that it is very important for a Cancerian man to resolve any "mother problems" before embarking on his own relationships. There is something of the mothering influence in male Cancerians as well as female. This is because you are a feminine Water sign, affected by the cycles of the Moon.

While you are not necessarily the most physically passionate of signs, you enjoy snuggling up in bed with the person you love, feeling that you are safe in your little nest. You will fare better in love when you don't give way to the touchy, moody, and ultrasensitive side of your personality. It can be awfully boring for your partner and certainly takes some of the excitement out of your relationship.

The typical Cancerian is an excellent husband and father. Because you are caring and kind, you do not usually shirk your responsibilities; you manage to have a demanding career and a good family life. However, you may be very demanding in the fulfillment of your own emotional needs, and you have to learn to be less selfish. Your partner requires more from life than simply being your partner and mother to your children.

You are often attracted to people you know are not right for you and are likely to hurt you. It is almost as though your subconscious wants to be hurt and to experience your emotions, including suffering. It is so necessary for the Moon-ruled Cancer to balance your fluctuating emotions and not creep into your shell. You have to admit to yourself what you are feeling, as well as come to terms with what you want out of your life. Therein lies the answer to fulfilling your emotional goals in the best possible way.

How to Achieve Your Material Goals

Even though you are a Water sign, there is certainly nothing wishy-washy about a Cancerian when it comes to practical goals. Those of you who are determined to succeed need very little advice. You inwardly sense the way to move ahead. You manage to control your emotions, even if you are perhaps sometimes seething inwardly.

Your idea of material success is not necessarily purely financial, although it is almost always related to your own idea of security. Typical Cancerians cannot bear the thought of having to live in situations that do not fulfill their need for comfort, whether this means acquiring a mansion or simply a one-bedroom apartment. Their home must be comfortable.

To attain success, you must willingly accept that you too easily display the moody side of your personality. If you don't like working in a certain atmosphere or among certain people, you will have to work harder to achieve a position in which you can call all the shots yourself. It is no use moaning about what you do not have if you are not prepared to do something concrete about it. I have found that some Cancerians are a little too adept at moaning when they should be going full steam ahead, showing they believe in their projects from the drawing board onward. This diffidence often stems from insecurity; once you have overcome it, there is no one more tenacious than you in your determination to rise to the top. Becoming more successful for you means being more secure both financially and emotionally. Within all of us there is something of our opposite sign that influences us. Hard-working Capricorn is the sign that opposes Cancer. You often work as hard as any Capricorn, and I can think of several Can-cerians who stay to work late in their offices when everyone else has gone home.

However, you Crabs sometimes create a somewhat too con-voluted route to your destination. You invariably move side-ways to avoid dealing with situations that may be best faced head-on.

The Powerful Assets at Your Disposal to Become More Successful

The Power of Your Element . . . Water

Cancer is the first of the Water signs, Scorpio and Pisces being the remaining two. The quality of Cancer is cardinal, which relates to enterprise and initiative. Born under a cardinal sign, it is not surprising that you are full of ideas and aspirations, but it is important that they don't get washed away in a sea of emotions.

Your element Water empowers you to follow your feelings strongly, to listen to your instincts and intuition. Where a Gemini thinks out situations, you feel them.

Try not to let a conflict develop between the soft, watery, sensitive side of your personality, and the side that yearns for greater power and success. The greatest success in your life can be attained by balancing your ideals and aspirations with acquiring greater self-knowledge and by accepting your par-ticular strengths and weaknesses.

Your Water element has blessed you with a caring and understanding nature. Combined with your intuitive side, this can lead to great success. It can guide you to flow with life's natural patterns, and show you a way of escape when you know something is wrong. This is why it is important to listen to those instinctive feelings but not to become carried away in fantasy or illusion when you want to believe something that you really know is not good for you.

The Power of Your Ruling Planet . . . the Moon

The Moon governs the tides of the sea and relates to birth, motherhood, and the nurturing side of your personality, and influences you to the very depths of your being. The Moon affects your unconscious state, your emotions, instincts, and habits. The Moon's twenty-eight-day cycle corresponds to a woman's menstrual cycle. Cancerians' moods fluctuate along with the phases of the Moon.

It is a powerful asset to have this planet as your ruler. To make it work in your best interest it is important to learn a little about the phases of the Moon, even just to make sure you know when it is new or full. Perhaps you have already discovered that you tend to feel more energized at the time of a new Moon, or somewhat moody and even depressed when it is a full Moon again. There should be nothing surprising about this, for the Moon affects your mood swings in the same way as she affects the tidal ebb and flow of the seas. When you choose to maximize your potential, it is a valuable asset to know when it is best to go full steam ahead, and when it is better to put something off for another day.

The Moon's influence adds to your allure, mystique, and the feminine side of your nature. This is not usually difficult for women Cancerians to understand, but it is sometimes hard for a man born under your sign to accept. Realize that there is nothing "weak" about having this feminine part in your personality. Men, this element sharpens your instincts and feelings in an extremely positive way.

Amazing displays of inspiration, a fertile imagination, and an abundance of creativity are all bestowed upon you by this planet. It enables you to see below the surface of a situation, and to protect the people and possessions you care for.

You are a sensitive soul, and often a very private one, too. Your ruling planet will certainly open your eyes and your heart to inspire you to greater heights. Listen when it silently tells you that you must fulfill your emotional and domestic needs.

The Power of Your Rising Sign

Your Ascendant, or rising sign, is the sign that was rising on the eastern horizon at the time of your birth. In many ways this is as important as your Sun and Moon signs. The way you play out your life is very much influenced by this rising sign.

In the table on pages 278–79, you will be able to determine your Ascendant sign. Below are some short descriptions of how you as a Cancer will be affected by the twelve different rising signs, and how they can help you to be more successful:

CANCER WITH ARIES RISING

Cancer and Aries are both cardinal signs, so you are more forthright, enterprising and outgoing than many other Cancerians. You are also more argumentative. Don't let your Aries ascendant overwhelm your sensitivity too much.

CANCER WITH TAURUS RISING

A Taurus Ascendant makes you even more domesticated and security-conscious than is normal for Cancerians. Working hard does not bother you, but don't indulge in too many moody spells just because you are in an excessively stubborn frame of mind.

CANCER WITH GEMINI RISING

Cancer feels while Gemini thinks, talks, and gets on with things! Hopefully your Gemini Ascendant helps you move ahead faster to get some of your ideas off the ground.

CANCER WITH CANCER RISING

Sweet, sensitive, and wonderfully compassionate, or moody at the slightest excuse—it's up to you, Cancer. You benefit from a double ration of instinct and intuition, and there is no stopping you in the success stakes if you use these powers wisely.

CANCER WITH LEO RISING

Wanting to be a star is one thing, believing in yourself whole-heartedly, knowing you will succeed, and charting your course is another. Your Leo ascendant enables you to confront rivals with the knowledge that you definitely have what it takes.

CANCER WITH VIRGO RISING

Please don't be moody and worry too much about things. That is definitely not the way to become more successful. The bonus of a Virgo Ascendant is that your powers of analysis and criticism can be wonderful assets when combined with your intuition.

CANCER WITH LIBRA RISING

A certain amount of Libran indecision is to be expected here, but make sure you are not too laid-back in how you deal with people and situations. Your diplomacy and charm can be an asset, and you will have an ambitious streak.

CANCER WITH SCORPIO RISING

A Scorpio Ascendant highlights your deepest emotions and gives you a need for privacy, especially when you are in a down mood! An intensity of purpose means your ambitious streak is show-cased. Your determination to succeed should not be ignored.

CANCER WITH SAGITTARIUS RISING

There is a happy-go-lucky attitude about you, and you have a much more open approach to life than the typical Cancer. Mood swings won't bother you too much, and you are more inclined to take a few risks if it means you can climb higher up the ladder of success.

CANCER WITH CAPRICORN RISING

With your opposite sign as your Ascendant, you have an even greater desire than usual for financial security and status, as well as a need to establish and maintain good traditions and a good family life, You don't mind working hard if it enables you to achieve your aims.

CANCER WITH AQUARIUS RISING

You don't fit into the textbook definition of a Cancerian. You are far too unpredictable and unconventional for that. There may be a stubborn quality along with those mood swings, but the Aquarius Ascendant tones down your ultrasensitivity.

CANCER WITH PISCES RISING

Definitely a Watery combination! Make sure you don't drown in a sea of emotions, losing sight of all those dreams you want to turn into reality. It is important to retain a practical viewpoint and not let your heart rule your head in business.

How to Create Greater Success

Creating Greater Success . . . in Your Everyday Life

Typical Cancerians share with your opposite sign, Capricorn, the ability to be structured and organized in your daily life. There is an amazing determination within your soft and sensitive Cancerian soul that enables you to work extremely hard. Often you combine a high-pressure career with being one of the most domesticated people in the zodiac.

However, your sensitivity is the one area that may let you down. You are far too prone to react to slights or disagreements by creeping away or becoming overly touchy and moody.

To become more successful in your everyday life, remember that everyone does not possess such fine-tuned sensitivity as you. While you are solicitous and protective of other people, you often find it extremely hard to be more protective of yourself. Try not to give way to any unnecessary feelings of self-pity when someone or something upsets you. The person upsetting you may be going through something difficult of their own and probably has no intention of hurting you. The tricky situation you may face has not been put there just for *you.* And if it is tricky, there are always ways to overcome it. Try to be more positive whenever one of your negative feelings takes over. Don't saturate yourself with your own emotions.

If you consider yourself worthy of greater success, yet through no fault of your own it eludes you, read the following checklist to get some pointers on how to create a better daily regime, without completely altering your Cancerian ways.

DO . . .
- try harder to control your fluctuating moods.
- be more optimistic about life and you will become more positive, too.
- use your imagination and instinct to help yourself get ahead.
- be kind, loving, and protective, while giving others their freedom.
- learn to find a sense of security within yourself as well as outside.
- make good use of your wonderful memory.

DON'T . . .
- be too touchy, defensive, or moody.
- crawl back into your shell rather than face up to things.
- hoard too many memories from the past.
- fill your home or office with things you never use.
- be overly possessive with family and friends.
- lose your sense of humor if a joke is directed at you.

Creating Greater Success . . . in Love

Because you are ruled by the Moon, your emotions have the utmost importance on all levels of your life, and especially in the area of love.

Love is everything to a typical Cancerian, whether it is love for your parents, husband, wife, lover, or children—and even if it is purely a love for people who need your help. Elisabeth Kübler-Ross is a perfect example of a Cancerian who embodies all the powers of caring and loving in her pioneering work with the fatally ill.

However, you do have a tendency to allow negative emotions to take over, especially when you feel unrequited in love. To be more successful emotionally, you must resist your innate tendency to try to enclose the object of your affections in your little world. Never make yourself—or another person—a prisoner of love! It won't help you to have successful relationships, as it can turn people away. You are blessed with wonderfully protective and caring ways, but make sure they don't turn into possessiveness of someone who needs to feel mentally free, even if they do adore you. It is important to make sure that emotional insecurities do not cast any unnecessary dark clouds over your relationships, especially on those that are founded on genuine mutual love and trust.

To be really successful in love, make sure you continue to grow as the unique individual you are. Don't lose yourself in love, no matter how wonderful that love may be.

Creating Greater Success . . . in Dating

Dating does not necessarily come easily to a somewhat shy and sensitive Crab. In your earlier days, you were probably the one who really disliked going out if the main object was to meet someone new, while all your friends were enjoying every minute of the dating game. Often you prefer to be formally introduced by someone else, perhaps to meet over a dinner with mutual friends, rather than to make the eternal round of singles bars or parties, hoping that Mr. or Ms. Right will appear.

The Cancerian personality may sometimes come across as somewhat cool and uninterested, when in reality this reserve is a cover-up for shyness. You can overcome this reticence by developing greater belief in yourself and what you have to give. Try not to sidestep questions you feel are an intrusion on your privacy, if they are simply a way of allowing someone interested in you the chance to know more about you.

And if you find yourself having to date all over again owing to the breakdown of a marriage or long-standing relationship or because you are bereaved, remember to utilize your powerful intuition. With this advantage at your fingertips, you should find it fairly easy to recognize a soulmate when one appears.

CANCER DATING TIPS
- Be a little more lively when you're supposed to be having fun.
- Be receptive to what (and who!) may be waiting there for you.
- *Don't* start trying to hem him or her in after the very first date.

Creating Greater Success . . . in Family Ties

Your home and family are extremely important to you if you are a typical Cancerian. By far the best way for you to keep up a good relationship with virtually any member of your family, whether a partner, parent, or child, is to make sure you don't suffocate the person with your desire to give your best.

When Cancerians become parents themselves, it often happens that your strong desire to take care of your offspring results in an inability to allow them to become adults. Naturally you want to protect them from any dangers and negative influences of the modern world, but being overly protective is doing them a disservice.

It is also important to remember that family ties can be extremely strong without living in each other's pockets. If you have family members who live far from you, it is useless to feel guilty if you cannot see them as often as you would like. There are always the mail and the telephone! You should never stop caring, but your expression of caring sometimes needs to be modified in order to fit individual circumstances.

To create more success in all your family ties, it is necessary to have understanding relationships on all sides. You need privacy, and you must accept it if any of your relatives feel the same way. Things cannot be one-sided, and the trouble with being a Cancerian is that you tend to go into a sulk if someone doesn't understand you. You must realize that some of your own little habits and foibles could be irritating to others, just as theirs can be irritating to you.

TIPS FOR SUCCESSFUL FAMILY TIES

- Make sure that your strong maternal or paternal instincts don't make you hold on to your kids far too long.
- Give your love and affection freely, without expecting something in return.
- Don't bring up memories of the past every time you're with other family members.

Creating Greater Success . . . at Work

I never fail to be amazed by how many domesticated, home-loving Cancerians are also highly motivated by their work and are extremely ambitious. Bill Cosby is a very successful businessman, as well as a top entertainer and family man. Rose Kennedy was the matriarch of the Kennedy family and continued to hold high ambitions for her family until her death. And while writing this chapter I read that Cancerian Sylvester Stallone had just negotiated for himself one of the highest-paying movie deals ever.

Just like your opposite sign, Capricorn, when you set your sights on something, your ambitious streak sends you hurtling along in the direction of success. Your instinct is a fantastic asset in the workplace, but don't let your sensitivity to atmosphere and desire for perfection make you overreact to situations, or skirt around them when confrontation is necessary. Don't worry if a chosen career eludes you, for whatever reason, and you have to switch to something else. The important thing is for you to believe that you can and will be successful, for when you believe that, you're halfway there!

If you are a typical Cancerian, it is extremely important for you to be paid commensurately with your skills and talents. You don't necessarily mind starting off at a low level of pay provided you know your pay will rise. Financial security is incredibly important to you, often because you have a hidden fear of being left without enough food in the future. I'm not joking. Cancerians often equate security with being able to fill their stomachs— or, rather, the stomachs of their nearest and dearest. I'm sure that in the days of the Great Depression, it was the families of Cancerians who survived in the best way. You cannot bear to think of anyone going hungry. If it is true that we are what we eat, then you have a head start on the rest of us: You know that by staying healthy we can achieve even more in our lives.

It is always important for you to balance your working life with sufficient time spent in your home, among your family— with the people you love most. Try to make sure that you go back to a place where you feel comfortable at the end of the day. They say that a Leo's home is his or her palace; for a Cancerian, home is your safe nest, where you can be shielded from the outside world.

The following do's and don'ts will also provide a guide for you to be more successful at work.

DO . . .
- listen to your intuition when planning your strategy.
- make your workplace as comfortable as you can.
- try to relate well to colleagues but don't mother them too much.

DON'T . . .
- become power-crazy or overly ambitious.
- be moody and jealous if others are more successful than you.
- lose yourself in your work to the exclusion of everything else.

Creating Greater Success . . . in Finding the Right Job

One of the first things to remember when looking for the right job is that you really need to care about what you do. Don't go for something that would put you in a rut, with few opportunities for promotion and expansion.

Look for a position that will enable you to make the best possible use of your fantastic memory and your excellent knowledge of virtually everything that has ever interested you. Not every job opportunity offers perfect Cancerian surroundings, with water flowing nearby and a peaceful ambience with near-perfect peers and colleagues. But you will definitely find it easier to fulfill your potential in an atmosphere that can, in one way or another, be considered peaceful—at least *sometimes*.

You are excellent in caretaking and service occupations—being a doctor, nurse, hotel manager, day-care attendant, teacher, social worker, real estate agent, caterer, or personnel director. You would also be a good artist, actor, musician, banker, or antique dealer.

Because security is so important to you, you will enjoy working in any sphere that involves making other people's lives more secure.

Creating Greater Success . . . in All Your Relationships

One of the most significant factors in leading a successful life is relating well to others. While your Cancerian instincts and intuition are a big plus, you can sometimes be a little too moody for your own good. Here are a few tips on how to relate even better to the other signs:

CANCER AND ARIES

Fun-loving Aries may find it hard to put up with the ebb and flow of your moods. The Ram lives in the present and the future, so you will have to make more of an effort not to linger in the past. You're both pretty determined about what you want.

CANCER AND TAURUS

The Bull definitely yearns for security just as much as you, and the sensuality of Taurus is very appealing to a Crab searching for true romance and a comfortable domestic life. This may not be the most exciting relationship ever, but if you want it, go for it.

CANCER AND GEMINI

To have a good relationship with Gemini, resolve to keep your conversations interesting, somewhat intellectual, and never boring! Make sure you don't overindulge your sensitive emotions, for Gemini often wants to keep things light.

CANCER AND CANCER

Two caring, sentimental Crabs together might sound like bliss. You might never get anything done, though, because you would be too busy empathizing with each other, or hiding away from the outside world in an oasis of domesticity.

CANCER AND LEO

Leo will enjoy being pampered and praised by you—for a while, at least. But avoid being too servile in your desire to care for and protect Leo. And resolve not to be too sulky and emotionally vulnerable when the Moon is full, as Leos don't have too much patience.

CANCER AND VIRGO

Both of you enjoy feeling that you make worthwhile contributions to the world. If you can do it together, that's great! Both of you are perfectionists, but your desire for material security may irritate Virgo, who will also be very critical if you are ultrasensitive.

CANCER AND LIBRA

Two very loving signs, both of whom appreciate being cared for and caring for others, too. Try to be more patient and understanding if Libra is slow to make decisions. Home and family are important to both these signs, but don't smother Libra with your possessive ways.

CANCER AND SCORPIO

Although you are both Water signs, there could be a big power struggle here. You enjoy the passion and intensity of Scorpio, but must resolve not to let emotional insecurity make you too jealous and tenacious. The latter reactions could cause Scorpio to run away from you.

CANCER AND SAGITTARIUS

You can learn a lot from the optimistic and free and easy ways of the Archer. But you will need to control your mood swings successfully if you want to build a lasting relationship.

CANCER AND CAPRICORN

You have a lot in common with your opposite sign, both being ambitious in your material and financial aims, and in appreciating tradition. Don't wear your heart too openly on your sleeve, for Capricorn can be much tougher than you.

CANCER AND AQUARIUS

If you don't expect an Aquarian to be anything other than unpredictable and unconventional, you can often be pleasantly surprised. Keep in mind that too much sappy sentimentality will drive this Air sign wild, as Aquarians prefer to keep deep emotions out of sight.

CANCER AND PISCES

Too many romantic dreams and not enough practical common sense could infuriate you when dealing with a Piscean. But if you really learn about each other's personalities and accept the other's capabilities, this could be an interesting duo in all sorts of ways!

Becoming a More Successful Leo

LEO

If you were born between July 22 and August 21, you were born under the sign of Leo. Leo is the fifth sign of the zodiac, a masculine, positive, fixed Fire sign, ruled by the Sun. Your planetary symbol is the Lion.

On the surface you are amazingly flamboyant and full of charisma, with a sunny and sparkling personality that makes you one of the easiest signs to guess. Male Leos sometimes sport a beard, almost always possess a powerful head of hair, and are definitely determined to look as attractive as possible for as long as possible—George Hamilton, Arnold Schwarzenegger, and President Bill Clinton are Leos. The hair of Leo ladies often resembles a lion's mane in its beauty, thickness, and appearance. Jacqueline Kennedy Onassis was the epitome of a well-groomed aristocratic and ambitious Leo lady with an abundance of charm.

The true key to who you are perhaps lies below the surface of your magnetic and flamboyant Leo personality. I think that when you become excessively outgoing and self-centered it is really only a cover-up because you would hate anyone to find the slightest trace of weakness in your dynamic personality. Underneath, you are often almost as much of a child as Aries, the first of the Fire signs, sharing a vulnerability and insecurity that makes you yearn for praise, and even sometimes demand it.

Leo is considered the sign of show business. Just think of some of those extroverted Leos, who even if they are not consciously searching for the limelight always seem to attract it: Madonna, Sean Penn, Roman Polanski, Robert De Niro, Arnold Schwarzenegger, Whitney Houston, and Mick Jagger. Can you imagine any of them being born under a different sign?

Each sign of the zodiac relates to a different area of the body, starting with the head and ending with the feet, from Aries to Pisces. Leo rules the heart, spine, back, and circulatory system. To cut down on your risk of heart disease, it is very important for you Leos to watch your cholesterol intake and not to overdo things.

Since the heart is ruled by Leo, it is not surprising that you are such an emotional person. You thrive on giving and receiving love, and you are one of the most warmhearted and generous signs around. This is one of your greatest assets in the success stakes, as it enables you to charm almost everyone with whom you come into contact.

If you are typical of your sign, you have a deep-rooted need and desire to prove to the rest of the world you are a bright and shining star. You have an incredible sense of pride, but if you really want to become more successful, bear in mind the saying "Pride goeth before a fall." Sometimes you become almost too demanding, and risk losing your popularity by insisting on being praised from morning to night. To make more of a success of your life, try to accept that you cannot always be in center stage, even if you do consider the position rightfully yours. I've often noticed with Leos that you seem unhappy when left out of a conversation, or if someone else is being praised rather than you! Success involves learning to step back sometimes and allowing other people to have their moment. Leo Andy Warhol said that *everyone* should have his (or her) fifteen minutes of fame.

There is also an extremely positive side in the way you consider yourself worthy of being a star, rather like a self-fulfilling prophecy with which you were born. To be truly successful and stay that way, it won't hurt you to practice a little humility once in a while.

If you're a typical Leo, there's an indolent side to your nature. Bursts of enormous energy when you are totally involved in something may be followed by periods of inertia, when you are happiest doing very little. If you want to keep up the momentum and be successful, you must balance your days. Don't sulk or indulge yourself in self-pity when things don't go your own way—that is definitely not the behavior expected from a bright and sparkling Leo.

Defining Your Goals

Naturally, not every Leo is destined to be a famous movie star, a President, or First Lady. You may not want to own a Beverly Hills mansion, your own private jet, or a fantastic yacht to take you around the Caribbean or Mediterranean. But it is typical of your sign to desire luxury in one form or another. You want your home to be your palace for you are the regal ruler of the zodiac. You invariably love gold, status symbols, designer clothes (even if your income dictates that they be copies), and dining out on gourmet food.

How to Achieve Your Emotional Goals

A world without love is a pretty sorry world for the average Leo. Most of you positively thrive on romance and are happiest when giving and receiving love. Your emotional goals reflect your need for an ideal partner who complements you in every way. Deep down you yearn for someone you can love, worship, and adore. But unfortunately, sometimes your own inherent need to be admired and praised can be exhausting for anyone involved with you.

Many Leos can be childish emotionally, demanding love as their rightful due. Don't be too insistent where love is concerned, nor allow the lazy side of your personality to prevent you from demonstrating your affections, and you will be rewarded with a great deal more success in this area of your life.

Leo is the fifth house of the zodiac, which is the house of love affairs and children. This is why you are so emotional, and are at your best when your emotional feelings are fulfilled. Since Leo rules the heart, it is not surprising that words such as "heartfelt" and "heart-warming" tend to fit so well into your vocabulary while also suiting your personality. You truly give from the heart. In fact, often you give so much you end up feeling drained.

Greater emotional success can be yours when you understand your personality better. As a fixed Fire sign, isn't it true that you sometimes hold on too long, or blow hot and cold in a romance? Are you too bossy and domineering? Do you sulk when praise doesn't come your way? Are you perhaps guilty of indulging a sometimes inflated ego? These are all common Leo faults, even though you are prone to deny them. Sometimes you are not certain of your emotional needs, although you know emotional success is extremely important for you to feel completely evolved as a Leo. Achieving this will be helped by balancing the plus and minus sides of your makeup.

Emotional success doesn't always come when you want it, which is a problem for typical Leos who subconsciously feel it is their due. But often you don't work hard enough to achieve it. You're a sparkling, playful party goer with a heart of gold, who on a bad day can easily turn into a domineering bore if you feel your need for admiration is not fulfilled. It's not that you are a selfish person. It's simply that sometimes you can't be bothered to do something for yourself if there is a loving person around to do it for you.

Leo is also the sign of creativity and show business. To achieve and maintain emotional success, though, you need to be more than a star: To keep your audience and your friends you must be as loving offstage as on. This means stepping down occasionally from your number one position and admitting that even the regal ruler of the zodiac has faults and vulnerabilities.

EMOTIONS AND THE LEO WOMAN

I used to think Leo women had it easier than anyone else in the emotional stakes. You possess a joie de vivre that makes you a woman who receives the kind of attention normally reserved for movie stars and princesses. You are wildly romantic and amazingly imperious and usually possess a great sense of humor. You can also be one of the most elegant hostesses in town.

Surprisingly, in my years of counseling clients and writing astrology books, I have discovered that many Leo women have a problem sustaining successful relationships. This is because you have failed to understand your Leo personality.

The typical Leo woman truly wants to love and be loved. You also desire to be a star, and prefer to dominate than be dominated, no matter how much you respect the object of your affections. This can lead to problems, because while you yearn for a strong partner, your own strength can sometimes be off-putting. You like to give orders but usually hate receiving any.

Often this means that you end up with a partner weaker than you, someone who may be happy to consider you a prized possession and put you on a pedestal to worship you but who fails to live up to your romantic expectations that love makes the world go around.

The fixed quality of your sign means you don't necessarily like to be given advice, or even listen to your own intuition. Sometimes you even marry the same partner more than once, hoping your initial problems can be overcome the second time round—as the Leo movie actress Melanie Griffiths did with Sagittarian Don Johnson. On the other hand, the Leo actress Helen Mirren has managed to continue a highly successful career, much of it in England, while enjoying a successful relationship with the director Taylor Hackford, who lives mainly in Los Angeles. To be truly successful emotionally, you must work hard for what you want. Don't just sit back and fool yourself into believing that simply because you were born under that most romantic, magnanimous, glamorous, and fascinating sign of the Sun, life will always be wonderful. It may not be, for strangely enough, Leos may be considered lucky in love by a lot of people, the opposite may be much nearer the truth.

The power of your Leo personality is not to be underestimated. There is a dramatic quality about you, even if you pos-

sess not the slightest drop of acting blood. Because you are flirtatious, capricious, yet possess deep emotions, you will throw
yourself wholeheartedly into a love affair, only to be bitterly
disappointed if it does not live up to your expectations—not
realizing that this may can be your own fault. You tend to be
attracted by what you see on the surface. Good looks, physical
compatibility, and, dare I say it, the possibility of financial
security with someone prepared to pander to your every whim
can be all too important to you.

I've often joked to female Leo friends that what they really
need is someone to boss them around a little—to get them to
scrub the kitchen floor, or to make them give all their baubles
and beads to charity. This may not go down too well with
you, though. But to attain greater emotional fulfillment, it is
immensely important for you to accommodate your deepest
emotional needs and not simply to those that relate to material things. Madonna may enjoying singing the lyrics to
"Material Girl," but does she sometimes feel lonely at the end
of the day?

As a Leo woman, you long for someone on whom you can
bestow your love. But don't forget the importance of respecting your partner for who he is, and not solely because of what
he can offer you. Love, respect and financial security can all
flow beautifully together. As an example, think of the Leo
Jacqueline Kennedy Onassis, who after two marriages, which
must at times have been far from easy, was able to spend the
last years of her life with a companion who obviously adored
her and also allowed her to be her own person.

You are a very powerful and positive Fire sign with a very
big heart. Within your character is the ability to achieve
extremely successful emotional relationships. A great deal is
up to you—you must convince yourself of your ability. There
is vulnerability within us all, but somehow it is difficult for
you to face up to your own. You often prefer to gloss over
past mistakes, since being unsuccessful in anything, espe-

cially in love, is something you hate to consider as one of your possibilities!

EMOTIONS AND THE LEO MAN

Romance is probably never too far from the mind of a Leo man. Sometimes you wear your emotions on your sleeve, or shining out of your eyes, just a little too obviously! There is an almost childlike glow of happiness in an emotionally fulfilled Leo man. On the other hand, just think about some of those Leo men mentioned earlier in this chapter—President Bill Clinton, Robert De Niro, Mick Jagger, Roman Polanski. I wouldn't say they have necessarily found it easy to "have and to hold, cherish and obey" the loves of their lives.

If you're a typical Leo man, I'm afraid you are terribly easily flattered. It's almost as though, no matter what profession you're in, you need groupies around you to tell you that you're a truly wonderful person, a fantastic lover, and that the world would be a duller place without you.

Your ego often creates problems for you. To become more successful emotionally, you need to stop pampering that Leo ego quite so much and focus on emotional relationships that will balance your life on every level. Then you won't feel the need to have constant confirmation that you are someone special, because you will believe in yourself on a deeper level. Interestingly enough, while you often come across as extremely self-involved and convinced that you too are worthy of presidential attention or of the publicity achieved by Arnold Schwarzenegger, you are just as vulnerable as the Leo woman. Your major pitfall is often your pride, and yet once you can overcome this, and admit that you are vulnerable emotionally, you become infinitely more successful. Try to forget about your image and think more about what your instinct tells you to do in order to achieve the best in your life.

From personal experience with my own Leo partner, I know that underneath all the show and bravado, you are one of the most warmhearted and loving men in the whole zodiac. Unabashed and playful, you are able to turn at a moment's notice from a roaring lion into a playful pussycat, wanting to do your very best for the love of your life.

There is a larger-than-life side to your personality, and your mental and physical energy is unbeatable. However, if you scatter your energies here, there, and everywhere, you will find you don't even have enough to give to yourself. Emotional maturity easily eludes you, although it is the one element you need to enjoy your life to the full. Although many Leo men are thought of as playboys—the sort of men who enjoy having fun and playing the field—there are just as many of you who are longing to settle down with a soulmate who is not there just to bolster your ego.

Your emotional success is all up to you, Leo. As the sign ruled by the Sun and possessing such a loving heart, you certainly have a great deal to give in a relationship. The best kind of partner for you is one who is self-sufficient and not too dependent on you; this will create a much better balance in your life.

How to Achieve Your Material Goals

If you are truly determined to achieve your material goals, which definitely involve attaining a fairly luxurious lifestyle in one way or another, then perhaps the most important advice I can give you is to warn you against overindulgence, overextravagance, overachieving, and sometimes even overconfidence! If Shakespeare's definition of the world as a stage where the men and women on it are merely players is true, then it is not difficult to imagine the only role available for you is as the star of the show! Of course, when you're in a good mood, those other players become like an extended family, but when you are not, they may be treated rather more like servants!

You sometimes make unnecessary problems for yourself by being unduly dictatorial and domineering. You are convinced that center stage is the only true position for you, but don't forget that you are also the proud possessor of an extremely generous and warmhearted personality that allows you to care about other people. Trying to be in the limelight all the time will also work against you, as it will be extremely exhausting and deplete your creative energies. It may also cause the very people whose help you need most to turn against you.

Success for you means not only achieving something you are proud of but also basking in a whole lot of glory; success requires other people singing your praises, both to your face and to others. I'm not being unfairly cruel to you Lions of the zodiac, I'm just stating the astrological facts. No one should ever doubt your prowess in the leadership stakes, although you need only to think about Leos such as Napoleon, Mussolini, and Castro to see what can go wrong when humility flies out the window and center-stage dictatorship takes over. As the regal ruler of the zodiac, Leo is a born leader, so when you do set your heart on achieving something there is a strong determination in your makeup that makes you an extremely powerful contender for success. I'm just asking you not to become a tyrant at the same time.

Strangely enough, for someone who can be such a committed overachiever, there is a side of you that never thinks you are good enough. You can be as self-critical and analytical as any Virgo, which is why you appear to need continual praise for your efforts. The thought of failure may be so horrendous to you that you overcompensate with arrogance and a tendency to boast about how great you are.

Learn to have greater inner belief and faith in your prowess and abilities. You are without doubt one of the most creative signs in the whole zodiac. It is important for you to learn and appreciate the value of working with others as part of a team and to share your center-stage position with others whom you respect.

The Powerful Assets at Your Disposal to Become More Successful

The Power of Your Element . . . Fire

The four elements, Fire, Earth, Air, and Water, all have a great bearing on Sun-sign characteristics. Leo is the second of the Fire signs, Aries and Sagittarius being the other two.

While Aries the Ram charges into battle, fighting to the end for its beliefs, Leo the Lion tends to roar loudly and wait, hoping that his position as king of the zodiac will command the respect due a leader. For you there is a lazy side that you must overcome.

It is the Fire element that produces in you the courage to accept challenges with optimism and vision, and to aim high in your ideals. At the same time, this fiery side of your personality encourages a negative tendency to be dictatorial, so that you give orders when you have no right to do so and treat colleagues, family, and friends in a tyrannical way simply because they do not bow to your will. With most Leos this is a rarely manifested side to your personality, since basically you are a loving and lovable Lion at heart.

Your Fire power enables you to look ahead with enthusiasm, to survive defeats with a smile, and to lead others into new fields. You demonstrate a bravery that enables you to start afresh when ventures fail and when your creative talents need to be redirected toward new channels. Use this fiery power wisely! Don't overreact if your Leo pride is wounded, and don't bitterly strike back if someone does get the better of you.

Try to avoid roaring if your ideas, ideals, and opinions some-times fall on deaf ears. Others have the right to that center-stage position sometimes too, so it will be to your political advantage to stand in the wings once in a while.

While your fellow Fire signs, Aries and Sagittarius, will argue vehemently to prove a point, many Leos tend to hate argu-ments. You are invariably convinced that you are right and that discussion is pointless. The trouble is that you seem to hand out orders that must not be disputed or disobeyed.

One way in which you resemble Aries is that like Ariens you are a child at heart—but try not to be a child who bullies all the other kids on the block when you don't get your own way. Prove that you can be magnanimous as well as magnificent, and you will be even more successful in life.

The Power of Your Ruling Planet . . . the Sun

The Sun as the cosmic masculine life force represents the wholeness of being and the power of self-integration. With such a powerful "planet" as your sign's ruler, it is not surpris-ing that you possess such a bright, shining, and charismatic personality. It endows you with a sunny disposition that makes it easy for you to be adored by others, and also enhances your warmth, passion, and enthusiasm for life. Depending on the details of your birth chart, it can, however, increase your desire for admiration and acclaim. Sun worship has existed throughout the centuries as a religious tradition, and on a lighter level perhaps this is yet another reason why so many of you feel the need to be worshiped yourselves. But don't forget that the Sun also scorches and burns, and its power needs to be carefully harnessed to avoid danger. It is important for you to respect and recognize the power con-tained within yourself.

Because the Sun is such a vital life force, its power as your ruling planet can never be underestimated. It truly will enable you to succeed where others have failed; and to explore new avenues creatively and with dynamic flair. The Sun influence ensures that you will stand out in a crowd, even on those rare occasions when you prefer to wait in the wings.

Your image and your sense of identity are given full rein by the Sun, and its strength enables your creative energy to flow through you with intensity. To cultivate the power of your ruling planet in order to become more successful, you need to focus on tasks that are for your highest good. This will prevent you from succumbing to lower temptations that can lead you into vanity, ostentatiousness, and an insatiable need for power.

The Power of Your Rising Sign

Your Ascendant, or rising sign, is the sign that was rising on the eastern horizon at the time of your birth. In many ways it is as important as your Sun and Moon signs in determining how you live out your life. Using the chart on pages 278–79, you will be able to figure out your Ascendant sign. Below are some short descriptions of how your Leo personality is influenced by the twelve rising signs:

LEO WITH ARIES RISING
Your fiery personality is unmistakable. You want immediate success in everything you undertake, and you are unlikely to be a lazy Leo! Be sure your impatience doesn't make you too dictatorial.

LEO WITH TAURUS RISING
The stubborn side of Leo is magnified by the Taurus influence, so take care you don't upset people by insisting on having your way too much. Your determination to succeed at turning dreams into realities pays off handsomely with this combination.

LEO WITH GEMINI RISING

You definitely have what it takes to be a real star. Your dynamically regal Leo presence, combined with Gemini's inborn ability to talk your way to the top with confidence will create magical opportunities for you.

LEO WITH CANCER RISING

A flamboyant, extroverted Leo, with a somewhat introverted Cancerian side, especially at full moon—that's you! Your Cancer ascendant gives you sufficient sensitivity to ensure that you don't offend other people with your imperious ways.

LEO WITH LEO RISING

Being bossy, domineering, holding on tight to a center-stage position, but smiling so brightly that hardly anyone seems to object—could that be you? Don't let the negative side of your Leo personality hold you back when you aim to conquer the world!

LEO WITH VIRGO RISING

When you start to act larger than life and try to rule the world, your Virgo Ascendant grounds you and explains to you your faults in a brilliantly analytical manner—without making you feel insecure.

LEO WITH LIBRA RISING

The calm and measured Libran approach to life brings a perfect balance to your usual flamboyant and extravagant gestures. You don't rush into situations on the basis purely of what your heart tells you, and you will find partnerships beneficial.

LEO WITH SCORPIO RISING

You are more secretive and less outgoing than many other Leos, but very determined to achieve your ideals and ambitions. Just

watch out that Scorpio Ascendant doesn't make you too manipulative and scheming when you aim for greater success.

LEO WITH SAGITTARIUS RISING

Both Leo and Sagittarius like to do things with style, but this rising sign could make you more extravagant than usual. Try not
to be careless by taking too many risks when making important
moves or you could lose out on what you really want from life.

LEO WITH CAPRICORN RISING

A Capricorn Ascendant endows you with more of a traditional
and conservative view of life. It helps you to achieve greater
material success by toning down your tendency to go for glit-
ter and gold! Don't become too stubborn, though.

LEO WITH AQUARIUS RISING

With your opposite sign as your Ascendant, it's unlikely that
you would be a typical Leo, and your success could be assured
in an unconventional and unpredictable way. Aquarius adds
flair and inventiveness to your creative talents.

LEO WITH PISCES RISING

A Pisces Ascendant means you will be more romantic than
ever. It will also make you less domineering when climbing
higher up that ladder to success. Don't look at life through
rose-colored spectacles too often, for you can't afford it.

How to Create Greater Success

Creating Greater Success . . . in Your Everyday Life

Being successful in every walk of life is important to most Leos,
but your determination to be the star of the show often needs

to be toned down. Once you have the right attitude toward the way you face every day, everything will fall into place much more easily.

Interestingly enough, it is not always immediately obvious that within your warmhearted and sparkling personality lurks a dictatorial side. Often your orders do not even seem to be orders, when they're couched in soft terms as if you were only asking a favor. But anyone who gets to know a Leo well will soon learn that you expect your requests to be acted on, or else you expect to get a very good explanation. You make good leaders—General Norman Schwarzkopf was born under your sign. The Leo personality often contains the deep urge to rule. Leo is the sign of royalty. In England the Queen Mother, Princess Margaret and Princess Anne are all Leos. Queen Elizabeth II has her moon in Leo, and Prince Charles has a Leo Ascendant.

Notwithstanding all of this, it simply isn't going to be possible for you to maintain a tame audience of admiring courtiers around you all the time. Everyone has to go through periods of uncertainty and even rejection at one time or another. While this may go against your Leo pride, it can also be a growing process. Besides, if you truly know you are on the right track, does it really matter much if you are not continually complimented by others for your brilliance and great talent?

If you consider that you are worthy of greater success but that it eludes you through no fault of your own, the following checklist will give you some pointers on how to create a better daily regime suited to your Leo personality.

DO . . .
- try to become more sensitive toward other people when telling them what to do.
- retain your pride without demanding adulation.
- be more like a playful pussycat in some of your ways, and less like a roaring lion.

- share the limelight with others who may also deserve it.
- keep your sense of humor along with your dignity.
- enjoy the luxuries of life without being greedy.

DON'T . . .
- be too domineering, dogmatic, and dictatorial.
- demand instant recognition for your talents—work for it.
- be too extravagant, even if you are in a generous mood.
- patronize other people, especially when they show they don't appreciate it.
- be too much of a show-off . . . vanity could be your downfall.
- become a snob, even if you *are* a star!

Creating Greater Success . . . in Love

Although you cannot bear the mere thought of rejection, you are more likely to retire sulking than to fight to win your loved one's affections. It is best for you to be more realistic in the area of love, and to find mutually compatible partners. The power of love is never underestimated by the typical Leo, and what you want, you feel you have to have, even if it seems impossible. However, life isn't always forthcoming, even for royal Leos!

Love truly does make the world a better place for you, and the perfect partner/bed mate is often your greatest dream. A major factor in creating greater success in love for most Leos is your willingness to accept a partner as an equal. All too often your dream is to be passionately worshiped and adored by the love of your life and to passionately worship and adore him or her—but on your own terms. Although you enjoy the feeling of pride when your loved one is admired by other people, sometimes you place a little too much emphasis on appearances and don't take the time to make sure you are fulfilling your beloved's desires. Creating greater success in love means a lot more than orchestrating an elaborate seduction and romantic little getaways in exotic faraway places.

It is not that you are selfish, just that sometimes you can be so busy blowing your own horn that you forget about anything else. To be truly successful in love, you must love and appreciate your loved one as much as you love and appreciate yourself. Being in the limelight is wonderful, but sharing it with someone special can be even more life-enhancing.

Let your warmhearted and fascinating Leo personality shine through, but don't become too much of a show-off, caring only about impressing others.

Creating Greater Success . . . in Dating

The art of dating often comes naturally for the typical Leo, who is very much a social animal. With your outgoing personality, enthusiasm for life, and love of company, it should be no problem for you to have many dates clamoring for your company. However, sometimes your Leo ego can lead you into major pitfalls, since you find it hard to believe you are not totally irresistible. Getting a first date may not be a problem, but if you want the date to be the prelude of a good relationship, it's best to leave any signs of an overinflated ego behind.

When you want to make a wonderful impression on a date, there is no one more successful than you. You inspire confidence and come across instantly as sexy, warm, and full of fun. And there is no doubt that you are one of the most generous signs of the whole zodiac. But, remember to show interest in the world around you, and not just in *your* world.

LEO DATING TIPS
- Be affectionate, tender, and humorous, but avoid the tendency to be too self-centered.

- Be prepared to take time to get to know your date properly.
- Don't insist on taking the lead in everything right away.

Creating Greater Success . . . in Family Ties

Your home is always your castle when you are born under the regal sign of Leo. But if you genuinely want to successfully sustain good family ties, don't expect the rest of your family to attend to your every whim just because you feel you have a right to give orders.

If you are a typical Leo, you enjoy your relatives, particularly when you have the opportunity to play host or hostess at large gatherings. It's not that you are especially domesticated (some of you could do with a maid to pick up everything you drop carelessly to the floor!), but you are usually extremely well organized. If you keep notes of birthdays and anniversaries, it is unlikely you will ever miss an opportunity to throw a party and give wonderful presents, even if you are pressed for cash.

While you enjoy having a captive audience at family get-togethers, it is important to allow younger members of your family to come into their own, rather than expecting them to bask in your glory. You usually love children and are extremely demonstrative and generous to your offspring. Watch out that you don't overindulge them so that they end up spoiled.

You take great pride in your family and love having them around, although you need to guard against intolerance when their views oppose your own. Leo mothers often find it hard to deal with a glamorous daughter coming into womanhood, for then you start to worry about being overshadowed. The same can apply to a Leo father who feels he is getting past his prime and has a teenage son who is obviously adored by all the neighborhood girls.

TIPS FOR SUCCESSFUL FAMILY TIES

- Remember, the little things in life count. Show how much you care.
- Fit into your schedule what other members of the family want to do, even when it means taking second place.
- Don't be a prima donna, even when your pride is injured through being ignored!

Creating Greater Success . . . at Work

Cecil B. De Mille, Alfred Hitchcock, Henry Ford, John Huston, Lucille Ball, Coco Chanel, and Carl Jung were Leos who were successful in their fields. Not every single Leo can be this successful, but you can try! Don't insist on running before you have done the necessary walking. It is all very well for you to stamp your foot and assert that the only place for a Leo is at the top, but first you have to prove you are worthy of the *numero uno* position.

The best leaders are those who realize they are only as good as those who follow them. No matter how ambitious you may be to achieve greater success for yourself, don't forget that the ability to work in harmony with others is a great asset. You have masses of charm and creativity. Use these attributes to bring out the creative individuality of your peers and colleagues. This will inspire them to appreciate and respect you even more, and offer you the loyalty you hold so dear. Bill Clinton won the nomination to become President, but he has had a difficult time since then, perhaps because he has been too flamboyantly Leo in some of his ways, instead of realizing the importance of team spirit.

Team spirit is one of the most important factors in greater success at work. Make sure you praise other people when praise is due, remembering how much you thrive on it yourself. And don't let your creative drive flag by spending too much time on an extravagant social life, as you certainly don't want to give an impression of being lazy.

The following do's and don'ts will also provide a guide for you to become more successful at work.

DO . . .
- dress well—it goes with being a leader!
- work as hard as you expect others to work.
- be proud of what you do but never exaggerate its importance.

DON'T . . .
- try to be another Napoleon or Mussolini!
- neglect important tasks because you feel like having fun.
- behave like a star until you *are* one.

Creating Greater Success . . . in Finding the Right Job

It is wonderful to be the proud possessor of Leo's vitality, creativity and enthusiasm, but a little humility will help the typical Leo when it comes to finding the right job. Since you are extremely goal-oriented, seek a position that gives you the chance to make your mark on the world, even if it does not give you overnight stardom and an expense account. Go for professional opportunities that utilize your creative talents, for enterprises that put you in the public eye, and for positions with a work environment that makes you feel at home.

Try to make sure you really love what you do, for then you will produce the best results. Even if you feel that fame is more important than fortune, subconsciously you will expect fortune to come your way, too. Working on your own is not always easy for the typical Leo, as you need a fair amount of feedback and praise for your efforts.

Ideal Leo careers include show business—especially the movie world—fashion, art, big business, public relations, and almost any kind of high-level management.

Creating Greater Success . . . in All Your Relationships

One of the most important factors in being successful in life is developing strong relationships with others. You are definitely one of the most sociable and pleasure-loving of all the signs, and genuinely enjoy mixing with other people, but even bright and shining Leo can benefit from some extra tips on how to get along with others.

LEO AND ARIES

Two powerful Fire signs together means that sparks could definitely fly. One of you will have to take second place once in a while. The boundless enthusiasm of Aries will spur you to even greater creative heights.

LEO AND TAURUS

On the pleasure-loving aspect of life you almost have an equal here. But working with Taurus the Bull means you will need to become more patient and not so anxious to take the world by storm. Both of you need to avoid stubbornness.

LEO AND GEMINI

Don't create too many dramatic situations if you want to relate well with Gemini, and don't expect to be feted with compliments from morning to night either. Sharing a sense of humor and stimulating conversations will make life great fun.

LEO AND CANCER

Since Cancer can provide you with the nurturing you love so much, don't spoil things by being overly pushy and domineering, especially when the Crab is in an ultrasensitive mood. Both of you need to respect each other's feelings.

LEO AND LEO

At least you know what you're up against here! Two of you fighting for that center-stage position will certainly allow you to recognize each other's faults. You're sure to boss each other around, but don't forget to show your wonderful Leo affection, too.

LEO AND VIRGO

Be prepared to have your every thought and action analyzed, so watch what you say and do. Both of you are insecure, and Virgo's conscientious approach to tasks will help you see it's not worth trying to cut corners when success is at stake.

LEO AND LIBRA

Librans don't like to have anything forced upon them, so don't be too pushy and domineering. The sign of the Scales can be the perfect balance for your flamboyant personality and a Libran will remain good-humored even when you behave like a child.

LEO AND SCORPIO

Don't try to manipulate this sign in any way . . . they will beat you hands down! Scorpio has a great need for personal privacy, but may not pay too much respect to your own privacy needs. Each of you should avoid becoming jealous.

LEO AND SAGITTARIUS

For the Lion and the Archer purely as a fun-loving, extravagant pair doing everything in grand style, things will work out fine. You can be wonderful friends, but don't try to force the Archer to fit in with all your plans. Sagittarians need to feel inwardly free.

LEO AND CAPRICORN

The Mountain Goat is far more cost-conscious than you. Capricorns also prefer to do things in traditional ways. You will really have to work extra hard to be praised by this sign, and while doing so you cannot afford to be too self-centered.

LEO AND AQUARIUS

Since opposites attract, you could be a good duo. Always talk things over and you won't be bored. The refusal of most Aquarians to let their feelings show may prevent you from going over the top with yours!

LEO AND PISCES

Try to understand that Pisces is the romantic dreamer of the zodiac. You both can be horribly extravagant financially. You will form a wonderful mutual admiration society if you make an effort to be sensitive to each other's positive and negative sides.

Becoming a
More Successful
Virgo

If you were born between August 22 and September 21, you were born under the sign of Virgo, the sixth sign of the zodiac. Virgo is a feminine, mutable, negative, Earth sign, ruled by Mercury, planet of communication. Your planetary symbol is the Virgin.

Known as the critic and analyst of the zodiac, Virgos often seem to be trying to pick holes in everything they see around them, including themselves. It is an astrological truth that your star sign has bequeathed to you the task of searching for perfection. It is also true that perfection is not easy to find. And somewhere along the way you seem to have forgotten it is human to err. The successful Virgo is one who realizes that it is not the end of the world if you cannot achieve your ideal of perfection every minute of every day. If you accept these points, you don't have to be such a nit-picker with yourself and others.

Resolve not to worry quite so much if everything is not as perfect as you would like. Your often serious view of life is not helped by the fact that astrology has deemed you "the sign of service." Is it any wonder that Mother Teresa was born under your sign? Or that sometimes you feel that you are up against a mammoth task that can never be accomplished?

Leo, the sign that precedes yours, treats life as more to be enjoyed than worried about. Libra, the sign following yours, tends to balance the good with the bad. If you find it hard to do either of these things, it may help you to borrow a few of the good points of these signs so that greater success can be yours! You usually possess a good sense of humor, and it will benefit you greatly to make use of it more often.

Each sign of the zodiac relates to a different area of the body, starting with the head and ending with the feet, from Aries to Pisces. Virgo rules the nervous system, the digestive tract, and the intestines, especially the small intestine. When you worry too much or get into a panic it is definitely not good for your nerves or your bowels, so it is extremely important for you to make sure this does not happen often. Many of you seem to try to carry the world's problems on your shoulders, and are often too hard on yourself.

To be more successful, start the ball rolling by being a whole lot more positive about yourself. Thinking about problems can almost create them—at least in your mind. If you are typical of your sign, you are exceptionally alert and bright.

I have often thought it was a big mistake to call Virgo "the sign of service," because you sometimes take this epithet too literally, and forget that you are also allowed to have time off to enjoy yourself. I knew a Virgo man who worked incredibly hard all his life, arriving at his office by 8:00 A.M. every day and never arriving home before 8:00 P.M. His only real hobbies were football and fishing, and he never allowed much time for either. On taking early retirement in his mid-fifties, he was given a large separation package and an extremely good monthly pension. He had no financial worries and plenty of time to enjoy himself. The problem was that he did not really know how to enjoy himself. He had spent so much time "serving" his career that his newfound freedom made him feel unsure about his purpose in life. To be successful, Virgo must not only enjoy working hard but also appreciate taking time off to enjoy other aspects of life.

Interestingly enough, on the surface there seem to be more extremes of personality born under your sign than any other. Famous Virgoans include such diverse personalities as D. H. Lawrence, H. G. Wells, Christopher Isherwood, Stephen King, Agatha Christie, Greta Garbo, Ingrid Bergman, Sean Connery, Michael Jackson, Frederick Forsyth, Jackie Bisset, Lauren Bacall, Raquel Welch, Sophia Loren, and Claudia Schiffer. Just think how successful Agatha Christie and Stephen King have been by applying their analytical minds to their writing. Think how obsessively determined Greta Garbo was to hide away, and how often Michael Jackson has done likewise.

Success will always mean different things to different people. Feeling that the potential to achieve success is within you is always important to the typical Virgo, yet success is often hard for you to achieve. This is why it is necessary for you to accept yourself as you truly are.

Defining Your Goals

Not every Virgo wants to be a best-selling writer, international movie star, or a top model, but every Virgoan has some goals. With Mercury enhancing your powers of communication, you must not give way to doubts and uncertainties concerning your talents and abilities. Just as leopards can't change their spots, you can't help that you are a Virgo and tend to worry too much. You can, however, take a more positive attitude toward your life. Oscar Wilde wrote, "Better to take pleasure in a rose than put its root under a microscope." Perhaps he was thinking of a Virgo when he wrote that!

Once you are able to define your personal goals, this guide to the different areas of your life will lead you to greater success.

How to Achieve Your Emotional Goals

Admitting you have emotions as well as emotional goals can sometimes be extremely hard for you. Your emotions are a serious part of your Virgo personality and are often hidden so deep below the surface that you come across as cool, cautious, and even calculating. You are a master of rationalization and intellectual discussion, but you tend to handle emotional issues differently.

To become more successful emotionally, you must start to develop more faith in yourself as a lovable and desirable person. If this seems strange, let me tell you that I've discovered that even the most beautiful Virgo women or handsome Virgo men often harbor major dissatisfaction with some minor point they hate about themselves, causing them to develop an inferiority complex over something the rest of us would not notice!

Some of the words often associated with Virgo do not necessarily help you achieve your emotional goals. You are said to be disciplined, fastidious, exacting, dutiful, dedicated, fussy, and pessimistic perfectionists. In addition, you tend to spend far too long on inconsequential details—not exactly the way to start off a sizzling love affair, for many people.

However, greater emotional success can certainly be yours once you stop dissecting, analyzing, and criticizing your every feeling. Feeling and showing emotion is natural, and since you enjoy emotional fulfillment just as much as any other sign in the zodiac, it's time you admitted it.

Don't forget that you are an Earth sign, and there truly is an earthy sensual sexuality buried underneath that mass of intellectual analysis. No one is asking you to drop your standards, at least not if those standards are reasonable and are not so impossibly high that only a god or a saint could achieve them.

If you do have unfulfilled emotional goals, don't sit around bemoaning the lack of suitable partners. Instead, constructively and with total honesty analyze who you are and what you want out of life. Or better yet, get an unbiased friend to do it for you. It could prove one of the most positive things you've ever done, showing you that you are someone special and that you can be infinitely more successful if you stop worrying quite so much.

EMOTIONS AND THE VIRGO WOMAN

There is no doubt that you have deep emotions, but you cannot really blame other people for doubting their existence. Amazingly thoughtful and caring, patient and persevering, at times you seem to distance yourself so far from the emotional side of your own nature that you would put off all but the most ardent admirer. Your apparently cool and aloof behavior makes you seem almost like a prim and proper maiden from the Victorian era. Is this to cover up your shyness, or is it to cover up your deep-rooted fear of being hurt?

There is definitely a certain purity about the sign of the Virgin. But not all Virgo women wish to lead a solitary existence, even though Greta Garbo certainly seemed to be the textbook Virgo personality in this particular respect.

Many of you need to realize you have something very much in common with your opposite sign, Pisces. Both signs are incurable romantics—the only difference is that Pisces admits this fact, and you usually use every trick in the book to hide it.

To be more successful emotionally, try harder to give rein to your feelings at the right time and in the right place. Don't be afraid to let yourself go. Your instinct, coupled with your powers of discrimination, can be a powerful ally in helping you decide when you should express yourself. You will soon know if you are being used or taken for granted. You don't have to lose your finely tuned sense of self-preservation or your instinct for caution in all things, but you could safely allow yourself to be more open toward people you feel would be receptive.

It is unlikely that you will ever cease to seek perfection in relationships, just as you do in all other areas of your life. But you will become less stressed out about it if you learn to appreciate other people for who they are and forget or overlook what you see as their shortcomings.

You must learn to balance your feelings with your rational side. I have often had Virgo clients who feel that they became martyrs to past loves, fulfilling their duties as wife, mother, and lover to someone who never understood their needs. In many cases I am sure this was true, but there's another viewpoint: With Virgoans, it is as though you contain your feelings in a locked box and hide the key. Perhaps some past relationships have failed because of your desire to hold back too much—but this tendency doesn't necessarily have to block your ability to have good relationships in the future. Once you learn to relax and unwind, you will often be as flirtatious, passionate, and sensual as a woman born under any other sign! Think of the sex goddesses born under your sign: Raquel Welch and Sophia Loren are just two of them. They are both extremely beautiful, with minds of their own and a great sense of style. Obviously they benefit from the positive Virgoan philosophy of taking good care of oneself in a healthy way, and they also give other women advice on how to do the same.

EMOTIONS AND THE VIRGO MAN

If you are a typical Virgo man, it is not always easy to understand your emotions. They don't exactly shine through like a beacon on a foggy night. You appear to be so concerned with what is supposedly right and proper and are so busy making sure that your life is orderly that anyone involved with you has to fit into your little world as it is. You don't like having to change anything, and you get into an awful state when something has to be changed!

I once knew a Virgo man who had every Virgoan characteristic in the book. He wasn't able to balance the contrasts within his personality, and consequently his deep feelings were hidden for much of the time, and usually surfaced as possessiveness and jealousy.

However, you can be wonderfully witty, with a dry sense of humor that adds to your sex appeal. Sean Connery was a wonderfully sexy James Bond! You are nowhere near as coldhearted as people make you out to be, especially when you learn to relax more and accept yourself for who you are. The trouble with many Virgo men is that you are so busy holding on to your to your cool outer demeanor that you forget there may be a passionate heart beating strongly within. But since some of the men born under your sign include Richard Gere, Tommy Lee Jones, Jeremy Irons, Charlie Sheen, and Hugh Grant, it is obvious that your sign is exceedingly attractive to many people.

Don't deny your feelings and emotions to yourself, let alone to others. Stop questioning yourself so critically and judgmentally. Admit that you enjoy loving and being loved as much as every other sign. Stop being quite so obsessional in your fussiness.

While you usually have a down-to-earth, practical approach to life in many ways, you may also suffer from emotional insecurity going back to your childhood. This often leads to a fear of failure in creating emotional ties in adulthood. Many other signs have also experienced emotional difficulties, however, and since you possess such brilliant powers of analysis, you must surely accept that you don't have to let the past control your future.

There is sometimes a feeling within a Virgo man that you get shortchanged in emotional relationships. You feel you have put everything you have into making something work and to provide for your nearest and dearest: devotion, care, and consideration. If you truly want to be more successful emotionally, don't forget to show your deepest feelings more, too. Don't analyze those loving words before you speak them, and don't be afraid to give a few hugs and kisses to go along with those words.

How to Achieve Your Material Goals

If you recall that Aristotle Onassis was born under your sign, then you really should not have to worry that perhaps Virgoans are too shy and retiring, or too full of insecurity and anxiety, to achieve material success. When you truly want to achieve something, you seem to overcome your worry of what other people may say. The Virgoan director Oliver Stone continues to make his controversial movies. D. H. Lawrence demonstrated that a Virgoan personality doesn't prevent someone from writing sexually explicit literature. And Michael Jackson seems to rise above the controversy that surrounds him time and again.

A challenge is intellectually stimulating for you, and your ruling planet, Mercury, makes you more than a match for any-one when it comes to the powers of communication. You simply have to rise above insecurity and the fear of failure.

To achieve your material goals in the easiest possible way, it is immensely important to utilize your skills at organizing, coordinating, and taking care of all the practical details in everything you undertake. Whereas Leo wants to occupy center stage, you are often totally happy working in the background. As an Earth sign, you have your feet planted firmly on the ground. No scatterbrained schemes are likely to figure in your plans, for you would worry far too much about their not coming to fruition. You must learn to place a higher value on yourself than you generally do, and not to continually question everything you do.

At the same time, it is essential for you to appreciate the importance of having a good backup team working with you; don't be unduly critical if other people do not always live up to what you expect of them. You don't have to stop being totally dedicated to what you do, but you must understand that unless you are with another Virgo, it will be hard for your team members to accept your sometimes blind devotion to your duties.

Your material success will be greater the better you understand the inner workings of your Virgo personality, and realize there are moments when a brief spell of rest and relaxation will help to calm your busy mind.

Your motivation in aiming for material success is often that you truly want to do something worthwhile for the world. You want to leave something behind that can be greatly admired, even if only by your family and friends. It's about time that you admitted to yourself that even Virgoans take great pride in their achievements, rather than almost punish yourself for doing something worthy of praise.

Virgo is the "sign of service," but don't ever make yourself into a servant locked into duty and routine without also giving yourself some time off to have fun and enjoy the lighter side of life. Expand your boundaries and really listen to what your visions tell you. Don't limit yourself to what you think you can do. Show yourself and everyone else that no one could do without your star sign in the world.

The Powerful Assets at Your Disposal to Become More Successful

The Power of Your Element . . . Earth

Virgo is the second of the Earth signs, Taurus and Capricorn being the other two. The Earth element contributes to your practical, down-to-earth approach to life. It means that you can be counted on to be extremely methodical, reliable, and steadfast in your everyday behavior.

Because of this practical side to your nature, it is unlikely that you would fall flat on your face if you were to fail. This makes it all the more difficult for others to understand why you often think the very worst is going to befall you.

The powerful element Earth provides us with a great deal in our lives. But somehow there are people born under your sign who appear to think of the Earth itself as a vast muddy brown or parched expanse, and even to think of their own lives in the same way—a vast expanse of time consisting of duty, routine, and service. However, the Earth is not simply brown. It is many different colors, and brings forth many different forms of life. Think of the wonderful colors of the trees, plants, and flowers, as you try to think of your own life unfolding in the same way.

Avoid letting yourself be accused of being boring, dull, or pedantic. Don't be so firmly rooted in traditions or beliefs that you fear taking control of your own life. Being practical is not always the best thing for you to do, but being honest with yourself usually is. I am sure that Virgo Richard Gere thought he was doing the best thing when he announced in the *Times* newspaper in London there were no problems in his marriage with Piscean (his opposite sign) Cindy Crawford. Opposite signs attract and can be wonderful together. Unfortunately, both people had to finally admit that their marriage was at an end. Was it fear of being labeled a failure that caused Gere to place that full-page announcement?

Don't you see, Virgo, that once you believe in your own strengths, and nurture your positive assets, you won't need to prove yourself to anyone but yourself. Your Earth power will help you to overcome your insecurities, but it is up to you to stop being sidetracked by trivial things, or to let your sense of duty create problems in your life.

A determined approach toward making a living and achieving your goals comes naturally to you, as one born under an Earth sign. Maximize the potential of this Earth power by letting optimism, not pessimism, be the ruler of your life.

The Power of Your Ruling Planet . . . Mercury

Both Gemini and you are ruled by Mercury, planet of communication and the winged messenger of the gods. In Gemini, an Air sign, the power of Mercury is expressed by an ability to switch ideas at the drop of a hat, to communicate with amazing and admirable ease with the world at large. If you're a typical Virgo, Mercury's influence enhances your pragmatic and realistic organizational approach to life because it makes you a brilliant analyst of people and situations. However, take care that you do not become overly critical of yourself or others.

To become more successful in your everyday life, it is important for you to realize that Mercury can enable you to broaden your vision and see further ahead with enthusiasm. You will then begin to enjoy greater clarity of thought without worrying so much about things that may never happen. You don't have to change your beliefs or lose your intellectual prowess. You don't have to stop analyzing either. I'm asking you to appreciate your ability to analyze, but to use it in a more positive way.

I once heard Virgo described as the "pessimistic perfectionist of the zodiac," and unfortunately, I do see the reasoning behind this comment. However, Mercury can inspire you to be bright, witty, and more "mercurial"—surprising—in your personality. If you don't insist on making your mind behave like an immovable object, it will lift you out of your earth-bound self and take you from your practical way of thinking up to even loftier heights of the imagination, offering inspiration. Even though you are an Earth sign, you share a mutable quality with Gemini, which means you can be adaptable and variable if you really choose to be so.

Never forget that Mercury is the planet that helps you to communicate your thoughts and ideas in the best possible way. In the same vein, if you insist on letting fear and rejection rule your life, Mercury will not be averse to helping your mind play games with you, for Mercury rules the mind. You definitely do not need to be a pessimistic perfectionist, and you must start to accept that a positive, discerning and imaginative perfectionist will always find opportunities to climb higher up the ladder of success.

The Power of Your Rising Sign

Your Ascendant, or rising sign, is the sign that was rising on the eastern horizon at the time of your birth. In many ways it is as important as your Sun and Moon signs, for it influences the way you live your life. Using the table on pages 278–79, you will be able to determine which is your Ascendant sign.

Here is a short example of how you, a Virgo, will be influenced by the twelve different rising signs.

VIRGO WITH ARIES RISING

An Aries ascendant could make you more headstrong and impatient than most Virgoans, as well as less critical. It inspires you to face life with a more positive and enthusiastic attitude, making you more successful in everything you do.

VIRGO WITH TAURUS RISING

You take life at a steady pace and aren't put off by negative situations or unexpected pitfalls. The Taurus Ascendant adds softness and sensuality to your personality, and you are concerned with your creature comforts as much as with working hard.

VIRGO WITH GEMINI RISING

A double lashing of Mercury's power means you win any battle of words! Mental stimulation and mental communication figure strongly in your life. Your analytical and critical views benefit from a chattier and friendlier touch.

VIRGO WITH CANCER RISING

The sensitivity of Cancer helps you to admit that even cool and fussy Virgoans have deep emotional feelings too. Watch out that you don't sulk too often if other people are not always appreciative of your sense of duty and worth ethic.

VIRGO WITH LEO RISING

A Leo Ascendant helps you lighten up amazingly, and even makes you enjoy the limelight more than you can imagine! You will cheerfully broaden your horizons, not be prone to criticize yourself as much as other Virgoans, and even be the star attraction of a few parties.

VIRGO WITH VIRGO RISING

You have the choice—to be a pessimistic perfectionist, or someone determined to prove you have what it takes to be a big success! With this combination, you have the ability to concentrate on priorities, and to weed out the inconsequential, with the wisdom to overcome your insecurities.

VIRGO WITH LIBRA RISING

Your Libra Ascendant helps you to balance and soften your critical, analytical, and discriminating ways. It also gives you the ability to see both sides of a situation with confidence and flair. You may be slightly more self-indulgent than other Virgoans, which could do you good!

VIRGO WITH SCORPIO RISING

Heaven help anyone who gets on the wrong side of you with this combination. Your ability to observe and discriminate goes hand in hand with a phenomenal memory, which enables you to beat any competitor aiming for what you want.

VIRGO WITH SAGITTARIUS RISING

You are a duty-loving, conscientious Virgo with great style. Outgoing and expansive, you might be more inclined to take a few more risks than most Virgoans. Just make sure you maintain your Virgoan powers of concentration and you can be a real winner.

VIRGO WITH CAPRICORN RISING

Capricorn Ascendant makes you doubly careful and prudent, and incredibly determined to live a secure and stable life. But watch out not to be too much of a stickler for the old ways of doing things, leaving you unreceptive to the new.

VIRGO WITH AQUARIUS RISING

You are more extroverted and unpredictable than many other Virgoans, which enables others to see you in a brighter and more sparkling light. You can also come up with some unique ways to express your creative talents.

VIRGO WITH PISCES RISING

Don't let Pisces Ascendant make you too impractical or vague concerning material issues. Appreciate the Piscean influence on your emotional life—resulting in a little more romance and less insistence on a life devoted to service.

How to Create Greater Success

Creating Greater Success . . . in Your Everyday Life

Don't worry, Virgo, I'm not about to admonish you for not being sufficiently structured and organized in your daily life. There is possibly no sign of the zodiac who is better organized than you!

To become more successful, consider the benefits of being less infatuated with an infinite number of unimportant details. Don't waste time and energy worrying so much about everything you undertake, or nervously wondering what other people think of your ideals. Maximize your powers of analysis and discrimination in a really constructive way, so that you enhance your abilities without feeling insecure about them.

Enjoy being more adaptable and versatile in the way you tackle everyday issues. Be more imaginative in your approach to problem solving. Learn to see more of the beauty in life without continually pointing out its flaws. You can still be critical, using your meticulous eyes and ears to perceive details, but try not to be quite so critical (especially of yourself).

Because you are so particular about everything, you can forfeit spontaneity. You may be used to thinking of yourself as a quiet, modest person who prefers to stay in the background and to let others take center stage. Maximizing your potential could involve changing some of that! Why don't you start to loosen up a little and stop being so tough on yourself. Don't insist on being quite so pedantic and unemotional and you will be amazed at how much more successful you will be.

It is typical of Virgoans to consider themselves worthy of greater success than they have and to feel that it eludes them through no fault of their own. You may find that the following checklist will suggest to you ways you can create a better daily regime, without having to alter your Virgo life too much.

DO . . .
- learn ways to relax so you become less stressed.
- start to appreciate yourself in a more positive way. Look at the brighter side of life and have more fun.
- be discerning and analytical, but don't go over the top.
- continue to look at details, but look at the overall picture, too.
- develop more compassion for those less perfect than you.

DON'T . . .
- be too nit-picking, discriminating, and intolerant.
- feed your mind with insecure feelings.
- be overly self-critical or too critical of the rest of the world.
- concern yourself quite so much with material values.
- insist on everyone's living up to your high standards.
- be quite such a stick-in-the mud when you *do* have time to party.

Creating Greater Success . . . in Love

If you're a typical Virgo, you may need to start believing that you are also allowed to love yourself—in addition to loving other people! It is also important for you not to think of love as a duty. Being involved in a good relationship can add a whole new dimension to your life. To maximize your potential for success in love, practice taking yourself a little less seriously and be a little less fastidious in your devotion to other areas of your life, too.

If you have had problems in past relationships, it will not hurt to analyze why they went wrong. You do not have to analyze them repeatedly, and of course you need not blame yourself if the problems were not of your own making. There are always two sides to a situation, though, and it's time you stopped making yourself a martyr in the name of love. Mother Teresa is a Virgoan who is doing amazingly good works in the world, but she made that her choice, and you are equally free to make your own choice. If you truly want to create greater success in love, you have only to open yourself up more and let love shine in.

I have always believed that we have a great deal to learn from our opposite sign of the zodiac, and your opposite sign is the romantic, sympathetic, and compassionate Pisces. Start to be more romantic, sensitive, and tender yourself, and you will be surprised how much brighter life will become.

Do learn to have more confidence in your personality and your body. Don't get all embarrassed when someone thinks you are fabulous!

Creating Greater Success . . . in Dating

To explain to you the importance of the above heading, perhaps it will be necessary to remind you that dating is not a complete waste of your valuable time, and something only indulged in by the very young or those who feel they have nothing better to do.

Since you are so caught up with the meaning of duty, it's time you considered the possibility that dating may be part of your duty to yourself. Dating can contribute to your having a full and enriched life on every possible level by bringing new people into your life. Sometimes, because of circumstance, you find yourself alone yet longing to find a compatible partner. Vow you won't be quite so cool and detached when someone interesting does catch your eye.

VIRGO DATING TIPS

- Be warmer, wittier and more aware of the potential of your charms.
- Take some time off from your other duties to socialize.
- Don't think of sexuality and sensuality as words, and qualities, to be avoided!

Creating Greater Success . . . in Family Ties

Make the most of the positive attributes of your Virgo personality, including the fact that you are a mutable Earth sign, which should give you both practicality and adaptability when it comes to the needs of others. So in theory you should be able to get on well with any member of your family.

In reality, however, you are not necessarily a very easygoing person, because you are often too obsessed with detail. Try to be more flexible so that you can get on better with people who aren't as neat and tidy as you.

Resolve to try a little harder to appreciate your family by encouraging them in their ideals and aspirations. Restrain yourself so that you don't offer too much unwanted advice.

Remember that you are by nature one of the most caring, down-to-earth and dependable zodiac signs, and often all that is necessary to create greater success in family ties is for you to show how much you care. Thus, if you know that certain members of your family find it difficult to cope with your critical and analytical ways, try to develop more of a sense of humor about this. Perhaps get your family to read up on the Virgo personality, to understand *you* better, too.

You will be positively brilliant at keeping notes of all the important dates that relate to members of your family—no matter how large nor how widespread it may be. On the other hand, sometimes you can be inordinately reticent at calling up or making time to see your relatives in person, probably because you already have a full schedule to maintain.

Relaxing with loved ones can be good for you—all the more so when you don't think of it merely as another one of your duties.

TIPS FOR SUCCESSFUL FAMILY TIES
- Be loyal, caring, and dependable without being overly demanding and critical.
- Try harder to accept your family members for who they are and who they want to be.
- Don't moan or nag about things that may irritate you but are not your problems.

Creating Greater Success . . . at Work

One of the important ways for you to create greater success in your work life is to stop being quite so obsessed with it. You possess admirable qualities such as being meticulous in your approach to work matters, and having a generous attitude toward putting in overtime. But then you sometimes go and ruin it all by complaining to yourself or to others that you are always being put upon. Needless to say, such situations are often your own fault since you will invariably convince yourself that no one can do a job as well as you!

Use your talents in a positive way. Try to accept that even a Virgo cannot do everything, even if you are brilliant at dealing with all the practical details and organizing projects from beginning to end. You can become more successful if you learn to stop incessantly fretting that perhaps you haven't worked hard enough or made enough sacrifices along the way.

I know many stressed-out Virgoans who worry so much about their work that they find it hard to drop off to sleep, and so it is important for you to find a way to relax before you go to bed. If necessary you can make lists of all the things you must do in the morning, and then remind yourself that recharging your batteries with a good night's rest will inspire you to be even more efficient the following day.

To become more successful and to feel more creatively fulfilled, too, it is necessary to overcome insecurities and self-doubts. Take a leaf out of Leo's book. You won't find much insecurity there. And *you* are quite prepared to work hard without taking center stage, too!

Because you invariably have high intelligence, it is important that you have opportunities to use your mental abilities to the greatest possible extent.

The following do's and don'ts will also provide a guide for you to become more successful at work:

DO . . .

- believe in your own worth and blow your own horn more often.
- make sure you are happy in your working environment. You achieve much more in the right environment.
- eat properly so your body has the strength to deal with your long hours.

DON'T . . .

- let other people take the praise when it should be yours.
- complain about your work without first taking steps to overcome any problems.
- panic in a crisis, because you know you will invariably find the right way to overcome it.

Creating Greater Success . . . *in Finding the Right Job*

Don't take just *any* dead-end job—unless you have absolutely no choice. Although you are an expert at organizing and analyzing, that doesn't mean you want to be a filing clerk all your life.

Believe in yourself and your abilities. This self-confidence will make it much easier to impress upon others that you really do know what you're talking about.

Don't always take behind-the-scenes jobs, hiding your light under a bushel and letting someone else take the acclaim for your efforts.

Many Virgo men and women are drawn to public service. Accountancy, the financial markets, stockbroking, pharmacy, science, bookkeeping, teaching, medicine and alternative medicine, publishing, and psychology are all professional fields where practitioners benefit from Virgo's eye for detail. Dieticians and nutritional experts, excellent craftsmen, first-class secretaries, and proofreaders benefit from the qualities of your sign.

Creating More Success . . .
in All Your Relationships

One of the most important factors in being successful in life is how you relate to other people. If you set impossibly high standards for yourself and for a prospective partner, you run the risk of becoming disillusioned.

Even though you, with your Virgo discernment, pride yourself on your ability to know who is for real and who is not, you can still benefit from a few tips on how to relate better to those born under each sign.

VIRGO AND ARIES

You may need lots of tolerance to cope with the Ram's head-strong attitude and impatient ways, but you could be fired with enthusiasm too. Don't be too critical. Underneath that aggressive exterior, hot-headed Aries often feels just as vulnerable as you do.

VIRGO AND TAURUS

Since you are both Earth signs you should have plenty in common. Don't accuse Taurus of being self-indulgent just because the Bull enjoys the sensual pleasures of life. Both of you want security and stability, so bask in it without always thinking of work.

VIRGO AND GEMINI

Always keep the mental stimulation alive in any relationship with Gemini. Don't criticize his or her high-flying ideas out of hand before you understand them or they have a chance to work. Don't be fussy over Gemini's occasional flippancy.

VIRGO AND CANCER

Cancer's nurturing capacity and ability to help you feel safe and secure by understanding your anxieties and innermost needs is a big plus. Don't spoil it all by continuing to worry unnecessarily; enjoy some domestic bliss.

VIRGO AND LEO

Stop looking for the crack in the mirror and enjoy what this bright and breezy sign has to offer. Leo's confidence and strength will empower you to maximize your talents and abilities. Just remember to give praise when it's due.

VIRGO AND VIRGO

At least you will know each other's pet neuroses, and perhaps you can even laugh at them together! If you resolve not to analyze and criticize each other too much, this can be a highly successful and workable relationship on every level.

VIRGO AND LIBRA

There is sure to be logic at work on both sides here. Libra is quite right in saying you need a social life to take you away from all that work, work, and more work! But since Libra is indecisive, you will need to make the beneficial decisions for you both.

VIRGO AND SCORPIO

Never underestimate the power of Scorpio. You dissect things in different ways, but are also both brilliant at getting what you want. On a physical level, Scorpio could bring out the passionate side of you as no one before—don't let that frighten you away.

VIRGO AND SAGITTARIUS

The optimistic free and easy ways of Sagittarius can be a big bonus to a Virgo in a negative mood. Don't be too critical or make the Archer feel hemmed in. Sagittarius will need to understand your sense of duty a little more, too.

VIRGO AND CAPRICORN

You share many of the same goals and aspirations, but will you ever stop working long enough to get to know each other better? Both of you need to lighten up and recognize there is more to life than material success.

VIRGO AND AQUARIUS

You will enjoy discussing everything under the sun, even if the two of you don't always agree. If you put too much pressure on Aquarius to see everything your way you won't have a chance, since you're both fixed signs with set opinions.

VIRGO AND PISCES

Romance can be wonderful, and your opposite sign can teach you a lot about this. This combination is the practical with the impractical, but both of you are caring and dedicated souls. You provide pragmatic advice on life while Pisces shows you how to dream a little more.

Becoming a
More Successful
Libra

If you were born between September 22 and October 22, you were born under the sign of Libra, the seventh sign of the zodiac, a masculine, cardinal, positive Air sign. You are ruled by Venus, the goddess of love, and your planetary symbol is the Scales.

Known as the sign of balance, peace, and harmony, you are supposed to be one of the most well-balanced signs in the whole zodiac. Without any doubt, you certainly make the most of your extremely fair-minded, tactful, and diplomatic qualities where other people are concerned. In your own life, however, the sides of those symbolic scales waver from side to side far too often and you become indecisive over far too many issues.

To become more successful, you will usually benefit from having at least one person in your life whose opinion you respect, whose advice you listen to, and to whom you can confide your innermost thoughts. The seventh house of the zodiac relates to marriages and partnerships, and many Librans feel more successful working in a partnership or as part of a team than on their own. This doesn't mean you always have to have someone around, especially since some of you may consider yourself totally self-sufficient. Those of you who have truly come to terms with who and what you are may also be perfectly capable of working in partnership with yourself. In any case, to achieve the greatest success, don't spend too much time dithering or jumping from one point of view to another; it will cause you to lose out on opportunities to climb higher up the ladder of success.

To present an even more positive face to the world, try making some firm decisions for yourself instead of impaling yourself on the horns of one dilemma or another. Stop yourself from weighing up the pros over and over, or asking your husband, wife, lover, friend, or boss for advice. If you are scared of making a terrible mistake, start with something minor. If everything goes well, as it probably will, you will soon progress to more important decisions. This exercise can be of great benefit to you, since one of the reasons many of you find it so difficult to make decisions is that you fear the consequences of making a wrong judgment.

The positive astrological attributes of your personality include being idealistic, refined, sophisticated, and romantic. Your negative traits include being changeable, snobbish, overly flirtatious, and unemotional. You can see how important it is to learn to create the right balance in your life, or you won't be able to define who you are, let alone give anyone else a clue.

Each sign of the zodiac relates to a different area of the body, starting with the head and ending with the feet, from Aries to Pisces. Libra rules the bladder and kidneys, organs that regulate the liquid in our body and eliminate waste. Both of these organs react to inner stress and overindulgence, which is all the more reason to endeavor to achieve balance in your life. Libra also relates to the nervous system, and Librans who do allow themselves to lose their equilibrium can be prone to ulcers. Let this be a warning to you to make sure that rest and relaxation are never neglected in your life.

I am convinced that every sign has something to learn from its opposite counterpart in the zodiac, and yours is Aries. Whereas Aries bursts forth with the first day of Spring and fearlessly rushes ahead with one project or another, your sign commences with the first day of fall and you tend to stand back as if contemplating what kind of winter lies ahead. Inwardly you want to know where you stand before you move on. I'm not suggesting you turn overnight into a fiery, headstrong Ram, but a little more energy and enthusiasm on your part could transform your life in a very positive way. Present yourself with a few challenges (just as Aries does), and fight for what you believe in. To become more successful in life, there is no time to sit on the fence debating on which side to lower yourself to the ground. It's not that you are always lazy and laid-back, even though astrologers often seem to accuse you of being so. When you believe in something you don't give up without a big fight.

Margaret Thatcher, Mahatma Gandhi, and Martina Navratilova were all born under your sign. Brigitte Bardot continually fights for her animal-rights causes, and Lee Iacocca didn't get where he is today by sitting back and doing nothing for Chrysler.

Naturally, success means different things to different people. Since Venus, Goddess of Love, rules your sign, to be liked and loved for who you *are* is an important component of success to you.

Defining Your Goals

Not every Libran reading this book wants to write best-selling books like the Librans John Le Carré or Jackie Collins, or aspires to become an acclaimed ice skater like Jayne Torvill, a renowned singer like Luciano Pavarotti, or a famous dress designer like Donna Karan or Ralph Lauren. Whatever your aspirations, this guide will give you some points on how to turn some of your goals into realities by means of balancing your Libran scales.

How to Achieve Your Emotional Goals

To become more successful emotionally, it is important for you to recognize that if you are like most Librans, you hate to be alone. If you feel incomplete when you don't have a partner, you sometimes end up with someone for the wrong reasons. Because you are extremely fair-minded, you are perfectly willing to take the blame for your own shortcomings and are usually prepared to work hard to create a good relationship. But if things break down irretrievably, you may be forced to make some decisions, which is not easy for you since you are not usually the type to simply walk out the door. Even so, remember you don't need to lose your balance if something goes wrong. You are fortunate in having an inborn ability to see things from a philosophical point of view.

To achieve your emotional goals, believe more in your ability to know inwardly when something really feels right. Resolve to become responsible for yourself and your actions. By doing this you will mature emotionally, and your ego will create its own inner identity. Stop telling yourself you can feel completely whole only when someone else is around. Being more independent emotionally will give you greater strength in every area of your life. Striving for outward harmony is all very well, but how can you expect to fully achieve this if your inner feelings are churned up? This is why Librans are prone to ulcers, and why I've decided over the years that many of you worry just as much as Virgoans, although you don't like to admit it.

Greater emotional success will come your way when you put more of your thoughts into actions, and don't just sit around waiting for things to happen. I've often felt that "Procrastination is the root of all evil" would be a good precept for your sign. You have to invest in life to get something worthwhile from it, and you sometimes spend an endless amount of time weighing things; if you were to listen to both your instinct and your intellect you would come up with the right answers with less agonizing.

Even though you are ruled by Venus, the goddess of love, as an Air sign you tend to talk about your emotions in a somewhat detached manner. To be more successful emotionally you will need to be more honest with your deepest feelings and to communicate more openly on every level. We all know that you hate arguments, that you much prefer to discuss problems in a calm and rational manner, but sometimes arguments are the only way to bring something to the foreground and sort it out. Don't be one of those Librans who sits back and simply accepts problems for fear of finding yourself isolated.

Your desire for peace, harmony, and beauty can make you hope for too much in a person. Nobody is perfect, and when you do achieve a good emotional relationship it will still need to be nurtured and worked at.

EMOTIONS AND THE LIBRA WOMAN

If you're a typical Libra woman you will throw yourself whole-heartedly into an emotional relationship as if it were truly the be-all and end-all of your life. Watch out that you don't become a human doormat, suppressing your own personality because of a deep need to be involved with a partner.

Remember that while you are without doubt one of the most wonderfully feminine women in the zodiac—sharing the Libra stage with Angie Dickinson, Britt Ekland, Deborah Kerr, and Catherine Deneuve—you are much tougher than you appear. Susan Sarandon, Barbara Walters, and Sigourney Weaver were also born under your sign.

Because you are a cardinal sign, you possess qualities of leadership, and because, astrologically, Libra is also a masculine sign, you possess male logic as well as female instinct. Nevertheless, it is your ruling planet, Venus, that endows you with your inherent need to give and receive love.

Sometimes you seem to come a cropper in the emotional stakes, because you are inspired not so much by falling in love with someone as by the thought process that goes along with the idea of love. Watch out that it isn't simply the idea of having a perfect partner that tugs at your heartstrings and leads you in circles, thus toward more difficult decisions. Trust your instincts when you meet someone—although it sometimes isn't such a bad idea to be a little indecisive before making a total commitment!

Don't give away your personal power by fooling yourself into believing you cannot live without an emotional tie. It is not always easy to be alone, but it is often better to be alone than with the wrong partner.

Be more honest with yourself about what you need to fulfill your emotions, and what you would like to achieve in your emotional life. We all know that you like beauty, peace, and harmony and dream of a soulmate with whom you can share a happy life ever after. But don't fall for someone because of your insecurities or because you need someone to bolster a fallen ego.

Although you appear on the surface to be someone who places love high on your agenda, I have always noticed that there are many Libran women who are also perfectly able to rationalize their feelings. You are the ones who are determined to remain in control, so that your head rather than your heart becomes the rule of your emotions. But then those Libran scales get out of balance once more, letting your heart play a larger part in giving more of your true self to emotional relationships.

You have something else to learn from your opposite sign, Aries, who is always ready for a challenge. Why not think of the challenge of achieving greater emotional success as something that goes hand in hand with the challenge of finding greater emotional security within yourself?

You can be extremely intellectual, and almost as analytical as Virgo. You are brilliant at seeing both sides of every argument, and of fighting for your beliefs, and you possess every feminine wile in the book. You're definitely not as fragile as you may look. Sometimes you are too self-indulgent for your own good and too keen to be wooed and won by a knight in shining armor.

Make an effort to achieve greater emotional success by accepting yourself fully and not simply by searching for someone else to build up your self-esteem. If you truly want to find yourself, start to believe in yourself as a woman with strong feelings and emotions, and don't be scared to let them show.

EMOTIONS AND THE LIBRA MAN

Many people have described the Libra man as having taste, an abundance of charm, a diplomatic touch, and a great deal of vanity. Perhaps the vanity part is a little unfair, but it is true that you often place great importance on appearances. On the other hand, you are wonderful at soothing other people's ruffled feathers and giving praise where praise is due, provided you receive the same favor in return. Your desire to please, your urge for peace and harmony, and your ability to converse on a variety of subjects with logic and wit can't be overemphasized.

I sometime think you are something of an enigma in the emotional stakes. Because the sign of Libra relates to marriages and partnerships, and because you definitely seem to function better when you are one of a pair, it would seem logical that you would be extremely successful in a marriage or long-standing relationship. But to become as successful emotionally as possible, open up more to what your heart reveals to you.

All too often, the typical Libra man is moved by what he *thinks* is right for him, and he knows he doesn't always want to live alone. But thinking that something or someone is right for you is very different from feeling it. It's not unusual for you to believe you are a romantic idealist, but it is more unusual for you to follow through on those romantic ideals to their logical conclusion. All too often you find yourself stuck in relationships that work well on a number of levels, but not on the truly romantic one.

Anyone who knows a Libra man will know that when he does really fall in love, even if he is already married, he falls hard. Because he is basically a law-abiding and fair-minded person, it is hard for him to make the inevitable and difficult decision to leave his spouse. Once it is done, however, Librans manage to take a philosophical view of what has happened, which enables them to move on without feeling guilt-ridden.

Sometimes one side of your Libran scales means that you end up taking the line of least resistance in your emotional life. So it is important to be aware of this tendency and not let yourself be pushed into something you don't really want simply because you are not prepared to stand on your own two feet and say it is not for you. Then again, one of your inconsistencies is that at times you refuse to be pushed into anything— least of all an argument or having to account for your behavior.

Librans have a talent for flattery and flirtation. But to achieve greater success in your emotional life, it is important to decide whether your brilliance at demonstrating your charming flirtatious ways truly fulfills your emotional needs. Once you admit to your innermost self that your emotional needs are not simply ideas of what a fulfilling life should be like, you will be far more in control of your own destiny. Try a little harder to let your understated sensitivity shine through, along with the rest of your Libran charm.

Julio Iglesias, Pierre Trudeau, Marcello Mastroianni, and Michael Douglas were all born under your sign.

How to Achieve Your Material Goals

The material goals of a typical Libran are as easy to define as having sufficient means to enjoy a peaceful, calm, and uncluttered life surrounded with beautiful people and beautiful objects. To achieve all of this, it is vital for you to remember the message "*Carpe diem.*" For you this means seizing not only the day, but also the moment to move closer to your goals. Maximize the potential of your inborn sense of timing, your logical thought process, and your ability to effectively communicate your thoughts to a wide variety of people.

Don't allow feelings of insecurity to prevent you from moving onward and upward. You can be your own best friend and partner if you are willing. Once you start to discipline yourself in a motivated way, there will be no stopping you. When you are sure of your objectives, the next issue will be to decide on your tactics. Decision-making is and always will be a dark area to many of you. There are some astrologers who say you Librans are not really indecisive, that you are merely weighing up carefully the possible repercussions of your actions. However, while one of your Libran assets is your ability to intuitively evaluate the pluses and minuses of each situation, I still think being decisive is not one of your best points. As I suggested earlier in this chapter, once you learn to trust yourself more and listen to and follow your instincts, you will find it easier to make decisions, whether they be large or small. Vacillation is what holds you back. Once you decide to commit yourself to your aims and ambitions, you will find that you are a master of strategy and can beat almost anyone at their own game. When someone tries to push you into a decision, don't panic; calmly state that you would prefer a little time to think things over. Your judgment improves the more you let your inner voice guide you.

Naturally, your material goals will be as varied as the individual horoscopes of a roomful of Librans. You may not see yourself as the next Margaret Thatcher or John Lennon, but you appreciate the comforts that material success can bring. You may be so fortunate as to have a limitless amount of money at your disposal. If not, though, you usually are more than willing to invest the time and energy necessary to become more successful. Financial insecurity plays havoc with your finely tuned nervous system, which is all the more reason to try to ensure that it doesn't become a problem in your life.

Don't forget that those Libran scales are capable of tipping both ways. Try not to allow yourself either to vacillate too much or to become overly anxious about failing to achieve your aspirations or being too dependent on other people. When you must to do things on your own, recognize that you have all the necessary talents and abilities at your disposal to create a more successful you.

The Powerful Assets at Your Disposal to Become More Successful

The Power of Your Element . . . Air

Each of the four elements, Fire, Earth, Air and Water, has a great bearing on your star sign characteristics. Libra is the second of the three Air signs, Gemini and Aquarius being the other two. The element Air makes all three of you communicative and mentally active, but in Librans this quality is expressed in a more tranquil way. Because you are also a cardinal sign, you have strong enterpreneurial abilities, and you must not simply sit back and wait for things to happen when you are on a quest for greater success. For Librans these enterprising qualities will be expressed best through mental and communicative activities.

It is your quality of Air that gives you your ability to reason calmly and carefully, to see both sides of a question, and to support your views with cool logic. When arguments arise, you can be a wonderful mediator—someone who creates calm and dispels the storm. The Air element also enables you to reject anything that does not appear reasonable and logical and to judge fairly when you are called upon to do so.

Don't place so much emphasis on your thoughts, though, that you forget all about your sense of feeling! Debating an issue and pondering lofty ideals and aspirations is something you do extremely well because of your Air element. You also have Venus, the goddess of love, ruling your sign, and she has an influence too. You must therefore pay a little more attention to what you feel deep down about life and listen to your senses as well as your thoughts.

I've often heard Librans described as being far too detached and unemotional, and this is a trap you can fall into when you don't pay more attention to your feelings. You are supposed to be the sign of relationships and the sign who hates to be alone for too long. You usually care a great deal about receiving approval from others, too. Try harder to balance your thoughts with your feelings and to balance your detachment with the ability to become more involved.

No one can dispute your ability to intellectualize brilliantly, and to circle around abstract ideas with ease, but to fully realize your potential you must allow your heart to have its say, and to listen when it does. You will achieve much more success this way.

The Power of Your Ruling Planet . . . Venus

Throughout the centuries, Venus, the ruling planet you share with Taurus, has been renowned and revered as the goddess of love and beauty. There is no doubt that both love and beauty are an integral part of your personality. You are deeply influenced by the aesthetic, and your taste is often very refined. You love to have beautiful people and objects around you. Your inability to say no to something beautiful means you sometimes spend far too much money.

The influence of Venus on Taurus enhances earthy Taurean sexuality and sensuality. With an Air sign like Libra, Venus tends to make you think more of the joy of love and the temptations and art of seduction rather than of actually throwing yourself into demonstrating your passions, body as well as soul.

When Venus is your ruler, you invariably have a strong attraction to the arts in general and music in particular. You may even possess great talent in these fields. John Lennon was a Libra, as are Sir George Solti and Luciano Pavarotti.

The benefits of Venus for you include your ability to see the brighter side of life and to envisage the sun shining through on a cloudy day. Anyone who is going through a difficult time and is uncertain what direction to take will benefit from your logical, philosophical, and fair-minded approach. Venus helps to make you ever more charming and diplomatic, easygoing and fun to be with, and also to balance your own Libran scales on those days when, even for you, the skies do seem a little too gray. Venus helps you maximize your ability to make the world a better place, not just for you but for everyone. Venus also enhances your eye for beauty, and my good friend, Libran agent and producer Bryan Bantry, has been instrumental in helping to change the perception of beauty for the over 35s, especially on the fashion scene. Your ruling planet will enhance your positive attributes and inspire you to overcome any negative ones. You may not hope to achieve sweetness and light every minute of every day, but Venus will make sure you try.

The Power of Your Rising Sign

Your Ascendant, or rising sign, is the sign that was rising on the eastern horizon at the time of your birth. In many ways it is as important as your Sun and Moon signs, since the way you play out your life is very much influenced by this rising sign.

Using the table on pages 278–79 you will be able to determine your Ascendant. Below are some descriptions of how you, a Libra, will be affected by the twelve different rising signs, and how they can help you to be more successful.

LIBRA WITH ARIES RISING

A Libran who wants things yesterday—that's the power of your headstrong Aries Ascendant! You enthusiastically enjoy putting your thoughts and ideas into action, rather than allowing them to remain as ideals and aspirations.

LIBRA WITH TAURUS RISING

Your desire for beauty is magnified by the Venus influence in both Taurus and Libra, and the will to achieve emotional and material fulfillment on every level will be strong. The Taurus Ascendant ensures that you don't give up on your endeavors halfway.

LIBRA WITH GEMINI RISING

This combination has the ability to convince the rest of the world that you have star quality. Don't simply talk about it—get out there and put all those scintillating ideas to work, without losing momentum along the way.

LIBRA WITH CANCER RISING

Cancer's influence increases your concern with trying to make everyone happy and causes you to truly empathize when others are going through a hard time. Your logic combined with Cancer's intuition is a great blend. Make sure you provide for a cozy nest where you can relax.

LIBRA WITH LEO RISING

You probably are more pushy, flamboyant, and outgoing than many Librans. Your creative flair and optimistic nature help propel you into the limelight, which you're bound to feel is your natural right. Make sure you don't spend money extravagantly.

LIBRA WITH VIRGO RISING

Your Virgo Ascendant highlights your ideals of perfection, and enhances your powers of analysis. You are brilliant at discerning what may be wrong with your life. Make sure you stay positive about all opportunities for success!

LIBRA WITH LIBRA RISING

The need to balance those Libran scales is all the more apparent here. A double dose of charm, tact, and diplomacy doubles your success potential, provided you make a compensating effort to be decisive and to do things on your own when necessary.

LIBRA WITH SCORPIO RISING
A lovable Libran with high-intensity emotions—you can be quite a powerhouse of energy and activity. Decision-making is easier with a Scorpio Ascendant, but watch out that you don't become too manipulative and greedy in your search for greater success.

LIBRA WITH SAGITTARIUS RISING
A Sagittarius Ascendant makes you more gregarious than most Librans and even prepared to take a few risks to achieve your objectives. Action speaks louder than words with this combination. You also possess an abundance of self-confidence.

LIBRA WITH CAPRICORN RISING
A Capricorn Ascendant brings material aims and ambitions to the fore, and the influence of the Mountain Goat inspires you to work long and hard. Don't let your working life put too much of a damper on your social life—remember that you need balance.

LIBRA WITH AQUARIUS RISING
Make sure you overcome the conflict created by your Aquarius side wanting to feel mentally free and the Libra side wanting a partner for everything. Greater success means not always letting your emotions take second place to intellect.

LIBRA WITH PISCES RISING
Romantic, sensitive, and sometimes horribly impractical—that's you! This combination can easily lead you on to creative success, provided you make yourself sit down and utilize your talents to the fullest. But you will probably need a good business manager, too.

How to Create Greater Success

Creating Greater Success . . . in Your Everyday Life

If you're a Libran who still thinks success means having someone to share everything with, I'm afraid I disagree. You really can balance your own Libran scales without anyone else's help. Certainly it is often so much nicer and easier to be part of a team and to liaise with allies and colleagues, and it's great to have one special person in your life with whom you relate fantastically on almost every level. If you are a typical Libran it is more than likely that you were born with the marvelous ability to relate well to almost everyone with whom you come in contact. But a partner is not absolutely necessary for your success.

One of your greatest assets is being able to see both sides of situations, and of having such a strong sense of equality and justice that you always do your best to make sure that no harm is done. Think about all the positive things you will do when you have made up your mind to overcome your indecision. Start to act more on your impulses rather than circling around your ideas (unless they involve indulging your expensive tastes too much!).

Be more alert to the possibilities around you, and not quite so laid-back in your attitude and approach to your everyday life. As an aunt once wrote in my autograph book when I was a child, "Do noble deeds, not dream them all day long."

If you feel you are worthy of greater success, and are making an effort to achieve it but without getting the right results, the following checklist will give you some points on how to create a better daily regime, without having to completely change your life.

DO . . .

- remember that your expectations can sometimes be *too* high.

- accept yourself for who you are without relying on what other people think.
- be diplomatic without saying things you don't mean.
- start to believe in your ability to make decisions.
- learn to trust your intuition more.
- show your feelings instead of just talking about them.

DON'T . . .
- be so changeable in your thoughts and ideas.
- sit on the fence if you want to move on.
- work on too many ideas all at once.
- upset your balance by involving yourself in arguments.
- hold grievances or grudges silently if they need to be aired.
- let a busy social life override everything else in your life.

Creating Greater Success . . . in Love

To become more successful in love, don't let your indecisiveness mean that you could lose out on having a wonderful emotional relationship because you didn't move fast enough. I have had Libran clients and friends who made that mistake, and I have also listened to the regrets and self-recriminations, especially when they had rejected my advice in the first place.

Don't imagine that I am asking you to become too much like your opposite sign, Aries, whose emotions sometimes race faster than the speed of sound, often propelling their owners into highly unsuitable relationships. I am merely reiterating that balancing your feelings with your idealistic thoughts can bring rewards.

It is not unusual for the typical Libran to fall in love with the *idea* of loving an individual who appears to be eminently suitable in every way. This is the *thought* of love, not the *feeling* of love. It doesn't mean you feel that tug at your heartstrings, that deep inner certainty that tells you you've found someone who could be a soulmate on every level. You have good instincts, Libra, so remember when love is involved it's that deep gut feeling that counts every time. Don't be afraid to say no if you truly feel you're in the wrong relationship. It's much better than ending up in the divorce court later on. And don't be afraid to make a quick decision when you know you've met the right person.

As a flirtatious charmer there is almost no one who can beat you, but if you are still searching without success for that perfect partner to help you balance your Libran scales, you will have to work harder to prove you have more than just a wonderful way with words. Venus, the goddess of love, is your ruling planet, so you do possess reserves of romance waiting to be set free.

Creating Greater Success . . . in Dating

Personally, I don't feel that many Librans need advice on dating, but for those of you who do, it may well be that you are too busy going here, there, and everywhere in your social life with a myriad of different dates, but never taking the time and trouble to know any of them on a more serious one-to-one basis. The trouble with you is that you hate to miss out on something that sounds fun, exciting, or even just vaguely interesting. It's usually easy for you to get a first date, but since you may ask someone out only because you don't want to be alone, you shouldn't expect such an encounter to develop into the most scintillating and romantically inspiring evening; the communication may simply not be there. Perhaps you should get to know people more as friends first, and let the potential partner of your dreams fall into place a bit farther down the line. Be aware that your desire for peace, harmony, and the companionship of a perfect partner tends to become greater as the years go by, which is all the more reason not to waste too much time dating the wrong people now.

LIBRA DATING TIPS
- Be flirtatious and charming, but never superficial and shallow.

- Look for mental compatibility and not just a pretty face.
- Don't take too long to make up your mind when you want to ask someone you really like for a date.

Creating Greater Success . . . in Family Ties

Because you enjoy company so much yourself, you are usually pretty good at keeping in touch with other members of your family, even if they live far away from you. Remember, you're a tower of strength under a seemingly soft exterior. Try to avoid being too laid-back or lazy in your approach to important domestic issues, or leaving them to other people to deal with them when you know the responsibility is yours. To become more successful in maintaining your family ties, you must also be practical. Although you are a wonderful host or hostess, and thoroughly enjoy entertaining on both a small and a large scale, watch out that you don't become so preoccupied with social gatherings and family get-togethers that you forget about some of the important issues involved in day-to-day family relations, especially if you have elderly relatives for whom you may feel responsible. Don't let yourself become lazy about remembering birthdays or anniversaries that you know are important to your family.

Make the most of your wonderful ability to mediate—without being *too* lax in your attitude—if there are any family disagreements to sort out. You are the one sign who can bring peace and harmony to the situation and restore the pride of a relative who feels hurt or left out. You are also great at helping to show children how to behave. Your calm and patient approach works extremely well with almost all young children, as they will sense instinctively that you care about what they think and feel.

Maximize your talent for communicating and spreading sweetness and light, and minimize your indecisiveness. This will put you on a winning track when it comes to establishing successful family ties.

TIPS FOR SUCCESSFUL FAMILY TIES

- Control your indecisiveness when quick decisions are needed.
- Be more organized about your domestic chores.
- Don't get stressed out if your peacemaking tactics don't always succeed in settling a family argument.

Creating Greater Success . . . at Work

The Librans who are most successful with their work are those who have realized early on how important it is to be able to make quick, concise, and well thought out decisions. You cannot expect to be successful at work if you are constantly indecisive about ideas, plans and projects, promotion possibilities, raises, and how to organize your office. You name it, there are a hundred and one things you can mull over if you haven't learned by now that deliberating too long is a definite loss-leader. You are a cardinal sign, and cardinal signs are not supposed to sit back. They are doers!

To be really successful, you need to achieve harmony in the workplace. You often like to think of your colleagues as an extended family. It would seem that open-plan offices would be perfect for such a social animal as you, but it is hard for you to give your best if there is too much noise and activity around you.

Relating well to people is definitely one of your best assets, but make sure you don't get talked into doing something against your will simply because you like the people involved. Taking the line of least resistance isn't the best thing if you want to be truly successful.

Make the most of your brilliant ability to strategize when this talent is needed. Bring your sense of fair play into boardroom or office discussions that erupt into dramas. Never underestimate your talents and abilities when you feel yourself worthy of reaching a higher rung on the ladder of success. You're not as soft as you sometimes appear.

The following do's and don'ts will provide a guide for you to be even more successful at work.

DO . . .
- stick to your decisions when you *do* make them.
- make sure you maximize your talents to the fullest.
- remember you have what it takes to be a leader.

DON'T . . .
- miss out on great opportunities by waiting too long to act.
- undervalue your talents and abilities.
- sit on the fence; decide on a course of action.

Creating Greater Success . . . *in Finding the Right Job*

With your natural ability to relate well to almost anyone, I'm sure you will be extremely presentable and capable of proving just what you're made of during job interviews. You may tend to be a little too laid-back when it comes to putting yourself out there, drifting somewhat aimlessly and hoping for the right opportunity to come your way. If things haven't always gone well and you want to become more successful, you must believe in yourself more and project greater self-confidence. When you maximize the potential of your creative talents and abilities, and are able to put them across to others, you will find that more offers come your way. Don't be afraid of the limelight—it suits you.

If you are a typical Libran, your eye for beauty often leads you into the arts. Writing, painting, and music all feature strongly in Libran careers. You make excellent art dealers, interior decorators, fashion designers, architects, judges, diplomats, counselors, stylists, hairdressers, personnel managers, flight attendants, public relations managers, and advertising executives. You are often drawn to the world of entertainment, too.

Creating Greater Success . . .
in All Your Relationships

One of the most important factors in being successful in life is relating well to other people. Although relating well is one of your finest assets, you might find you can benefit from a few extra tips on how to get along better with each sign.

LIBRA AND ARIES

Opposites definitely attract, and this combination will never be dull. Make sure Aries doesn't get too bored when you become too laid-back. Show your emotions more, and teach Aries the value of patience.

LIBRA AND TAURUS

With this Venus-ruled sign there will be plenty of romantic bliss. Be calm when Taurus is stubborn, patient when the Bull is possessive, and never too extravagant financially. Both of you appreciate the beauty in life.

LIBRA AND GEMINI

Don't try too hard to pin Gemini down and this intellectual and mentally stimulating sign will definitely add a sparkle to your life. Make sure you keep up with all the news, gossip, and latest technological information.

LIBRA AND CANCER

Whereas being rational and logical is your forte, empathy and sensitivity are a Cancerian's strong points. You think things through, but Cancer feels them. Try to be more understanding of the Crab's ups and downs.

LIBRA AND LEO

Give Leo lots of love, affection, and praise when it's deserved, and you've got the Lion for life! Never upstage the Lion, making him or her feel you could possibly be more popular than them. In return let Leo show you how to become more self-confident.

LIBRA AND VIRGO

When Virgo criticizes you, it's often for your own good. Don't upset a Virgo by being too lazy, untidy, or disorganized, as they simply can't cope with any of that. Your ability to be fair-minded is appreciated by this sign.

LIBRA AND LIBRA

A combination of the two of you together sounds perfect, but watch out that you don't spend too much time being so charming and kind to each other that you don't get anything done. Both of you need to organize yourselves on a practical day-to-day basis to live well.

LIBRA AND SCORPIO

Scorpio people can be possessive, jealous, and secretive, while demanding their own private space. Don't be too fickle, flirtatious, or just plain overly sociable, unless you want to discover the sting in the Scorpion's tail.

LIBRA AND SAGITTARIUS

Where you are tactful, the Archer is outspoken and frank. Don't ask for compliments unless you know you deserve them. This is a fun-loving duo if you can both rise above your extravagant tendencies and get down to business.

LIBRA AND CAPRICORN

Both of you long for a perfect world, so don't look askance at Capricorn's determination to work long, hard hours to get to the top. You need to put your social life on the back burner from time to time if you want to stay in step with the Mountain Goat.

LIBRA AND AQUARIUS

Understand and accept that Aquarius likes to be unpredictable and somewhat detached, and doesn't want to change. Appreciate your mental compatibility, and having fun at social gatherings, but don't try to turn the Water Bearer into someone else.

LIBRA AND PISCES

Pisces will provide a wonderful shoulder to lean on, just like you! But both of you will need to be disciplined and resolute on financial issues, and must encourage each other to become more forthright and decisive, too.

Becoming a More Successful Scorpio

If you came into this world between October 23 and November 21, you were born under the sign of Scorpio, the eighth sign of the zodiac. You are a feminine, negative, fixed Water sign, ruled by both Mars, the god of war, and Pluto, the lord of the underworld. Your planetary symbol is the Scorpion. The Serpent and the Eagle are also linked with Scorpio.

I wonder how many of you have sensed that some people seem to draw back hesitantly and almost fearfully as they mutter about the sting in the Scorpion's tail when they first hear that you are a Scorpio. I have often thought you are the most maligned and misunderstood sign in the whole zodiac, because it is so often forgotten that you can be immensely caring and loyal, prepared to do everything in your power to help loved ones or friends who need your help.

To become more successful, perhaps some of you need to recognize and accept something unfortunate but true—there can sometimes be a dark and brooding side to your magnetic personality, one more chilling than charismatic. This trait brings to mind the Scorpio Charles Manson, rather than the brilliantly creative and emotional Scorpio actor, Richard Burton. Some of you will have to find a way to lighten up, be a little less intense, and take life less seriously. You don't have to become a comedian, but you don't always have to place so much emphasis on the darker side of life, either. Through comedy, Roseanne Arnold and Whoopi Goldberg have both proved—and without losing their power—that your sign has the ability to make people laugh. If you can do just a little of the same, I'm sure you will not hear the scorpion's sting mentioned so much.

Because you are invariably extremely psychic, you have the ability to steal a march on the rest of us. You often know what other people are thinking before they say a word, and therefore, deep down, you know what you need to live a satisfying life. However, there is often a self-destructive side to your personality that can make you feel frustrated, jealous, and resentful of other people who appear to be achieving more than you. Few people seem to think of the average Scorpio as insecure, yet it is your hidden insecurity that holds you back. Because you are such a private person, it can be extremely hard for you to reveal your fears and yearnings to anyone else. You are usually described as the sex symbol of the zodiac. You can certainly be mean, moody, and magnificent, too. To become more successful you must be a whole lot more positive in your day-to-day life.

Each sign of the zodiac relates to a different area of the body, starting with the head and ending with the feet, from Aries to Pisces. Scorpio rules the reproductive system and the genital organs, in general, and the bladder, urethra, descending colon, anus, rectum, and prostate gland in particular. It has been said that problems can arise in these areas when your deepest feelings are held back and you refuse to release negative patterns. Scorpio also rules the nose, making nosebleeds common in those born under your sign.

There is a tendency in your Scorpio personality to go to extremes, especially in sexual excess. To become more satisfied with your life, you need to create and maintain balance. With Mars and Pluto ruling your sign, you possess great energy and wonderfully recuperative powers whenever you fall sick. However, this doesn't give you the green light to exhaust your mind, body, or soul.

When you are positive and use your instincts to help you decide on the kind of success you want from your life, you will rise above insecurity like a phoenix rising from the ashes and go forward fearlessly. Watch out that you don't become reckless. Remember, the scorpion will even sting himself to death when he is surrounded by a ring of fire! I'm not suggesting you would go to those lengths, but it will help you to be a little more flexible, and to modify your strong will. You are often described as invincible, but even you can benefit from a few words of advice.

Please don't be like one of my Scorpio clients, who during his first consultation with me confirmed he had indeed gone through all the relationship problems I saw in his horoscope: He was involved deeply with two women, yet was not totally sure about his feelings for either. He told me he would resolve the situation and never make the same mistake again. He appeared a few months later, not only having failed to take my advice to sort out his love life, but having acquired even more problems from charting his own course to destruction, since each woman was putting pressure on him to marry her, and he had also met someone new.

It is obvious that you hate the thought of being in someone else's power, but it often surprises me that you seem to lose out by not appreciating the benefits of your own power. Some of the people who were born under the sign of Scorpio include Marie Curie, Billy Graham, Theodore Roosevelt, Dr. Jonas Salk, Nehru, Indira Gandhi, Dostoyevsky, Trotsky, Dylan Thomas, Dr. Christian Barnard, Carl Sagan, and Michel Gauquelin. These personalities would never suggest the notion that Scorpios are weak! The Eagle, another symbol of your sign, represents your power to rise above the temptations of your own lower nature. Resolve to be more like an eagle soaring to the heights, not the secretive scorpion that hides away out of the light and stings those who surprise it.

Defining Your Goals

Naturally not every Scorpio reading this book wants to be a world leader, a scientist, surgeon, physicist, or a religious minister, even though you might be great at these careers. And you may not aspire to being the next Picasso, Bizet, Joni Mitchell, or Mort Sahl—Scorpios all. However, your high energy level, both emotionally and psychologically, makes you yearn for a goal or challenge to pit yourself against. This book will give you pointers on how to hone your Scorpio personality traits to lead a more rewarding life.

How to Achieve Your Emotional Goals

Do not negate the power of your emotions. Your burning intensity, passionate beliefs, and sometimes almost violent mood swings are the very things that make lesser mortals back away. To achieve your emotional goals, especially if they include having a good relationship with someone else, you will often need to examine a little more carefully your effect on others.

While you yearn for mental and physical compatibility on a grand scale, you are not always the most romantic of souls. Sexual ecstasy is of major importance to the average Scorpio, but you can lose out on really good relationships because you think that sex is the only issue at stake.

Unless you try harder to balance your life on more of a mind-body-soul level, a preoccupation with sex can lead you into more erotic and promiscuous ways.

You have within you the power to enlighten yourself, and to transform yourself emotionally into a more openly loving person. But for this to happen, you must allow yourself to become more vulnerable emotionally, enabling another person to reach deep into your heart and touch you in a place that may always have been locked. Since some of you seem to find it hard to fathom your own deep emotions, is it any wonder that other people may find it equally difficult to understand them?

To achieve your emotional goals, of course you must first admit you have them. You may consider your goals to be adding up sexual conquests, living for the moment, and not caring about the consequences. You may decide you are fine the way you are, or you may throw your emotions wholeheartedly into a religious crusade. Having emotional needs is an important part of being a Scorpio. When they are unfulfilled you can feel very lonely, depressed, and even angry. This is tough for a Scorpio because it means that you have to fight against the self-destructive side of your sign. All the more reason to work toward achieving your emotional goals in a truly positive way.

As a Water sign, you tend to feel before you think. If you continuously block your feelings there is a part of your personality that could explode. Harness the power within you with love rather than anger. You are a sign of great extremes, of immovable strength, and seething turbulent emotions. When you find your own personal way to balance those extremes you will at the same time find it much easier to achieve greater emotional balance with other people.

EMOTIONS AND THE SCORPIO WOMAN

If you're a typical Scorpio woman, it's ten to one that you know you are possibly the most sexually magnetic, charismatically fascinating, shrewd, intuitive, and powerful femme fatale. Whether it's the ice-cool look of Grace Kelly, the smoldering sexuality of Vivien Leigh, the unabashed ease with which you show off your pregnant nude body on the cover of *Vanity Fair,* like Demi Moore, or the ability to call off a wedding at the very last moment, as Julia Roberts once did—the Scorpio woman is more than a match for any man who tries to possess you!

True to your Scorpio personality, you are a law unto yourself—comedienne Roseanne certainly is. Scorpio women really use their power! Jodie Foster refuses to allow the press to intrude into her emotional life. Meg Ryan will not be drawn into discussions about her mother. Lauren Hutton certainly was not going to allow advancing years to prevent her from continuing a successful modeling and acting career. Hillary Rodham Clinton, the magazine editors Tina Brown and Anna

Wintour, and the actresses Katharine Hepburn, Linda Evans, Goldie Hawn, and Sally Field were all born under your powerful sign, as were Tatum O'Neal and Marla Maples.

In spite of your magnetism, I know from Scorpio clients and friends that you don't always find it easy to achieve a harmonious emotional life with a husband or lover. While you appear to have the art of seduction at your fingertips (no wonder Mata Hari was born under your sign!), the ability to differentiate between lust and love seems to be less simple for you. I do not wish to imply that every Scorpio woman is a sex maniac between the sheets, but sex is of paramount importance to your sign and for this reason you do need a relationship that is going to fulfill your sexual needs as much as your emotional ones. The trouble is that finding the proper balance often seems to be a problem for you.

As a feminine, fixed Water sign, you are very emotional, and with both Mars and Pluto ruling Scorpio, you are also very strong and determined and you inwardly yearn for control and power. For a relationship to be truly successful, you need a partner who is also strong and whom you can respect. Learn to control your possessiveness and jealousy, though. Since you insist on protecting your own private space, you must also learn to respect a partner's similar needs. Try to forgive and forget mistakes a little more often. This may not be easy for Scorpios of either sex, but it is an integral part of most rewarding relationships.

You invariably possess an abundance of intuition—why don't you intuitively get more in touch with yourself, so greater emotional success can come your way.

EMOTIONS AND THE SCORPIO MAN

If the truth be known, it is probably only fair to say you are the smoothest chatter-up in the zodiac. One look from your deepset smouldering eyes seems to send half the female population into a swoon. Rhett Butler surely was a Scorpio! And if not, at least we know that Margaret Mitchell, who wrote *Gone With the Wind,* was. Richard Burton, Alain Delon, Burt Lancaster, Rock Hudson, Lee Strasberg, Martin Scorsese, Lucchino Visconti, Roy Scheider, Sam Shepherd, Prince Charles, and King Hussein of Jordan are all Scorpio males.

One of my closest friends is a Scorpio actor. Heaven help the women involved with him—he possesses every single Scorpio characteristic and has never found it easy to settle down, even when he was deeply in love. I often feel that Scorpio men must have been taught the game of chess from an early age, since they are masters of every strategy in the book. However, while your personal magnetism is not in dispute, your macho, manipulative, possessive, and intensely calculating ways can be almost impossible to deal with.

To have a more successful emotional life, you need to be more honest, not just with a partner, but with yourself. If Britain's Prince Charles had expressed his emotions more openly years ago, Princess Diana and the rest of the royal family, let alone Camilla Parker Bowles, would not have been hounded by the world's press over that famous marriage breakup. Don't be so involved with your own ego and so convinced you can control the rest of the world. If you would only admit that underneath your seemingly invincible exterior there beats the heart of a somewhat self-destructive small boy, you would achieve far greater success in the emotional stakes.

When you fall head over heels in love, it hits you hard, and is not necessarily easy. Richard Burton's relationship with the Piscean Elizabeth Taylor showed the Scorpio male's need for a soulmate. The trouble is that most of you don't realize that you need a partner who is not just a sensual and seductive lover, but has the ability to reach your soul, too.

With your insatiable curiosity and psychic ability, you are brilliant at unearthing the mysteries of life, so it cannot be too difficult for you to decipher your own personality, however complex it may appear on the surface. Accept that you are ruled by your emotions, and learn to express them in a more positive way. Don't consistently seek to manipulate anyone with whom you become involved, unless you're prepared to accept the same sort of behavior in return—remember, though, that you tend to seethe with rage when anyone tries to cramp your style.

Sometimes you hold on far too long to things best forgotten, and suffer tremendously for past mistakes. It is not easy for you to forget anything, but try not to hang on to any negative emotional patterns of the past. Release them, let them go, and open your heart to more positive and lighter feelings. You will be far more successful emotionally once you do this.

How to Achieve Your Material Goals

When you are determined to achieve something, you go about it with great intensity and passion, just as you do with almost everything else in your life. However, to be successful, you must examine and define exactly what you want to achieve. Scorpio is the eighth sign of the zodiac, which relates to business issues, death, and regeneration. If you're a typical Scorpio, your goals will invariably involve reaching a position of power. You are very much ruled by this urge for power and control, and you intensely dislike the idea of being subservient to others, especially to those for whom you have little respect.

As a deep-feeling Water sign, you are quite prepared to throw yourself heart and soul into what you believe. Watch out that you don't completely exhaust yourself by letting your ambitions take over at the expense of everything else. If you have a thirst for power, don't become too ruthless, manipulative, and controlling. Acting this way will make you enemies along the way.

If you want to be more successful, you will almost certainly need some help and understanding from other people. Don't alienate them by becoming too consumed with your own importance and need for gratification. Avoid being so fearful that others will gain an advantage over you that you become more secretive than ever.

To achieve the most success, plan carefully. Things don't have to happen overnight. You will achieve more with the slow-but-sure approach, utilizing your clever mind and brilliant memory as you move along. Spend the necessary time searching out the facts and information you need. You have the patience, and you certainly have the inclination to succeed.

Power struggles will never bother you, since in maximizing your potential, you know deep down you are invincible. Stamina, endurance, and a warrior spirit—you have them all. As a fixed sign, you certainly won't be pushed away from a goal on which you have set your heart. As a Scorpio your instincts and intuition will help lead you in the right direction. There is no need to become bitter or obsessive if you encounter setbacks, as they will not deter you for very long.

With the benefits of your highly tuned intuition, together with your phenomenal power, drive, and concentration, you will be able to tune into what is happening around you, and see how you can exploit your own talents and abilities to achieve greater material fulfillment. Your material goals do not necessarily involve making a fortune, or being the chairman of the board, but they do include satisfying your hunger for power, even if it's behind the scenes. The benefit of your power is that even if you fail to achieve a particular material goal, you won't give up. Like the proverbial phoenix rising from the ashes, you will lift your head and start again.

Don't ever give up, Scorpio. You have the power within you to succeed, so get rid of any fears and frustrations that may be left over from past experiences. Your invincible determination will always win through. You thrive on crisis—it's all part of the regenerative energy that flows through your sign.

The Powerful Assets at Your Disposal to Become More Successful

The Power of Your Element . . . Water

The four elements, Fire, Earth, Air, and Water, have a great bearing on one's star sign characteristics. Scorpio is the second of the three Water signs, Cancer and Pisces being the other two. The element of Water makes all three of you caring and sensitive, but in your case your emotions are far more powerful and intense. You will be powerfully directed to follow your feelings, instincts, and intuition, as you will be extremely psychic and sometimes telepathic. You will also discover that learning to balance your inner and outer self will help you achieve greater success in life.

Because you are also a fixed sign, and ruled by Mars and Pluto, you will not be deterred from your chosen path without a struggle. A typical Scorpio will usually win, no matter how great the challenges.

As a Water sign, it will be immensely beneficial for your personality if you try harder to let your emotions flow more gently to balance the strong and unpredictable ebb and flow of feelings, which can almost be scary to anyone involved with you. While there is no doubt that your emotions are incredibly intense, if you are a typical Scorpio you often tend to repress them in some way, and to brood silently. Just because your element is water, there is surely no need for the rest of us to feel as though the water has changed from boiling hot to icy cold in a split second.

Since you care greatly about the suffering of others, I'm sure you do not consciously mean to be cruel, but sometimes you come across that way. Do try harder to be a little more like the other two Water signs, Cancer and Pisces, and be more compassionate. Sometimes you are very hard on other people, especially if they do not live up to your expectations. You almost seem to punish yourself after allowing others to see that you can't control your tears.

Continue to be strong, but don't be afraid to show humility, too. Think of these words by the seventeenth-century French priest St. Francis de Sales: "Nothing is so strong as gentleness; nothing so gentle as real strength." Therefore, allow your Water element to contribute to your gentleness, for then your Scorpio strength will become even greater.

The Power of Your Ruling Planets . . . Mars and Pluto

With both these planets ruling your sign, it is hardly a surprise that you are seemingly invincible and possess an abundance of inner strength. Mars, who is also the ruler of Aries, was the Roman god of war, and the power of this planet will enable you to fight for what you believe in, to challenge all opponents in the success stakes, and to rise above adversity. Your energy will seem limitless and you will not be averse to taking a few risks when necessary, although you will use this Martian power in a more controlled and less headstrong and immediately aggressive manner than Aries. Used in a positive way, Mars is a powerful ally for those of you keen to survive and climb higher up the ladder of success.

Your passion and sexual drive are also given added impetus by Mars. Watch out that the god of war doesn't also make you too aggressive, competitive, ruthless, manipulative, and too much of a power-player. Beware also of becoming insatiable in your desires, especially sexual ones. There is a tendency within you to become too obsessive and paranoid over inner fears and insecurities, and to give in to drug or alcohol abuse. Scorpios have even been driven to suicide by the torments they can build up inside them. Pluto can help you to bring things to the surface.

In Greek mythology Pluto was linked with Hades, who ruled the Underworld with his wife, Persephone. His astrological associations are with the regenerative and creative forces of the body, with enforced change, and with the beginnings and endings of life phases. It is Pluto you have to thank for your regenerative powers—your ability to rise above any problems that might devastate some of the other signs. Pluto's influence also lets you see beyond the here and now, and you must use Pluto's powers to take you above the mundane if you want to be truly successful.

Pluto's power will enable you to unearth the mysteries of life, to get beneath its complexities. It is Pluto that will always spur you on to greater heights, reaching for the light of profound knowledge, and lead you toward greater communication with your own higher mind. Bear this in mind whenever you feel dragged down by circumstances or your own negativity, and you will soon rise up again with an even stronger understanding of life and a stronger belief in your own power, too.

Pluto's influence as your co-ruler will make many of you interested in religion (Scorpio Billy Graham is a well-known crusader), the occult, and reincarnation.

The Power of Your Rising Sign

Your Ascendant, or rising sign, is the sign that was rising on the eastern horizon at the time of your birth. In many ways it is as important as your Sun and Moon signs in influencing the way you play out your life. Using the table on pages 278–79, you can determine your Ascendant sign. And the brief descriptions below tell you what your Scorpio personality would be like with the twelve rising signs, and how they can help you to be more successful:

SCORPIO WITH ARIES RISING

Definitely a combustible combination. You have an unbeatable amount of energy to make dynamic decisions, and the ability to rise fearlessly to any challenge that comes your way. Watch out that your Aries Ascendant doesn't make you too headstrong and impulsive.

SCORPIO WITH TAURUS RISING

Determination combined with an amazingly patient Taurean approach enables you to scale great heights with ease. Your opposite sign as Ascendant also helps you to realize that emotional and material security are both worth attaining.

SCORPIO WITH GEMINI RISING

Your Gemini Ascendant gives you an altogether lighter view of life than is usual in Scorpios, though you still can't resist delving below the surface. An abundance of creative Gemini ideas, combined with your powers of intuition, can bring great success.

SCORPIO WITH CANCER RISING

Your Cancer Ascendant helps to make you more compassionate, sensitive, and sympathetic, so no one can accuse you of being a ruthless power-player who breaks any rules to gain greater success. Cancer makes love and romance more important, too.

SCORPIO WITH LEO RISING

Let the Leo sun shine in so that you lose some of your brooding Scorpio intensity and thirst for power. You will enjoy having fun and coming up with creative ideas that can help you become more of a star and be loved by everyone.

SCORPIO WITH VIRGO RISING

Scorpio intuition combined with precise and critical Virgoan analysis makes you a winner in the success stakes. Don't let the Virgo influence make you start worrying that you don't have what it takes to reap life's rewards. Take some time off to rest your overworked mind.

SCORPIO WITH LIBRA RISING

You may appear to be more lightweight than the usual Scorpio, but all that Libran charm, tact, and diplomacy can be an incredible asset to your unique brand of power strategy. With Libra rising, you find it easier to relax in the company of others than many Scorpios.

SCORPIO WITH SCORPIO RISING

Heaven help an adversary who comes up against you. You truly will be the most invincible of all the Scorpios around. But remember, being cold, calculating, and ruthless isn't going to win you too many friends up there at the top.

SCORPIO WITH SAGITTARIUS RISING

A friendlier and more optimistic Scorpio would be hard to find. Your Sagittarius Ascendant helps you to view life's brighter hues, and your enthusiasm and enterprising ways help you to convince just about anyone that you're a real star.

SCORPIO WITH CAPRICORN RISING

No one could ever accuse you of not working hard to reach your goals. Watch out that you aren't too materialistic and conservative in your approach to life. Your sense of duty, combined with your insight, will definitely bear fruit.

SCORPIO WITH AQUARIUS RISING

Fixed in your opinions, fixed in your feelings, and consequently somewhat detached defines this combo. When you stay detached from life most of the time, there are bound to be occasions when you become too unpredictable for your own good. Try to express yourself a little better, and be responsive to those around you.

SCORPIO WITH PISCES RISING

Your Pisces Ascendant gives you the ability to empathize far more easily with friends as well as foes than is usual with Scorpios. Allow your sensitivity to shine through, for it will enable us to see a much softer and more tolerant you.

How to Create Greater Success

Creating Greater Success . . . in Your Everyday Life

If you're a typical Scorpio, the idea of structure and organization is unlikely to worry you, since you realize that they can be useful for increasing your own importance. You are invariably determined to create greater success, no matter where you stand at present. However, you must try harder to be more forgiving when other people, perhaps unwittingly, do something that offends or upsets you. Make the most of your brilliantly retentive memory for the things that really are important and not just to nurse slights that most other signs would shrug off in a second.

You may feel that being asked for too many details about your personal life is an infringement of your privacy; start to accept also that your prying too much into other people's lives is also intolerable. Since you hate to feel possessed and constrained in any way at all, remember that it works both ways.

You have the power to rise above obstacles and achieve greatness. Try learning to relax. Putting the maximum effort into each day will certainly help you to become more successful, but life does not have to be a continual crusade with no time off for good behavior.

Use your power in a constructive way, not to make others feel scared and insecure because they've heard so much about the sting in the scorpion's tail. Instead, use your personal magnetism in your everyday life to draw people to you. You want them to like you and feel comfortable with you.

If you feel you are worthy of success, yet somehow it seems to elude you, the following checklist will give you some pointers on how to create a better daily regime, without having to completely change your life.

DO . . .

- recharge your emotional and mental batteries once in a while.
- remember that love and compassion are always worthy assets.
- try to see yourself as others see you.
- listen to your instincts—they won't let you down.
- stick to your ideals and be secure with your thoughts.
- try to be more honest with yourself and others.

DON'T . . .

- be too obsessed with every little issue.
- be a control freak with other people.
- let your power-playing get out of control.
- make sex the only thing that really makes your world go round.
- become paranoid about that sting in your tail!
- take things to such extremes that you become a martyr.

Creating Greater Success . . . in Love

The rewards of your keenness of mind, power, and control should not become substitutes for a properly balanced emotional relationship; this will only create complications in your life. Your feelings are extremely intense and passionate, and sometimes so overpowering that you might scare off someone you desperately want to attract to your side.

To become really successful in love, you need to examine your feelings with total honesty. Often you fall hook, line, and sinker for someone—become obsessed with them—because of a strong sexual attraction. It's as if you were regenerated through the sex act. On a deep soul level, though, you may feel frustrated if your relationship continues to be based solely on sex.

The art of sexual seduction is rarely difficult for a Scorpio, but deep down you hope for the sort of mind, body, and soul relationship that doesn't happen every day. When it does, you must work harder than others not to spoil it by your excessively jealous and possessive ways. The fiery heat of your passion will sometimes switch to icy-cold behavior for no apparent reason. Intense one moment and totally remote the next, your feelings are not easy to understand. Stop taking things to the extreme and avoid battling with your own emotions.

To become more successful in love you need to try opening yourself up more, to trust in your intuition, and to overcome your innermost fears and insecurities. When you can do this successfully you will also be able to love someone else without fearing rejection. You need a partner with an inner strength you can respect, for someone who is weak will tend to bring out your own negative qualities.

Visualize yourself as more than a sex symbol. Be a sensitive, compassionate soul, too. Don't be so jealous, possessive, and domineering.

Creating Greater Success . . . in Dating

Do you go dating like everyone else, or are you rather like a vampire searching for the next neck to bite? Sorry, Scorpio, that question probably sounds horribly unfair, but it does often seem that way when you are on the loose looking for a new conquest upon whom to unleash your passionate emotions!

To become more successful in dating, I suggest you lighten up a little. Don't make it quite so obvious you are sizing up a person's physical attributes and wondering what he or she would be like in bed, when they are trying to conduct an intellectual conversation with you.

It's often true that one intense glance from your deep, smouldering Scorpio eyes can send shivers down the spine of any recipient of such a glance. And it's also true that you rely on your instinct, intuition, psychic powers—call it what you will—to flash you the green light when the sexual chemistry seems to flow between you and another. Try to take things a little more slowly. Get to know the mind beneath the body, discover whether you can communicate on more than one level, and don't frighten people away by coming on too strong.

SCORPIO DATING TIPS
- Be sexy and sensual, but make sure you can converse well.
- Show you're a good listener, too, and not just thinking of sex.
- Don't relentlessly chase someone who doesn't want to become involved with you, even if your pride is at stake.

Creating Greater Success . . . in Family Ties

I'm not sure you're the most brilliant sign at dealing with family ties, because you are such a private person, keeping so many of your emotions to yourself. At the same time, you often demand that others reveal their innermost thoughts and secrets to you. If people want to tell you things, fine, but you will be much more successful if you stop trying to pry and probe.

Since you are deeply sentimental, you are an expert at remembering significant dates such as birthdays and anniversaries. You are also amazingly loyal and supportive of the people you love. But this isn't always obvious—try to be a little more outgoing and openly unselfish so you can maintain enjoyable family relationships. Don't be so manipulative when it comes down to other people's time schedules, especially if you are not prepared to be more flexible with your own. Try not to be controlling with family members who do not fit into your idea of how they should act. After all, you intensely dislike anyone telling *you* what to do.

Your strong sexual urges may have led you into unsuccessful relationships that produced children. Even if, for whatever reason, you part with the father or mother of that child, try to keep the relationship with the child going, so that your offspring never feels abandoned by you. Not that you would ever forget anything, especially a child of your own flesh. But being forgiving is not always easy for Scorpio, and by not forgiving a partner you may also inflict unnecessary pain and suffering on the child.

Try not to allow power struggles to play a role in your relationships with members of your family, especially parents who have always tried to do their best for you.

TIPS FOR SUCCESSFUL FAMILY TIES
- Try to create a good and realistic understanding between yourself and your relatives.
- Let your sentimentality shine through a little more often—it's sometimes buried too deep.
- Don't hold grudges for anyone's past mistakes.

Creating Greater Success . . . at Work

Determined to prove your invincibility, you will usually strive courageously to reach the pinnacle of your chosen career. Scorpio is the sign of big business, joint financial ventures, inheritances, and investments. You excel at dealing with all these, and it is important to remember your own financial security is extremely important—which you have in common with your opposite sign, Taurus. Be thankful you possess such a shrewd mind, uncanny intuition, and a phenomenal memory. These traits will help you to be in the right place at the right time.

To become truly successful, you need a goal, something of a crusade to pit your steely determination and strong will against. Think of Billy Graham's determination to bring his religious message to the public, of Pablo Picasso's need to show the world what was happening in Spain through his painting *Guernica*, Dr. Christian Barnard's pioneering heart-transplant techniques, and of course Marie Curie's radiation research.

Since both Pluto and Mars rule your sign, you have to keep in check your tendency to try to overthrow anyone who stands in your path. Competing for your chosen goal does not mean you need to alienate the very people whose support you need. Don't make adversaries out of potential allies, and don't show your resentment if a colleague receives the praise you feel should be yours.

The best way to achieve greater success in your professional life is to throw your energy wholeheartedly into something you believe in; make it your mission. Watch out, though, that you don't burn up your energy and end up feeling angry and stressed out when things are tough. Holding on to negative feelings and memories will only hold you back.

The following do's and don'ts will also provide a guide for you to become even more successful at work.

DO . . .
- continue to enjoy challenges, but don't create unnecessary fights.
- endeavor to feel passionate about your work.
- try to relate well with everyone you work with, even if it involves some compromise.

DON'T . . .
- demoralize colleagues by pointing out their inadequacies.
- block your creativity by giving way to hidden insecurities.
- be an obsessive megalomaniac.

Creating Greater Success . . .
in Finding the Right Job

The perfect job for you will always be in a profession that is mentally and emotionally stimulating and fulfilling. Try not to go for anything that is lackluster and likely to leave you bored and frustrated. Make sure the remuneration will be up to scratch, so you don't resent having to put in long hours for too little in return.

Since Scorpio is the sign of transformation and regeneration, you may be happiest performing tasks that give you the chance to create something that transforms other people's lives—like the moving poetry of the Scorpions Sylvia Plath and Dylan Thomas, the sculpture of Rodin, the paintings of Francis Bacon, and the powerful acting of Richard Burton. Always try to make use of your investigative talents, and trust your intuition. If a job opportunity sounds right for you, it probably will be.

If you are a typical Scorpio, not only will you be exceedingly good at anything related with finance, but also your capabilities can be effective in psychiatry, psychology, research, police work, and in the professions of orator, politician, pharmacist, debater, scientist, healer or medium, lawyer, gossip columnist, surgeon, or religious leader.

Creating Greater Success . . .
in All Your Relationships

One of the most important factors in being successful in life is to relate well to other people. The following information offers you a few extra tips on getting along with all the signs.

SCORPIO AND ARIES

With a double dose of Martian energy and plenty of passion, this duo makes a fiery relationship on every level. Aries is a child at heart and emotionally more vulnerable than you, so don't be too cold, calculating, and manipulative.

SCORPIO AND TAURUS

Whereas you're fascinated by mystery, intrigue, and perhaps the darker side of life, earthy Taurus wants security and an uncomplicated life. But opposites do attract, and you are both sensual, stubborn, and eager to make money.

SCORPIO AND GEMINI

Enjoy Gemini's mental dexterity, flights of fancy, and sense of humor, but don't try to pin down this free-as-air and flirtatious sign. Neither jealousy nor the sting of your tail will have the slightest effect, so just enjoy things moment by moment.

SCORPIO AND CANCER

A mutual understanding of moods, emotions, and deep, deep feelings will make this a good combination. Whether you are colleagues, friends, partners, or lovers, you will know just how to nurture each other's needs and desires.

SCORPIO AND LEO

Leo can be just as strong-willed and stubborn as you, and Leo needs to take center stage at least once a day. Try not to be intensely emotional or to chastise the Lion for being too flamboyant and extravagant.

SCORPIO AND VIRGO

Don't be too critical, for Virgo is more adept at criticism than you. A working relationship will be successful, since you both involve yourself passionately in achieving your goals. Keep in mind that Virgo can blow as emotionally hot and cold as you.

SCORPIO AND LIBRA

Libra is the sign of peace and harmony, but don't forget that Librans can also be as coolly manipulative as you. Try to control your complex mood swings and in return ask Libra to promise to try to be less indecisive. Libra likes company, but you also need some privacy.

SCORPIO AND SCORPIO

Surely you won't need much advice to understand someone just like you! With another Scorpio, it's even more important to avoid being overly jealous, possessive, controlling, power-playing—in fact, overly *anything;* otherwise it will be a power struggle to the bitter end.

SCORPIO AND SAGITTARIUS

Don't try telling the Archer what to do. This sign is convinced he or she has all the answers. Don't be too brooding or intense, either, for Sagittarius wants to enjoy seeing the bright and positive side of life.

SCORPIO AND CAPRICORN

You two share an ambitious streak and a desire for financial security. You have much to learn from the Mountain Goat's determination to scale the heights to greater success, but don't expect Capricorn to go for sex as much as you.

SCORPIO AND AQUARIUS

Your passionate intensity could be just too much for this emotionally detached Air sign, so you'll need to simmer down. Don't try to control an Aquarius, even if you truly think it is for his or her own good.

SCORPIO AND PISCES

This Water sign can fulfill your deepest emotional needs if you're prepared to be a little more romantic. A working relationship could be harder unless you are both truly committed to your goal and you can convince Pisces that being more practical isn't a sin.

Becoming a
More Successful
Sagittarius

If you came into this world between November 22 and December 20, you were born under the sign of Sagittarius, the ninth sign of the zodiac. You are a masculine, positive, mutable Fire sign, ruled by Jupiter, the planet of good fortune. Your planetary symbol is the Archer.

Sagittarius is known as the sign of the higher mind, the sage, or counselor, as well as the long-distance traveler of the zodiac. You love to explore fresh avenues, conquer new fields, and you do love to bequeath advice to others, in your frank, honest, and even sometimes tactless manner. However, you are not always open to receiving words of wisdom from other people, because you appear convinced you know yourself best. To become more successful, you should acknowledge that advice can be extremely worthwhile. It is also true that you are one of the most positive signs in the whole zodiac. You possess masses of optimism, an adventurous disposition, and a sense of humor. Thanks to the influence of your ruler, Jupiter, it can also be said you receive an almost unfair amount of lucky breaks.

One of your less positive traits is your insistence on moralizing to everyone else, because they do not see things your way. Why should you present yourself as an example for the rest of us to follow? If other people don't want to trust to luck as much as you do, who are you to say they are wrong? To become more successful in life, you need to be a little more considerate of others' points of view.

One of the marvelous qualities of those born under your sign is your strong sense of survival. You can suffer setbacks that would send the rest of us reeling, but you manage to come up smiling, ready to start again. Don't ever lose your wonderful belief in life and all the good things it has to offer, for this truly is one of your most positive characteristics.

Each sign of the zodiac relates to different areas of the body, starting with the head and ending with the feet, from Aries to

Pisces. Sagittarius rules the hips and thighs, the veins and sciatic nerves, the femur and ilium, and the coccygeal and sacral regions of the spine. Many of you are extremely conscious of the importance of exercise (keeping those hips and thighs in good shape!) and you are often highly successful in sports. Jane Fonda was born under your sign, as were Joe DiMaggio, Lee Trevino, Chris Evert Lloyd, and Imran Khan.

With Jupiter ruling your sign, your potential for success is high, boosted by your innate belief in your own talents and abilities, often since childhood. Take the case of the Sagittarian Steven Spielberg, who, I feel, had no doubt that he would be famous one day. To become truly successful, it is also important to have the ability to convince other people you have what it takes to get ahead. This should not be a problem, given your natural self-confidence and good judgment.

While you are invariably brilliant at thinking great thoughts and coming up with amazing ideas to help you conquer the world, you are not always so fabulous at coping with the nitty-gritty side of putting those ideas into action. It's certainly not that you lack either the will or the inclination, but far more that your restless mind is always moving on to something new before you have accomplished the task at hand. Watch out that your restlessness does not become a drawback, especially when you have major things to accomplish. If greater success is your intention, you need to become more disciplined and less irresponsible and reckless. The symbol of Sagittarius is the centaur (half man and half horse) shooting a bow and arrow. Concentration is vital for the centaur's sure aim, and it is equally important that your concentration does not falter when you aim for your goals. In many ways your life is a perpetual quest, although I feel that some of you do not even know what you are searching for. There is a wanderlust, a need to travel far and wide to seek out your goals. If you're a typical Sagittarian you will usually not need to be told to broaden your horizons, as this comes easily to you. However, it is important for you to focus on what is right in front of your eyes, too. Some of you are even extremely philosophical. Laurens van der Post, Aleksandr Solzhenitsyn, Nostradamus, and Bhagwan Rajneesh were all born under your sign.

Along with your philosophical side, you have a good sense of humor, which is usually an integral part of the Sagittarius personality and can be an extremely useful asset. To be able to laugh at life and yourself is a wonderful way to overcome problems. Considering that you manage to find a humorous side in almost everything, it is hardly surprising that Sagittarian Woody Allen is able to turn his own neuroses into many brilliantly funny skits while nonetheless handling serious themes in his movies.

If you are a typical Sagittarian you have the potential to rise above even the most tremendous odds to achieve greater success. Think of the obstacles faced by the artist Toulouse-Lautrec, who overcame the tragedy of crippled legs to paint wonderful works; the unhappiness in the personal lives of both Edith Piaf and Maria Callas, who captivated us with their voices; and the way José Carreras continues to delight us with his voice, having successfully overcome serious illness.

Defining Your Goals

Naturally not every Sagittarius reading this wants to travel the world, become a brilliant philosopher, or be a movie producer like the Sagittarians Walt Disney and Steven Spielberg. But if you are a typical Sagittarian you are bound to have some goals, even if they are currently just ideas flitting around in your ever restless mind. Once you conceive the ideas, you will always look for ways to turn them into reality. This guide offers you advice on how to use your Sagittarian personality to attain greater emotional and material success in your life.

How to Achieve Your Emotional Goals

On the surface you seem to be self-confident, bright, breezy, and free as a bird. This makes you appear as if you wouldn't have a problem in the world in achieving your emotional goals. However, I have known Sagittarian clients and friends who have found it extremely difficult to balance their freedom-loving ways with a need for emotional security. To get what you want out of life, you must get over your deep-seated fear of commitment. This applies not only to your attempts at building long-lasting relationships, but to every aspect of your life. It is sometimes hard for you to contemplate a permanent relationship or staying in one place for very long.

Attracting admirers to your side is not usually the problem, but deciding whether you're ready to take a fun and happy-go-lucky friendship or relationship on to a deeper level can totally confuse you. Then again, because you seem to be born with a gambling streak, you will sometimes go full steam ahead without feeling one hundred percent sure of your feelings. People born under your sign tend to marry more than a few times—and may be totally convinced it is forever each time.

To achieve your emotional goals without a whole lot of hassle and upsets all round, you must first be sure of what you want. If you value your freedom above all else and want to travel the world unhampered by any emotional ties, it is hardly sensible to declare undying love to someone who will never understand what you're all about. While this may be an extreme case to use as an example, take the interesting fact that while Woody Allen was involved with the Aquarian Mia Farrow, he always kept his own apartment. This represents the Sagittarian need to feel inwardly free—and, interestingly enough, the Aquarian need, too.

As a Fire sign, you tend to rush in with fiery optimism, and can be almost as headstrong as Aries, and as charismatic as Leo. But try to control your restless ways and consider possible outcomes before you enter into yet another relationship where you may fall short of your goals.

Your overriding need for freedom may make it difficult for you to take responsibility for a deep emotional commitment. If you do so, though, I think you will find you can be just as idealistic about love as any other sign.

EMOTIONS AND THE SAGITTARIUS WOMAN

You're a cheerful bundle of fun, with a heart of gold, and an open mind. Your sense of humor is truly wonderful, so it's not surprising that Bette Midler was born under your sign.

Emotionally, many of you are idealistic about relationships. You probably fell in love early with the star basketball player at your school and were devastated when he treated you like one of the guys. Many Sagittarian women may find themselves in this predicament because half of you wants to be one of the guys and the other half wants to be a femme fatale. If you would only learn to balance the two, life would be much easier.

In addition to being idealistic, you are often very independent and outspoken, with an incredible love of life, which enables you to be perfectly happy without a permanent partner, just as long as your life is exciting. However, if you genuinely want a long-standing relationship in your life and have previously found it hard to sustain one, then it's time to ask yourself whether you are willing to give up your freedom. Freedom is one of the most important words in the Sagittarius vocabulary. Freedom of speech, freedom of action, freedom at all costs! But what happens when you fall in love? Admittedly some of you change; Jane Fonda used to speak out passionately for her political beliefs and is now very happy being Mrs. Ted Turner. But those of you who refuse to change anything about your freedom-at-all-costs personality usually find it much harder to have a successful one-on-one relationship. You often drift from one person to another, getting out when the going appears to get tough, or rather when some kind of commitment is needed.

Those of you who cling tenaciously to personal freedom sometimes have a shock when you fall deeply in love. You may discover something about yourself you don't like—that you can be as jealous and possessive as a Scorpio, or as dreamily romantic as a Pisces. Be careful when this happens, because there is a tendency for you to have become so used to living your free and easy life-style that you genuinely don't know how to deal with reality.

I have known both friends and clients who have literally become emotional wrecks waiting for the telephone to ring, especially if you have been used to having things your way. Remember, you don't have to lose your independence just because you're in love. You can remain strong-willed and have a partner at the same time. Sagittarian Kim Basinger's relationship with Alec Baldwin has survived.

It is important for a Sagittarian woman to admit she has emotional needs, even if they are so often glossed over by your quest to find greater excitement in your life. Since you believe so strongly in giving love to others, you must accept and believe you also have the staying power to sustain a good relationship without losing your individuality.

EMOTIONS AND THE SAGITTARIUS MAN

Think of an amusing, open-minded, generous, fun-loving best friend, and you have summed up the personality of a typical Sagittarian man. Okay, there is the other side of your makeup, too, for the Sagittarian painter Edward Munch does not portray too much happiness in his paintings, and the actor Don Johnson hasn't had an easy time with his personal life in the last few years. However, the chances are that as a Sagittarian man you have an amazing ability to go through your life as though it truly were one big adventure and you believe in your ability to make your dreams come true. But why do you sometimes fail in your emotional life, finding it difficult to commit? (Would John Kennedy, Jr., have settled down with Daryl Hannah if he had been born under a different sign than Sagittarius?)

A typical Sagittarian man often has a difficult emotional life because of his innate fear of being hemmed in or pressured into making a total commitment—total commitment doesn't come easy for you. To become more successful emotionally, you must be prepared to trust more in your feelings, to take a blind leap of faith to realize that life can be an even more exciting adventure with the right person by your side.

Your restless mind, eternal optimism, ever youthful image, sometimes make you feel you can get away with anything in the emotional stakes, and, indeed, a few of you do! But most of you don't because it is quite difficult for you to tell a lie. Being unfaithful doesn't necessarily make you any happier, for I can think of more than a few Sagittarian men who, on reaching a certain age, realize they have missed out a lot by having a great social life and no real partner. It's not that you always see yourself as the playboy of the Western world—you sometimes play the field a little too often.

Because both you and your opposite sign, Gemini, are dual signs (the Gemini Twins and the half man, half horse Sagittarian Centaur), you both have restless and flirtatious personalities, and you have an inner fear that life may become dull. When you start to have even more faith in your eternal optimism and your joie de vivre, you will realize the voyage of life can be more exciting when you have a partner. Just be sure she shares your ideals and aspirations without making you feel like a prisoner in a cage. The perfect partner is one who is also your very best friend.

How to Achieve Your Material Goals

If *all* Sagittarians were guilty of being careless, irresponsible, wildly optimistic, and overly ambitious with grandiose expectations of what life has to offer you, I don't believe people such as Nostradamus, Beethoven, Jane Austen, Louisa May Alcott, Walt Disney, Aleksandr Solzhenitsyn, and Edith Piaf could have been born under your sign!

To become successful in the material world in which we live today, you need to concentrate fully on your aims and objectives. Your mutable quality tends to make you intellectually restless, and to achieve your material goals many of you archers need to find a far more disciplined approach to life. Disciplining yourself will enable you to become far more organized and create a much better structure to your life. This, in turn, will maximize your potential to achieve greater success.

While the advantage of having Jupiter, the planet of good fortune, as your ruler means you often tend to be lucky, the disadvantage is that because of this you're more than willing to take unnecessary risks. There are probably as many Sagittarian gamblers as philosophers in the world, so don't rush into schemes without making sure you possess the full knowledge of what they will entail. On one level it is wonderful to be as optimistic, open, and trusting as you tend to be, but blind faith in material matters is not the best idea and can lead you into difficult situations.

Invariably, your material goals are not necessarily making a fortune, but making enough money to enable you to lead a fairly free and easy life. Often your goals will also include having the opportunity to impart your knowledge to others, because your sign is the sign of the "higher mind." They will also involve allowing your creative powers to flow in your chosen direction. Achieving your material goals, no matter what they are, requires that you accept that you don't always know all the answers. It is extremely positive to have the courage of your convictions, but it is also positive to be more open to counsel from others when it is proffered, especially when it is from someone whose views you respect.

If achieving some kind of material goal has a high priority for you, be prepared to balance your life so there isn't a lot more play than work, and always keep your options open. I have known Sagittarians who have successfully switched paths when their ideals and aspirations were no longer fulfilled by what they were doing. Even though you can be as impatient as the two other Fire signs, Aries and Leo, even with Jupiter's beneficial influence, you cannot expect to become an overnight sensation. Take for example, Steven Spielberg, who has a brilliant track record for making successful films—but it took a long time for him to be the recipient of a much-deserved Oscar.

Keep in mind that your sense of humor is a blessing. It will enable you to rise above any obstacles, and to see light at the end of a dark tunnel. Combined with a philosophical approach to life, you have a winning streak, so you have every right to feel good about achieving success in your material goals. Don't let this make you careless, though.

The Powerful Assets at Your Disposal to Become More Successful

The Power of Your Element . . . Fire

The four elements—Fire, Earth, Air, and Water—have a great bearing on your star sign characteristics. Sagittarius is the last (but equally important!) Fire sign, the other two being Aries and Leo.

You share with Aries and Leo your positive, outgoing temperament, and an optimistic vitality. The Fire signs tend to be leaders, but unless you are careful, there is a tendency in the typical Sagittarian makeup to sit back and let life lead you, convinced that everything will work out in the end. Meanwhile, since you can number General Custer, Winston Churchill, and Charles de Gaulle among your fellow Sagittarians, you obviously have the ability to lead when necessary.

As a mutable Sagittarian, you are invariably more relaxed and flexible than Aries or Leo. This means that while like Aries and Leo you are prepared to fight to the end for your principles and beliefs, you are more successful when you do it in a philosophical, less aggressive way. You rarely deplete your energies by fighting for anything in which you do not totally believe. Like the other Fire signs, you are extremely honest; in your case, you must learn to be more tactful, too. The fiery side of your personality sometimes means your desire to tell someone what you think of their behavior can cause sparks to fly. Remember, letting your feelings rip can be incredibly upsetting to a sensitive soul. Choose your moments and your words carefully.

However, just like Aries and Leo, it is also your Fire element that provides you with the ability to rise above the challenge of adversity with an amazing degree of optimism and an indefatigable sense of humor. Unlike Aries you don't usually argue a point without defining your strategy before you speak. You also manage to survive without worrying about your ego, like Leo.

You will always achieve the greatest success when you maximize the potential of your Fire element by cooling its flames with your philosophical approach to the ups and downs of daily life.

Your Fire power helps you to make your adventurous journey through life an even more exciting event, but don't exhaust yourself by doing so many things that you run out of steam along the way.

The Power of Your Ruling Planet . . . Jupiter

You are extremely fortunate to have Jupiter ruling your sign. In mythology this planet was the great benefactor who represented growth and expansion on the earth. Jupiter will be *your* benefactor, if you use its power wisely.

Astrologers always talk about the "lucky" planet Jupiter, but I prefer to think of it as the planet of good fortune. This good fortune can be yours when you make the most of the good opportunities that come your way. Jupiter influences your search for higher knowledge and your desire to learn more of the deeper meaning of life. It inspires you to aim your Sagittarian arrow higher, helping you to achieve greater success in your undertakings. Jupiter endows you with your optimism, self-confidence, and enthusiasm for life, giving you the spirit of adventure that lives within every Sagittarian I have ever met! Jupiter is also conscience in the deepest sense. It brings you an inner sense of law and order. Through Jupiter's influence you will be able to expand your consciousness on every level, becoming more aware of the need to preserve, heal, and protect.

But take care, for Jupiter's influence can also make you too extravagant, careless, and optimistic. Make sure you aim your Sagittarian Archer's arrow in the right direction. Think carefully before you race off into something new, whether it is a new career, an impulse marriage, or a trip to an exotic location! Plan your moves in a practical way, and try not to make too many gambles in your life, for this planet of good fortune can also tempt you to excesses, dissipating your energies along the way. Be more aware of the need for responsibility in your life, for sometimes you are a little too quick to let other people pick up the pieces if something goes wrong. Jupiter was known as the protector of humanity, but if you want to benefit from its security, you have to do your fair share by watching out for yourself, too. There are moments in life when even a Sagittarius has to stop and think before moving forward.

The Jupiter influence empowers you with an extrovert personality, the ability to make people smile and laugh easily. You're not afraid of an audience; in fact, many of you believe the more the merrier. Sagittarian Bette Midler embodies this characteristic, as does Frank Sinatra, who still packs them in at his performances.

Used constructively, the expansive influence of Jupiter will inspire you to achieve greater success and to broaden your horizons, both mentally and physically. In addition, it will undoubtedly provide you with what the rest of us consider to be your winning streak.

The Power of Your Rising Sign

Your Ascendant, or rising sign, is the sign that was rising on the eastern horizon at the time of your birth. In many ways, it is as important as your Sun and Moon signs, influencing the way you play out your life. Use the table on pages 278–79 to determine your Ascendant sign. Below are brief descriptions of how your Sagittarian personality can be influenced by different Ascendants:

SAGITTARIUS WITH ARIES RISING
A powerful, fiery combination. Go easy! Your Aries Ascendant makes you even more enthusiastic and enterprising, but sometimes far too headstrong and impulsive. Moderation in all things is needed here if you want success.

SAGITTARIUS WITH TAURUS RISING
You find broadening your horizons a whole lot easier with practical and dependable Taurus as your rising sign. You are optimistic and realistic, and temper your adventurous spirit with the realization that greater security is good, too.

SAGITTARIUS WITH GEMINI RISING
With your opposite sign as your Ascendant, you could be even more restless than other Sagittarians. Look for ways to organize yourself and practice great self-discipline. Write everything down and concentrate.

SAGITTARIUS WITH CANCER RISING
Cancer Ascendant makes you more domesticated than most Sagittarians. You still have a love of travel, but you work hard to create a cozy domestic setup and appreciate the value of good family ties.

SAGITTARIUS WITH LEO RISING
Everything you do is done with great style! This Ascendant makes you determined to be a real star. Watch out you don't get carried away with an excess of flamboyant living and over-the-top extravagance or all will be lost.

SAGITTARIUS WITH VIRGO RISING
Your Virgo Ascendant will curb some of your happy-go-lucky attitude toward life and make you determined to work really hard to achieve what you want. You are realistic about some of your high-flying ideas and therefore have a greater chance of success.

SAGITTARIUS WITH LIBRA RISING
Libra rising gives you the ability to see both sides of every situation, and to rationalize with greater clarity before jumping to conclusions. You are even more of a "people" person and not quite as tactless as some Sagittarians we all know.

SAGITTARIUS WITH SCORPIO RISING
Your Scorpio Ascendant gives you a greater intensity of purpose and determination to succeed in everything you undertake, plus plenty of sex appeal. Avoid becoming too jealous and possessive with loved ones and friends.

SAGITTARIUS WITH SAGITTARIUS RISING
The life and soul of almost every party—that's you. But don't be too lackadaisical in your approach to life, or trust to luck too

much. Believing in yourself will be no problem, but make sure others believe in you too.

SAGITTARIUS WITH CAPRICORN RISING

Your Capricorn Ascendant may make you wise beyond your years, and your maturity enables you to become even more successful. Traditional values are important, and you're not inclined to take any risks in order to realize your ambitions.

SAGITTARIUS WITH AQUARIUS RISING

Freedom-loving and unpredictable—that's bound to be you with this combination. Your Aquarius Ascendant makes you a searcher for the truth, a believer in worthy ideals, and someone determined to make the world a better place for everyone, not just for yourself.

SAGITTARIUS WITH PISCES RISING

Make sure you're not too much of a romantic idealist, spending long hours talking over your grandiose ideas but forgetting about reality. Your Pisces Ascendant makes you more sensitive, compassionate, and intuitive.

How to Create Greater Success

Creating Greater Success . . . in Your Everyday Life

If you're a typical Sagittarian, I'm sure you already know that your positive attitude toward life in general is incredibly important.

To create even greater success in your everyday life, it won't hurt you to be a little more understanding toward other people who find it extremely hard to be as positive as you. I've noticed some of you tend to lose patience rather too quickly with your problems, probably because of your ability to rise above misfortune with great ease.

Try not to be too much of a moralizer. Don't insist on passing judgment on other people's behavior; others may consider you too extreme in your happy-go-lucky way of life. It may be great to be a Sagittarian and almost incapable of being dishonest, but telling other people the reasons you feel their lives are a disaster when your opinion has not been requested is definitely not on!

Encouraging other people to try to be more positive is wonderful. Learn to be considerate toward others and don't assume that your way is always right. Sometimes you need to go deeper inside yourself to relate better to others, since you are often inclined to see things superficially.

One of the marvelous aspects of being a Sagittarian is that you are definitely a survivor. Always remember this, for you can suffer setbacks that would send the rest of us into a state of shock and might take us months to get over. When you use your positive and optimistic Sagittarian characteristics in a balanced way, you are able to pick up the pieces and start all over again quickly.

If you feel you are worthy of success, yet it seems to elude you, the following checklist will give you some points on how to create a better daily regime, without having to completely change your life.

DO . . .
- remain free-spirited and independent, but be responsible too.
- stand up for your convictions.
- try harder to be more tactful when you're telling others what you think.
- look on the bright side of life, but remember to be realistic.
- always retain your wonderful sense of humor and ability to laugh at yourself.

- deliver what you promise; put your great thoughts into action.

DON'T . . .
- ever become too reckless and too much of a gambler.
- upset other people by insisting on having everything your way.
- be blindly optimistic without knowing the facts.
- travel so much you lose out at home.
- waste valuable time talking when you have a schedule to keep.
- search for new horizons without conquering those close at hand first.

Creating Greater Success . . . in Love

Because you are such a freedom-loving sign, it is sometimes hard for you to commit yourself emotionally. However, I have many Sagittarian friends and clients who have managed to control their desire for independence, once they were fulfilled by a loving relationship. Unfortunately, it is also true that your sign has an especially high number of divorces. At least if you're a typical Sagittarian you have an ability to almost shrug your shoulders and feel you will be lucky next time around— and often you are.

To create greater success in love, you must first be totally honest with yourself, get in touch with your deepest felt emotions. If you're happy leading an independent life and have no wish to be with a partner, there is no earthly reason you should conform to what other people think you should do. But if you have an unfulfilled yearning for someone to share your life with, try to stay in one place long enough for someone to really get to know you, and for you to get to know them.

Since Sagittarius is a Fire sign, you are hardly likely to deny that you have a strong sex drive, but motivating yourself to become totally involved with someone can be something else. I sometimes think you are erratic more than erotic, with many of you being far more successful at relating to best buddies than to lovers! Often you will enthusiastically fall for someone who complements your own personality perfectly and who shares your intellectual interests and sense of humor. But without any apparent reason, your enthusiasm wanes and suddenly you're off on a new helter-skelter voyage of discovery.

Believe in your own optimism, and you will soon see that losing a little of your freedom could bring greater emotional success your way. Do be aware of your emotional needs and let them come to the surface, and don't be scared of being fenced in.

Creating Greater Success . . . in Dating

If you're a typical Sagittarian, dating will invariably be fun, since you tend not to take the whole thing very seriously. You can consider it a blessing that you have such sublime confidence in your ability to chat up anyone you fancy. Since your nature is as restless as that of your opposite sign, Gemini, you often need to try harder to keep your attention directed toward one person at a time.

Make the most of your lighthearted approach and free-and-easy attitude to life by all means, but remember that some prospective dates may not be looking for a new best friend and may jump to the conclusion that you're not a good prospect!

Learn to demonstrate that you can be serious about life in general and your emotional life in particular by being more in tune with your feelings. Give anyone you date a fair chance to know the real you. I'm definitely not suggesting you must commit yourself to anyone or anything on the first date, but being totally nonchalant can sometimes ruin your chances of a really good relationship developing later on.

Never be scared of dating, even if it is the first date in years, after a breakup or for some other reason. Believe in your charm and your ability to converse about a thousand topics equally well, and you won't go far wrong.

SAGITTARIUS DATING TIPS . . . IN CASE YOU NEED ANY!
- Relax and have fun, but be romantic, too.
- Remember that honesty is a virtue, but tactlessness is not.
- Don't be so edgy that you see a follow-up date as committing yourself for life.

Creating Greater Success . . . in Family Ties

You're the sort of person who is always there if you're really needed. To become more successful at sustaining really good family ties, you sometimes need to be far more disciplined about keeping in touch on a regular basis, or even on an irregular basis.

Many Sagittarians leave home at an early age, determined to seek your own independence. And you have no doubt had quite a number of different homes since then! However, no matter how far you travel, don't forget your family responsibilities, from elderly relatives to your own offspring.

Since you are so keen to retain your free and easy lifestyle, show empathy with family members who want to do the same. Control your tendency to be narrow-minded and disapproving, especially as you hate to be criticized.

We all know that while we cannot choose our relatives, we can certainly choose our friends. You are brilliantly adept at making friends, so why not make the most of that particular talent with your relatives, too, and that includes in-laws. It will invariably make life easier for everyone.

Writing letters is not one of your strong points. You prefer chattering away on the phone. Either way, make sure you organize yourself well enough so that important anniversaries are not overlooked.

If and when family conflicts arise, always try to understand the other person's point of view, and vow to be more sensitive, too.

TIPS FOR SUCCESSFUL FAMILY TIES
- Keep in mind that tact and diplomacy work wonders when conflicts arise.
- Enjoy being with your family and think of them as friends.
- Don't moan about how you hate to feel tied down.

Creating Greater Success . . . at Work

Aided by your boundless enthusiasm and optimism, your belief in yourself and in your abilities will propel you in the direction of success.

You need to believe wholeheartedly in what you're doing. A big plus for you is a position that allows you the chance to travel and broaden your horizons. Even if this is not possible, hopefully it will be at times exciting and always mentally stimulating, giving you the opportunity to make the best possible use of your breadth of vision, and giving you a certain amount of freedom.

Creating greater success does mean being more prepared to listen to your peers and colleagues. Even though your ruling planet, Jupiter, helps to bring good fortune your way, it does not mean you can afford to become overly optimistic and think you will achieve instant success in your chosen field just because you are a Sagittarian. Be careful never to promise the impossible. Sometimes you are far too inclined to agree to deadlines that no one could make and to land yourself with heavy work schedules that leave you exhausted.

In many ways you are a born winner, but reading such a description time after time can make you careless and inclined to risks that aren't always fruitful.

As the sage and counselor of the zodiac, you were born with a great desire for knowledge. You enjoy instructing others, but watch out that you don't moralize too much. Keep an open mind, and be alert to opportunities to learn and discover even more about life and technology.

To become even more successful at work, pay attention to the following do's and don'ts.

DO . . .
- make sure you utilize your talents to the fullest.
- remember to look at details and not just the big picture.
- be open to input from other people without feeling you always know best!

DON'T
- scatter your energies too far and wide.
- make unrealistic and extravagant promises you may not be able to keep.
- avoid commitment when you know it will be good for you.

Creating Greater Success . . . in Finding the Right Job

Like your opposite sign, Gemini, who shares your restlessness and dislike of feeling confined, you must try to find something that does not tie you down in one place.

Adaptable and versatile, you have the ability to fit into almost any surroundings. You are not always the most practical sign where money is concerned, so make sure you receive a fair salary for your work. Don't rely on your Sagittarian optimism if you have to work on a commission basis, for you could end up losing out.

Many Sagittarians are attracted to philosophy, law, teaching, sports and sports promoting, social administration, politics, travel-related careers (the anthropologist Margaret Mead was a Sagittarian), writing, publishing, involvement in book stores, and library work. Since you are so good at entertaining people, it is no surprise that many of you also gravitate to the entertainment industry—just consider the careers of fellow Sagittarians Richard Pryor, Sammy Davis, Jr., Tina Turner, Phil Donahue, Andy Williams, Kirk Douglas, Jeff Bridges, Ellen Burstyn, John Malkovich, and Rita Moreno.

Creating Greater Success . . . in All Your Relationships

The way one relates to other people is one extremely important factor of success in life. Even if you are an amazingly friendly Sagittarian, and no matter how well you may think you get along with someone, it can never hurt to have a few extra tips in this area:

SAGITTARIUS AND ARIES
A winning combination between two impulsive, adventurous, and enthusiastic Fire signs—but remember, sparks will fly if Aries thinks you want *too* much freedom! Make sure you both find time to discuss what you really want from life.

SAGITTARIUS AND TAURUS
Never push the Bull too far. This sign is far more stubborn and resistant to change than you could imagine. If you want loyalty and security, Taurus will be there to help you, while sharing your good sense of humor.

SAGITTARIUS AND GEMINI
Your opposite sign is like a mirror image of you. If you hate feeling hemmed in, remember that Gemini feels the same way. Enjoy the mental stimulation and flirtation provided by this sign, but keep things light.

SAGITTARIUS AND CANCER

Always remember that Cancer likes to feel cozy and secure, and can find it hard to put up with your free and easy attitude toward life. Don't upset the Crab by being too outspoken, tactless, or intolerant, as you are dealing with a highly sensitive personality here.

SAGITTARIUS AND LEO

Don't forget Leo's ego! Wounded pride does not sit happily on the average Lion of the zodiac, and you may have to power-play in a fairly understated way if you're in any kind of competition with this sign.

SAGITTARIUS AND VIRGO

You can provide the confidence Virgo needs to move higher up the ladder of success, and in turn you will receive constructive criticism and advice to help turn your own dreams into reality if you are prepared to listen.

SAGITTARIUS AND LIBRA

The sign of balance can help you even the scales in your own life. But Libra thrives on peace, harmony, and refinement, so strive not to be too outspoken. Don't expect too many quick decisions from the average Libran.

SAGITTARIUS AND SCORPIO

You're open and easygoing but Scorpio is closed and intense. Don't be too tactless and upset this sign. Scorpios will always remember the slight and may not forgive you. Scorpio wants privacy and can be very jealous, which could be difficult for someone who wants too much freedom.

SAGITTARIUS AND SAGITTARIUS

You can be best friends but will probably criticize each other's faults without realizing they are yours, too. Encourage each other with all your schemes, but make sure they're neither wildly impractical or extravagant.

SAGITTARIUS AND CAPRICORN

An interesting duo—the optimist combined with the pessimist of the zodiac. You will help Capricorn to see the brighter side of life, and you will learn from the Mountain Goat's resolute determination to do things in a practical and money-saving way.

SAGITTARIUS AND AQUARIUS

While you are both creative and adaptable, the Water Bearer is far more detached emotionally than you, and more unpredictable, too. However, you could do wonderfully well together on a mission to save the world.

SAGITTARIUS AND PISCES

Don't assume this romantic and sensitive Water sign is too wishy-washy for you. Pisces will open up your eyes to the beauty around you and tug at your heartstrings in a very gentle way, but you will need to be especially considerate in return.

Becoming a
More Successful
Capricorn

I f you were born between December 21 and January 19, you were born under the sign of Capricorn, the tenth sign of the zodiac, a feminine, cardinal, negative Earth sign, ruled by Saturn, the planet known as "Old Father Time." Your planetary symbol is either the Goat with the curling fish's tail, or as is more usually portrayed, the Mountain Goat.

If you are a typical Capricorn, your determination to be successful most likely became a part of you with your very first breath. Achievement is what life is all about for you, and astrologers think of you as the natural builder of the zodiac, always working hard to get your ideas off the ground, and willing to learn new things along the way. You possess a great sense of responsibility, patience, and the ability to persevere. Just as the Mountain Goat picks its way carefully up a steep and craggy mountain, determined to reach the top, you set yourself goals that may seem impossible to attain for most of us—but you do not give up until you have achieved them!

To become more successful, it is necessary for you to get your priorities in order. In your desire to be a great tycoon, don't become so concerned with the material side of life that you lose out on personal happiness. To create greater balance it is also important to have a sense of humor. You will find life bestows greater rewards when you are able to relax and be more willing to take some time off. Hard-working Capricorn needs some moments of leisure!

Each sign of the zodiac relates to a different area of the body, starting with the head and ending with the feet, from Aries to Pisces. Capricorn rules the structural elements in the body—the bones, joints, ligaments, spine, and knees—as well as the teeth and skin. The importance of the joints makes you vulnerable to arthritis or rheumatism resulting from crystallization when you become too set in your thinking. So appreciate the benefits of relaxation to help your body and mind to unwind.

Your ambition is often coupled with a pessimistic view of life. To achieve greater success, it is imperative for you to be more positive about life. Don't view the world only with a pessimistic eye, for there are truly beautiful things to see if you open yourself up to them. Don't be too rigid in the demands you make yourself, on others, and on life; a little more flexibility will enable you to achieve your goals without giving yourself such a hard time.

Within your personality there is an in-built determination to succeed at anything you set your heart on. You are fortunate in appreciating the value of good timing and hard work; you are possibly the most conscientious sign in the whole zodiac, aside from Virgo. When you believe in your aims and aspirations there is no stopping you! Dr. Martin Luther King, Jr., and President Anwar Sadat were both Capricorns who tried through their work to make the world a better place; Capricorns Joseph Stalin and Idi Amin are considered to have abused their power and ambition for their own purposes. Capricorn is very much the sign of ambition, but when power and ambition become too intertwined and your ego takes over, disaster can strike, as Richard Nixon discovered during the Watergate scandal.

You don't have to think of yourself as someone only concerned with achieving greater success on a material level, for there are many Capricorns with great spiritual leanings who have taught us a lot: Joan of Arc, Louis Pasteur, Albert Schweitzer, Maharishi Mahesh Yogi, Gurdjieff, Swami Sachidananda, and Paramhansa Yogananda.

Success will always mean different things to different people, but you have an incredible potential to turn your ideas into reality. For you, sheer hard work and the conviction that you can succeed will allow you to do so. You don't just talk about what you want in life; you get out there and go for it.

Make sure you have done the groundwork necessary to achieve your aims and ambitions. Listen to your common sense (which you have in abundance!), and appreciate the value of your inborn sense of timing. With these elements in place, you can start climbing up the success mountain, happy in the knowledge that for you its peak is never as daunting as it might appear at first sight!

Defining Your Goals

Not every Capricorn wants to be a millionaire, a politician, a business tycoon, a movie star, the owner of an island in the Caribbean, or "the King," as the Capricorn Elvis Presley was known. However you define success, Saturn adds to your powers of concentration and your sense of timing, so you will be on a winning streak when you decide what you do want.

Keep in mind the advice of the Capricorn Paramhansa Yogananda: "Inner harmony is a prolific source of power; it breeds strength." You possess strength and determination in great abundance, but you are sometimes short on inner harmony and can worry almost as much as Virgo if you don't feel you are fulfilling your ambitions as quickly or successfully as you believe you should. When you are better able to balance your inner and outer strengths, you will find it even easier to define and achieve your personal goals.

How to Achieve Your Emotional Goals

If you're a typical Capricorn, your emotional goals tend to be overshadowed by your material ones. For example, you are generally highly self-disciplined in your working life but hardly allow yourself the opportunity to show any emotion. This gives other people the impression that you are cold and unfeeling.

There are no hard and fast rules for achieving your emotional goals, but it will certainly help you to do so if you present yourself as less driven and allow a smile to cross your face more often. Telling a Capricorn to lighten up is more likely to produce a scowl than a grin, but I can assure you that lightening up will produce encouraging results if you're striving for greater success in the emotional stakes.

You often appear to equate emotional success with finding a partner who belongs to the right social stratum. I would hate to accuse you of being a snob, but you do place enormous importance on the background, family, position, professional prestige, and social standing of a prospective partner. Love does not necessarily involve any of these, and it would be sad if you were to miss out on emotional success by being too calculating in your approach to your emotional life.

You are an Earth sign, like Taurus and Virgo, and there is an earthy sensuality and passionate sexuality hidden beneath your cool exterior, just waiting to be tapped. Believe more in yourself, and realize that you have the charismatic power necessary to convince a partner of your choice that you are right for him or her.

One of the best ways for you to achieve greater emotional success is to be honest with yourself right down to your soul. Don't be afraid to show you have a heart! And don't be scared to let down those barriers and allow love to shine in.

There is certainly nothing wrong with not wanting to commit yourself to anyone too quickly. But if you do have unfulfilled emotional goals, you need to ask yourself if it could be your own fault. Perhaps you are not being open to potential opportunities to get to know someone on a true soulmate level. If so, resolve to adopt a different approach.

EMOTIONS AND THE CAPRICORN WOMAN

The personality of a typical Capricorn woman contains an amazing strength and sense of purpose. Think of some of the people born under your sign: beauty tycoons such as Elizabeth Arden and Helena Rubenstein; actresses like Marlene Dietrich,

Ava Gardner, Ingrid Bergman, Mary Tyler Moore, and Diane Keaton; and personalities like Sophie Tucker and Dolly Parton.

When you come up against an obstacle in your life, you fight to remove it, especially if you feel you have been wronged. Actress Faye Dunaway did just that when Andrew Lloyd Webber dismissed her from *Sunset Boulevard.*

However, I have noticed many times with Capricorn friends and clients that emotionally you often find it difficult to find a partner who brings you what you need. I'm convinced that this frequently occurs because you find it extremely difficult to admit to your needs.

On the surface you are sometimes very preoccupied with material security and stability, but having achieved this very successfully through a long-term relationship or marriage, you also may discover that you have very little else. Naturally, I am generalizing, but there is certainly something within the typical Capricorn personality that makes it extremely difficult for you to admit that passion, sensuality, and sex all form part of a love relationship.

If you want to be more successful emotionally, don't be scared of giving in to your feelings on a deeper level. While I'm certainly not advocating that you should jump into bed with everyone who makes a pass at you, I really do not think it is below your dignity to indulge in some gentle flirtation a little more often.

Don't be quite so serious about everything in general, and your image in particular. Sometimes you can be almost as self-critical as Virgo, and as stubborn as Taurus. You seem to be terrified of letting anyone see that you have deep feelings or that you could be insecure. Often there appears to be an icy determination about everything you do, a cool and calculating approach that can be very off-putting to potential admirers. Once you develop greater belief in yourself you will realize that you have the ability to captivate anyone you choose and to admit that you are passionate about achieving a successful love life, not only about reaching your professional aims and ambitions. Admitting that you need emotional intimacy just as much as any other sign will make it much easier to find it.

It is wonderful to be as practical, well-organized, and hard-working as the typical Capricorn woman. But as a feminine Earth sign, you must never ignore your sexual desires in the interest of material security. Don't be so hard on yourself. Once you become more in touch with your emotions, you will achieve greater success in relating to a partner who really *is* good for you in every way.

Your rating in the overall success stakes is high, but it will be even higher in the emotional ones once you become more romantic and decide that external power is not the only important thing in life.

EMOTIONS AND THE CAPRICORN MAN

The Capricorn man is not always thought of as the easiest of males. You tend to come across as shy, insensitive, introverted, or intolerant, and sometimes a combination of all of these. While Scorpio is often described as being mean, moody, and magnificent, you are more likely to be described as strong, silent, and somewhat stern. Meanwhile, deep down, I'm sure you want to love and be loved just as much as every other man.

You are usually fairly conservative about almost everything and definitely take life seriously. Because material success is so important to your sign, and because you are highly disciplined in your approach to work, you sometimes lose out emotionally. This is because you don't allow yourself any time to think about what you need emotionally, let alone how to show your feelings to someone else.

It's almost as though you feel it's a weakness to display any emotion. Consequently, if you're not careful you come across as very cold, cynical, and even selfish in your desire for power. Your opposite sign is Cancer, one of the most sentimental signs

212 / *Success Through the Stars*

around. Every sign has something to learn from its opposite, so stop hiding behind your self-built wall and start to achieve greater success by showing your own sensitivity and senti-mentality.

As a sensual Earth sign, remind yourself that plenty of fasci-nating men have been born under your sign: Aristotle Onassis, Humphrey Bogart, Kevin Costner, Michael Crawford, Robert Duvall, Mel Gibson, Cary Grant, Anthony Hopkins, Ben Kings-ley, and Rod Stewart are just some of them.

To become more successful in emotional matters, it will help if you can learn to be more demonstrative and open with your affections. I know this doesn't necessarily come easily to you, because you seem to have been taught from childhood on to be seen and not heard. But, it is difficult for someone else to inter-pret what you feel about them if you are determined not to give the slightest clue.

A further difficulty is that you may have suffered much rejection in the past, or endured a difficult childhood, and you may subconsciously build up an even higher wall around your emotions. Once you learn to let go of the past and believe you are worthy of love, it will be much easier for you to achieve emotional success.

Capricorns are extremely status conscious, searching for a partner who will help them climb higher up the ladder of suc-cess. Do not make the mistake of losing someone who could be an ideal soulmate, simply because they do not have the background you hoped for.

How to Achieve Your Material Goals

A typical Capricorn is driven by goals. If you come from a poor background, like Aristotle Onassis you become even more resourceful and determined to succeed. Often your success is almost entirely self-made, and you thrive on seeing tangible results of your efforts—although often, the more you achieve the more you want! There can be something insatiable in your thirst for success and material security.

It is usually unnecessary to give a typical Capricorn advice on how to achieve material goals. Sometimes it seems almost as though you were born with a sense of responsibility and a highly developed business acumen. In fact, if one were able to conduct a real conversation with a Capricorn baby, it would probably be about the stock market and business accounts!

Good timing is essential when you are aiming to achieve your material goals, and as a practical and pragmatic Earth sign ruled by Saturn ("Old Father Time"), timing is usually not a problem for you. It's all there in your symbol, the Mountain Goat, carefully picking his way up the mountain. Provided you take things cautiously, you will invariably arrive at the top of your own mountain. You are born under the sign of the empire builder—for example, the Capricorn Conrad Hilton successfully developed a chain of hotels. The trouble starts when a Capricorn takes risks and desires more and more power—as both Richard Nixon and John DeLorean found out. Richard Nixon's desire for absolute power obscured his higher instincts, both personally and politically.

I don't think Capricorns are terribly good at cutting corners or taking risks. You excel when you stick to the tried and true, and when you stray from what you know best you often seem to land yourself with problems.

Life for a typical Capricorn can often be difficult for the first twenty-eight to thirty years. This can be traced to the influence of your ruling planet, Saturn. This is one of the reasons I feel you have an inborn determination to make your life even better as you grow older, and why those Capricorn babies look so very serious.

To achieve your material goals in a happier and more productive manner, plan to let some rest and relaxation go hand in hand with all your hard work. This will recharge your batteries and make you even more efficient. You know you will reach your chosen position, but do you really want to be burned out when you get there? It is said that Capricorns are only happy when they are at the top, but I've known many of you who, when you reached the top, appeared to have lost sight of the pleasures of life. This because you have committed yourselves solely to achieving material success at the cost of your happiness. Capricorn Howard Hughes's millions didn't seem to make him happy.

More important than telling you how to achieve material success is advising you to enjoy it when you do! Don't lose out on all that life has to offer by focusing yourself too intensely on making your dollars grow.

The Powerful Assets at Your Disposal to Become More Successful

The Power of Your Element . . . Earth

The four elements—Fire, Earth, Air, and Water—have a great bearing on the characteristics of the star signs. Capricorn is the third of the Earth signs. As a cardinal Earth sign, you possess boundless persistence and determination, and are extremely resourceful in your enterprises. You also have a strong sense of timing and are quite happy to live by the one-day-at-a-time theory, because you believe anything worth having is worth waiting for.

The Earth element grounds you in a practical way, and helps you to focus on achieving the respect and esteem that makes you feel all your hard work is worthwhile. You're also prepared to seize good opportunities when they come your way. The benefit of your Earth element is that it will enable you to see the practical side of every issue, thus preventing you from forging ahead with something unsuitable or unpromising.

Your Earth element always ensures that you will speak out and act positively if you feel there is a threat to your security or, indeed, to the security of loved ones. It also endows you with your dependability so that other people are certain they can rely on you when they really need you. To become more successful, don't let yourself be *too* grounded to the earth, narrow-minded in your outlook, or rigid in your approach to everyday situations. Learn to open up your mind more and see beyond what is in front of you.

Your Earth power enables you to be strong in your beliefs, and strong in your determination to do your duty. It helps you to plan your actions meticulously and to avoid the possibility of last-minute problems. Just watch out that it doesn't also make you too rooted to the past and present, and not interested enough in the future.

The Power of Your Ruling Planet . . . Saturn

One of the major influences on you is your planetary ruler, Saturn, Old Father Time. In Greek mythology Saturn was Cronus, the oldest of the gods. As well as being the keeper of time, he was also the lawgiver and taskmaster of everyone on earth, teaching, testing, and representing the highest forms of justice and human attainment.

Astrologers always tend to call Saturn "the task master of the zodiac," but the benefit of Saturn's influence on you is that he brings you the greatest rewards if you are self-disciplined and have faith in yourself, through all the demands that are sometimes placed on you and the obstacles you encounter.

Earlier in this chapter I mentioned that people born under your sign often seem to have a difficult start in your lives and don't really flourish until you have reached your late twenties. These early challenges can make you even more determined to succeed. Saturn takes roughly twenty-eight and a half years to go round the zodiac. When it returns to the place it occupied at your birth, it usually coincides with an extremely important time in your life, sometimes even a crisis point. After this first Saturn return, your life starts to become easier and your resourcefulness and determination are rewarded so that you continue to achieve greater success as you go through life.

To become more successful in your everyday life, it is worth remembering that Saturn helps to give you the structure necessary to turn your ideas and proposed projects into reality. It helps you to concentrate on everything down to the finest detail, and to ride out the storm when obstacles and delays occur. Saturn-ruled Capricorns are often drawn to spirituality, with a message to give the world. However, Saturn also has a dark side that is almost satanic than saturnine. J. Edgar Hoover, Mao Tse-tung, Joseph Stalin, Al Capone, and Hermann Göring were all Capricorns.

One of the most positive effects of having Saturn as your ruling planet is that it represents the structure and order necessary not only in your own personal life, but for society as a whole. With Saturn's influence you can always put your house in order, no matter what struggles you may have been through in the past. Saturn helps to bring stability into your life, and teaches you self-preservation, discipline, and duty.

Saturn is a powerful planet, and its strength can help you to be more successful, wiser, and more knowledgeable about life.

The Power of Your Rising Sign

Your Ascendant, or rising sign, is the sign that was rising on the eastern horizon at the time of your birth. In many ways its influence is as important as your Sun and Moon signs on how you live out your life.

Using the chart on pages 278–79, you will be able to determine your Ascendant sign. The following information lets you know how your personality would be influenced by the twelve different rising signs.

CAPRICORN WITH ARIES RISING

You are a real go-getter with this combination—more impatient than most Capricorns, but more enthusiastic about life, too. However, Aries energy combined with Capricorn restrictiveness can be a combustible formula, so you need to balance yourself well.

CAPRICORN WITH TAURUS RISING

You're well starred for success here, as there is absolutely no way you give up on something you believe in. Your understanding of good timing, responsibility, and determination to succeed is magnified and made more powerful by the Bull.

CAPRICORN WITH GEMINI RISING

The Gemini influence gives you a brighter and more exciting view of life, and also enables you to come up with inventive and original ideas. This combination makes it easier to put your views across to others in a dynamic way.

CAPRICORN WITH CANCER RISING

A Cancer Ascendant confers on you greater sensitivity, sensibility, and sentimentality. These attributes lighten the generally more somber Capricorn personality. Achieving material security will be of paramount importance, and you *will* achieve it!

CAPRICORN WITH LEO RISING

You enjoy aiming for greater success, and enjoy even more the chance to flaunt it! Watch out that your ego doesn't get too inflated or that a busy social life doesn't prevent you from getting on with all the hard work on your Capricorn agenda.

CAPRICORN WITH VIRGO RISING

This combination makes you the most dedicated workaholic in the entire zodiac. You leave no stone unturned in your search for perfection on the way up that ladder of success. But to be successful in your emotional life, you must take *some* time off!

CAPRICORN WITH LIBRA RISING

You benefit from the ability to see both sides of a situation, and to balance the pros and cons before making major decisions. You also place importance on working in partnership in most areas of your life.

CAPRICORN WITH SCORPIO RISING

This is a combination of great strength, but do watch out that you aren't too controlling and manipulative in your dealings with other people. Your emotional intensity makes you even more determined to be powerful and successful.

CAPRICORN WITH SAGITTARIUS RISING

You are more open to new ideas and benefit from a more optimistic view of life than is generally Capricorn's lot. Don't scatter your energies and take on more than even you can do in a day, and pay attention to a predilection to be extravagant with money.

CAPRICORN WITH CAPRICORN RISING

This combination means you never shirk your responsibilities—just remember that the whole meaning of life doesn't reside in work. Try to relax and add a little sparkle to your personality as it will make you more successful.

CAPRICORN WITH AQUARIUS RISING

An Aquarius Ascendant gives you a more freedom-loving approach to life than usual, and you also benefit from Aquarius's innovative and ingenious approaches to increasing your prospects for success. Make sure you maintain self-discipline.

CAPRICORN WITH PISCES RISING

Your pragmatic approach to situations is helped by some Piscean intuition, which boosts your success potential. You also find it easier to relax and let your sentimental feelings show through more than many other Capricorns.

How to Create Greater Success

Creating Greater Success . . . in Your Everyday Life

While your devotion to duty is almost worthy of a medal, and no one could criticize you for being insufficiently structured and organized, you can come across as being almost too cool, calculating, and self-sufficient for words.

Learning to relate better to other people will make you more successful in your daily life. Don't be quite so conventional in your attitude, so insistent on presenting a public face that shows little emotion; it makes you appear to distance yourself from the rest of us.

You tend to take every little thing unbelievably seriously. Ease up! I've discovered that beneath the surface, many of you have a wonderful sense of humor and are bright and sparkling individuals, but it's almost as though you feel guilty if you laugh, as though you were convinced you are neglecting something that could go dramatically wrong if you don't give it your immediate attention.

Your engrossment in achieving your material goals can lead you to forget about your hobbies, going to the movies or the theater, and taking a well-deserved vacation once in a while. Don't drive yourself so hard that you end up stressed out and neurotic. You needn't feel that you have to carry the world on your shoulders.

If you are a typical Capricorn you tend to feel insecure when you're not in control, because you want to prove you're the boss. Keep in mind that using too many power- and control-leased maneuvers to achieve your goals could turn you into a dictatorial type.

It is widely acknowledged that typical Capricorns always worry about whether they will have enough in the bank to live on when they are old. You probably do this even if you have a million dollars! The typical Capricorn always has something stashed away for emergencies and for your old age. So why not vow not to worry so much!

Being more successful in your everyday life involves being more tolerant of other people than is your natural bent. Go easy on those who don't see eye to eye with your rigid and overly conventional views, and don't be so hard on yourself, either.

DO . . .
- let your sense of humor start to show through.
- resolve to learn how to laugh at yourself.
- be a little frivolous and even extravagant once in a while.
- develop some interests besides your material aspirations.
- become more aware of other people's feelings.
- be conscientious but caring, too.

DON'T . . .
- be so pessimistic.
- lose your sensitivity in your thirst for greater power.
- be so obsessed with your material aims and ambitions.
- end up lonely because you've put up too many walls around your emotions.

- place too much emphasis on social status.
- be a wet blanket when everyone else wants to have fun.

Creating Greater Success . . . in Love

To become more successful in love and to achieve emotional fulfillment, you must first admit that you have emotional needs. Many of you seem extraordinarily self-contained and unemotional in your behavior—even cold and scheming where your love life is concerned—so admitting vulnerability may be challenging.

You may be far more concerned with finding a "suitable match" who satisfies your social and financial expectations rather than a soulmate. Yet the "suitable match" may be a life sentence to a dry, unromantic existence. Try not to be so concerned with the practical considerations of finding a partner and let some romance shine in your life.

Ruled by Saturn, that old task master of the zodiac, you feel it is your duty and responsibility to marry well and have children—a perfect family—but don't sell yourself short on true love because of this ambition. I'm certainly not advising you to start having wildly passionate affairs, just for the sake of kicking over the traces. I am counseling you against settling for a secure and stable partnership that may not fulfill your emotional needs.

As a Capricorn, you find it hard to admit that the fires of passion burn within you, but it's quite conceivable that you possess strong emotional feelings just waiting to be unleashed. Some astrologers consider you one of the most highly sexed signs in the zodiac, and I've often thought that if you were not such a conformist and confirmed workaholic you could have quite a Casanovalike reputation!

Your opposite sign of the zodiac is the emotional Water sign Cancer, who cares for security and stability just as much as you

222 / Success Through the Stars

do. We all have something to learn from our opposite signs, and you will soon find you can achieve greater success in love if you incorporate some of Cancer's qualities and become a little more sensitive and romantic.

Start to lighten up. Stop thinking about the serious side of life, and of working all the time, and don't pretend that love doesn't interest you.

Creating Greater Success . . . in Dating

If you are a typical Capricorn you may dismiss dating as something far too unimportant for such a serious, hard-working person as you. Perhaps even when you were young you had the parents of a prospective partner vetted to make sure you were moving in the right social stratum. I'm sorry to say this, Capricorn, but sometimes you are an awful snob!

To have greater success in dating—and more fun!—make sure you are with someone who is amusing and who doesn't simply discuss stocks and shares and the state of the world economy during dinner.

It's no use saying you have no time for dating; it may happen that you suddenly realize that you are alone and feel the need for someone to share your life. While Saturn's influence brings a great deal of self-discipline into your life, this does not mean that you're supposed to deny yourself spontaneity and fun—even silliness. It's not easy for Capricorns to let down their hair and enjoy themselves without worrying about what others think, but you will be a whole lot more successful in the dating game if you start off by doing just that.

CAPRICORN DATING TIPS
- Let your sense of humor and your sex appeal shine through.
- Relax, unwind, and become more spontaneous in words and actions.

• Don't be so serious all the time. Remember, Rod Stewart, Cary Grant and Tracy Ullman were all born under your sign.

Creating Greater Success . . . in Family Ties

You are not the sort of person who would ever willingly neglect your responsibilities, but for you to create more successful family ties, it is sometimes necessary to remind you that providing material security isn't the only thing involved in family bonds. You need to be more demonstrative sometimes and show the affection you feel, because it can be difficult for others to tell how much you care about them. This is especially relevant if you are one of those typically hard-working and serious Mountain Goats who always end up coming home late from the office.

Try a little harder to be around on important anniversaries. Use your talent for organization to make notes of them so as not to schedule meetings on those days. If you have young children, resolve that you won't always come across as a stern parent who insists that they remember their duties every single moment of the day. Teach them responsibility in a realistic but not overbearing manner. It is sometimes necessary to bend some of your self-inflicted rules and regulations when dealing with family members. You also set great store by traditions and by how you think things should be. Some of these ideas are limiting to you and others. Vow that you won't look down on any of your relatives, or a partner's relatives, if they don't come from the same background or vote the same way as you!

If you are a typical Capricorn you drive yourself extremely hard, especially in your working life. It is important that you not let this get in the way of your family relationships. Always make sure that you find time to relax and enjoy your family without letting relatives become yet another pressure in your already busy life.

Your traditional, status-conscious view of life leads you to place a great deal of importance on living in "the right place, among the right people." But you may find yourself isolated from kinfolk who are very much a part of your life. If you end up living a great distance from loved ones, don't let work be the excuse for failing to keep in touch.

TIPS FOR SUCCESSFUL FAMILY TIES
- Be truly caring as well as conscientious.
- Be more demonstrative in showing affection.
- Don't cut yourself off from your family, even if you are busy at work.

Creating Greater Success . . . at Work

Your persistence and determination to get ahead can never be underestimated, and you can be counted on to steer your life to accomplish great things! Even if you start at the very bottom you will use your self-discipline and tenacity to reach the top of the mountain.

The way you set about achieving your goals is often admirable, provided you don't get so carried away with your quest for greater power that you make enemies along the way. Genuine success is generally partly a result of relating well to peers and colleagues in the workplace, and of not appearing to be so afire with ambition that nothing and nobody else counts. Don't become so insatiable and ruthless in your determination to be up there at the top that you alienate the very people whose help you need to get there. Be optimistic and harness your energy, and that of others, in a positive way. A Capricorn wants to be in control, but it is worth remembering that you are often more successful when you are working with people whose expertise and trust can be relied upon implicitly. Even a Capricorn cannot do everything alone!

It is rarely necessary to advise you to organize yourself better when it comes to work—but it is worth mentioning that organizing yourself better on a total mind, body, and soul level can make your drive even more inspiring to your colleagues. In other words, don't neglect the other areas of your life and your psyche just because you insist on being such a workaholic. If you encounter a few failures along the way take them in stride for you will always learn a great deal from your mistakes, as well as the mistakes of others.

There is an old saying "All work and no play makes Jack a dull boy." The person who first said this must have had a Capricorn in mind! Remember to give yourself a break at times so you can recharge your batteries.

The following do's and don'ts provide you with some more ideas for becoming even more successful at work.

DO . . .
- remember your amazing ability to overcome obstacles.
- stick to your principles and be true to yourself.
- balance all your hard work with some hours of relaxation.

DON'T . . .
- let yourself become corrupted by your desire to achieve power.
- allow empire building to leave you no time to fulfill your emotional needs.
- become stressed out by spending *too* many long hours at work!

Creating Greater Success . . .
in Finding the Right Job

Never fear, Capricorn, even if do you have to start way down the bottom of the mountain, you will soon start climbing right up to the top and you will get there!

You are probably the most career-minded and business-oriented sign of the zodiac. Capricorn occupations include politician, business tycoon, entrepreneur, teacher, statesman, scientist, banker, administrator, accountant, tax collector, insurance broker, and private secretary. You are often drawn to anything connected with construction and are able to organize almost anything. Some of you have made your mark in show business, utilizing your unique brand of determination; Patricia Neal's determination enabled her to recover from a stroke. The former boxing champ Muhammed Ali also proved he has what it takes to reach the top.

Choose a profession and a position that has the potential to fulfill your ambitions; otherwise you may find yourself becoming bitter and dissatisfied in later years. And if you need further study to achieve your aims, don't say you have no time—as if you would!

If the financial situation is extremely important to you, try to choose something that pays good overtime, since staying late will never bother you. Don't hide away your creative talents just because you feel real money can be made only in the business world.

Creating Greater Success . . .
in All Your Relationships

One of the most important factors in successful in life is relating well to other people. You may be so busy climbing up the ladder of success that you lose sight of this. Here are a few tips on how to relate better to everyone:

CAPRICORN AND ARIES
The Ram provides passion and enthusiasm for life, while you provide practicality and bossiness! However, if you're too pessimistic you will dampen all that Aries fire and lose the benefit of seeing life with a more optimistic eye.

CAPRICORN AND TAURUS

While Taurus is as practical and dependable as any Capricorn, the Bull has a stubborn side and simply won't be pushed too far. You can learn a lot about relaxation from this sign, who will teach you sensuality too!

CAPRICORN AND GEMINI

Although you may not always approve of Gemini's flirtatious ways, this sign will show you that having a fun social life doesn't have to mean losing your sense of control. Some of Gemini's inventive ideas could help you to be even more successful!

CAPRICORN AND CANCER

Rather like looking in the mirror, you'll see some of your good and bad points in your opposite sign. This moon child will help you become aware of your emotions and become more sensitive, compassionate, and caring. With all these benefits, I think you can put up with the Crab's moods in return!

CAPRICORN AND LEO

Like you, Leo loves power, and being in the limelight. Deflating a Leo's pride is like letting the air out of a balloon, so remember to give praise when it's due, and try to be much more demonstrative in your affection.

CAPRICORN AND VIRGO

You two will understand each other from the start, since you are both workaholics. But you'd better be prepared for someone who is even more of a perfectionist and slave to duty than you. Both of you could benefit from having some time off!

CAPRICORN AND LIBRA

Both of you appreciate style and comfort, but don't start forcing Libra to make any quick decisions or you will be disappointed. Libra can bring some balance to your life, and you will benefit from the peace and harmony you feel.

CAPRICORN AND SCORPIO

A powerful duo with lofty ambitions and intense determination to succeed. Scorpio is very jealous and possessive, and has deep emotional needs. Try not to turn a Scorpio against you—this sign never forgets!

CAPRICORN AND SAGITTARIUS

If you really want to appreciate the lighter side of life, you could have no better guide! Sagittarians can inspire you to greater heights of success, so don't negate their words of wisdom, even if they are sometimes tactless and downright extravagant.

CAPRICORN AND CAPRICORN

This can be a great bond, provided you are both working with the same end in mind! You will have a mutual support system with another goat. But one of you will have to make the decision that enough work is enough, allowing you *some* time to play.

CAPRICORN AND AQUARIUS

You restrain and control yourself, while Aquarius is unpredictable and unconventional. You will learn plenty from the Water Bearer's innovative ideas, and you share with Aquarians a reticence over revealing your deepest feelings. But don't try to fence in an Aquarian . . . ever!

CAPRICORN AND PISCES

Reality and dreams don't always mix, but Piscean intuition could help you find easier ways to climb your mountains. Try to understand that it's hard for the sign of the Fish to be as organized and practical as you, especially financially.

Becoming A More Successful Aquarius

If you were born between January 20 and February 18, you were born under the sign of Aquarius, the eleventh sign of the zodiac. Aquarius is a masculine, fixed, positive Air sign ruled by Uranus, the planet of invention. (Before Uranus was discovered, in 1781, Saturn was associated with your sign.) Your symbol is the Water Bearer.

Because your symbol is the Water Bearer, people often think your element is Water. The meaning of the water pouring out of your jug is more like a blessing on the earth, for water in ancient times was the symbol of life and spiritual baptism. Your true Aquarian gift is to serve as a vessel for higher truths, distributing the water of life itself.

You are the truth seeker and the humanitarian of the zodiac, as well as an idealist with a social conscience, determined to leave your imprint on the world. If you're a typical Aquarian, you will fight long and hard to get your truths across, even if you don't always find support. People born under your sign include Abraham Lincoln, Franklin Roosevelt, Thomas Edison, Sir Thomas More, Galileo, Charles Lindbergh, Charles Darwin, Boris Yeltsin, D. W. Griffith, Betty Friedan, Ronald Reagan, Germaine Greer, Yoko Ono, and Vanessa Redgrave.

To achieve the highest degree of success in your everyday life, you need to strike the right balance between your sense of duty to the world in general and your responsibility to yourself and the people closest to you. Often you are aloof and emotionally detached, which makes it almost impossible to know what you are thinking or feeling. People may believe that you're simply not interested in them. Concentrate more on people and issues close at hand, rather than becoming too heavily involved in "causes" that may make you lose sight of what needs to be done on the home front.

If you are a typical Aquarian, you are without a doubt the most unconventional and unpredictable sign in the entire zodiac. After being an astrologer for many years now, I have to admit I don't think there *is* a stereotypical Aquarian. You are the sort of person who behaves wonderfully when those around you fear the worst—you may behave like a monster when others expect everything to be sweetness and light!

To create a more successful life for yourself you could try to make yourself easier to understand by being less erratic—not to mention even sometimes eccentric—in your behavior. To do this you don't have to completely change your personality.

Each sign of the zodiac relates to a different area of the body, starting with the head and ending with the feet, from Aries to Pisces. Aquarius rules the ankles and the legs from the knee to the ankle. These body parts can be weak if you are not careful. Aquarius also rules the circulation of blood throughout the body, so that in really cold weather it is important for you to keep yourself warm enough.

Your ruling planet, Uranus, bequeaths to you a unique brand of flair, inventiveness, and originality. You do, however, have a tendency to allow your mind to go off on high-speed tangents. So force yourself to concentrate on the task at hand—especially important since you typically create a life where you have a million and one things to do. Saturn also influences your sign, and this influence makes you an interesting blend of the traditional and the radical. Your lesson in life is to learn to balance the two so you can benefit from both.

As a fixed sign, you can sometimes be incredibly irritating because just when others think they are beginning to understand you, suddenly you demonstrate an amazing stubbornness, or a rigidity in your outlook, that seems to go totally against the rest of your Aquarian personality. This is why it is important for you to try to understand *yourself* a little more, for only then will you realize why it truly is difficult for everyone else to do so. Besides, for the truth seeker of the zodiac, it only makes sense to start with yourself and reap the benefits of greater self-understanding.

Success means different things to different people. If you are a typical Aquarian, it means having the personal freedom to express yourself and to bring knowledge and truth to the rest of society, even if the rest of the world doesn't always want to hear what you have to say. But remember, while sticking to your own opinion is fine, sometimes your way of forcing your opinions on others is not. Of course you can go through life being the original rebel with a cause—if that is truly what you want—but you will often achieve more success if you are tolerant of those who choose to go a different way!

Defining Your Goals

Not every Aquarian wants to be an outspoken humanitarian, or to change the face of society, although many of you are extremely concerned about the needs of the world. But I am sure that each one of you does have some goals you wish to fulfill, and your inquiring mind and independent character will certainly help you to go all out to achieve them. Ask yourself what you truly want out of life, and then focus your Aquarian intuition and inventiveness uncompromisingly on your goals.

What *is* important is believing wholeheartedly in what you set out to do, whether it be for yourself or for someone else. You have the courage to rise above any setback or obstacles, and the integrity to follow your goals through to fruition. Just bear in mind that your ideas may well be ahead of their time, and that it may take others awhile to believe in their validity and to accept them. As long as you combine your positive Aquarian traits of idealism and inspiration with reality and practicality, the good news is that you will more than likely convince the skeptics in the end.

How to Achieve Your Emotional Goals

If you are a typical Aquarian, your emotional goals may be difficult to fathom, simply because you are such an unpredictable sign: At times you yearn for a soulmate, at other times you yearn to be alone, and often you don't know *what* you want. Sometimes you moan that other people don't understand you, but perhaps this is because you don't totally understand yourself. To achieve better emotional balance, start by getting more in touch with your own feelings. Although your emotions run as deep as those of any other sign, yours are such a private part of your personality that you may not be aware of their strength and depth. My father was a wonderful Aquarian man, a true humanitarian and always fair in his judgments. However, he couldn't express his feelings well with words of love, which is typical of Aquarius.

To become more successful emotionally, it is important to conquer your emotional weaknesses. In your case, it is often necessary for you to begin by admitting that you *do* have a deep-rooted problem expressing your emotions. I think that many of you genuinely don't believe this, and you inadvertently give others the wrong signals. By not understanding your own emotions and accurately conveying them to others, you can so easily end up blaming those around you for misunderstandings, especially after a break up that occurred because your partner did not realize you really did care. It's wonderful to be able to burst forth with passionate expressions of your beliefs, but expressing passion on a one-to-one basis is often much harder for you to do. Air signs certainly talk a lot, but not always about what they should. Start to open up a little more on a deeper level because that is what true emotional success is all about.

Aquarius is the sign of friendship, and as a friend you are one of the most loyal, stimulating, effervescent, and interesting people around. However, this part of you is most enjoyed by others when they have learned to accept your erratic behavior and your cool, emotional detachment. Occasionally, with your far-out ideas, it appears as though you live in your own world, or in space. But, you are amazingly intuitive, and you probably suspect that getting in touch with your emotions and sharing them with others isn't one of your strong points.

When I think of my Aquarian friends and clients, it is interesting to observe that many of them are loners and prefer to be so. They enjoy the freedom of not being tied down to a partner, and could certainly not be described as lonely. If you are a typical Aquarian you are extremely independent and are not willing to settle for anything less than what you really want.

However, if you have unfulfilled emotional goals, try to let your feelings show more often. Don't hide behind that cool, aloof exterior just because you may feel scared of losing your emotional perspective. Deep down, you know you're far too bright and intellectual for that. You will find yourself more successful emotionally on every level with partners, coworkers, family members and friends, when you are in tune with yourself on every level, too.

There is invariably a great longing within your Aquarian personality to make the world a better place for everyone, even on days when everything seems to go wrong and you find it hard to visualize yourself as a humanitarian. Getting more in touch with your inner feelings makes it easier to fulfill your own emotional needs and goals. This is a stronger basis for solving the problems of the rest of the world.

EMOTIONS AND THE AQUARIUS WOMAN

Even if the Aquarian woman is emotionally unpredictable, it is crucial for anyone involved with her to find the magic key to her emotions, in order to sustain a successful relationship with her.

There is something incalculable about your personality. Mia Farrow, Helen Gurley Brown, Zsa Zsa Gabor, Gypsy Rose Lee,

Eva Braun, Ayn Rand, Gertrude Stein, Lana Turner, Carol Channing, Jeanne Moreau, and Angela Davis were born under your sign, so you see it is extremely difficult to make generalizations about the Aquarian woman, other than you are *all* truly unique!

Since every zodiac sign gains something from its opposite sign, and yours is Leo, the sign that thrives on both giving and receiving love, perhaps you should also read the chapter on the Leo woman's emotions to discover what *she* does to be more successful emotionally!

Aquarian women are often more prepared to be a man's good friend than the love of his life. When you are in a love relationship, though, you are determined to retain your independence. It's not that you are against romance, but you tend to shy away from total commitment. To be sure, there are times when you hate to be alone, but they are infrequent.

This kind of emotional pattern makes sustaining a successful relationship difficult. You may be willing to give up a bit of your independence for the rewards of finding someone who shares some of your ideas, stimulates you mentally, and shows you that passion is not simply a load of hot air!

To be more successful in a love relationship, you must realize that you don't have to insist on always doing things your own way; this leads nowhere, unless you are involved with someone who is prepared to give in to your every whim. And would you really want this? Try to be more intimate, and don't be quite so worried about letting someone get close to you, mentally or physically. By playing too hard to get you may miss out on attracting someone you could really care about.

Don't ignore your emotional and sexual needs because of your deep desire to feel free. Not every potential partner is a threat to your civil liberties. Start letting your heart dictate a little more, rather than listening to your head. You often meet others who have the potential to be someone special, but instead of enjoying them for who they are, you begin worrying about what to do if you start to care about them, and how you don't want to tie yourself down when you have so much else happening in your life.

I know a few Aquarian women who have managed to successfully sustain excellent relationships, without feeling they have lost a part of themselves. A special friend of mine has been married for twenty years to the same man and they have both told me they feel they are on a perpetual honeymoon. And he is an Aquarian, too. I also have an Aquarian client who decided not to remarry after her husband died, but she has not cut herself off from a wide circle of friends and feels extremely fulfilled emotionally as a result. Success can always be yours if you are prepared to balance your inner and outer needs.

EMOTIONS AND THE AQUARIUS MAN

There are Aquarian men who manage to retain their individuality and also fulfill their emotional needs—and indeed stay with the same partner for many years. Aquarian Paul Newman has been married since 1958 to Piscean Joanne Woodward, which for Hollywood stars sets quite a record! Paul Newman isn't the only show business male born under this sign who is recognized as a real charmer: Clark Gable, James Dean (the original rebel with or without a cause), Humphrey Bogart, Jack Lemmon, Mikhail Baryshnikov, Nick Nolte, Burt Reynolds, Tom Selleck, and Robert Wagner.

Aquarian men tend to be charismatic, exciting, unpredictable, and quite often, nonconformists. In addition, you appear to think of yourself as the most elusive of all men, or at least that is how you like to present yourself. To be more successful emotionally, you need to open up more to some old-fashioned romance, rather than rationalizing about how much happier you are with a best friend rather than a lover. You tend to become almost tongue-tied with embarrassment when it's time to utter a declaration of love, or when simply admitting that a particular person is important to you.

You needn't be quite so terrified of showing your emotions. Ask yourself why you fear letting yourself go quite so much, and then rationalize your feelings rather than trying to ignore them. Having known more than a few Aquarian men and listened to their tales of woe when a relationship was going wrong, I'm not so sure you are really so detached, deep inside. One man was determined to remain free for as long as possible, and when he did decide he wanted to settle down his prospective partner had grown tired of waiting for a marriage proposal. He realized too late that she would have been his ideal soulmate, but he had refrained from telling her this, fearing he would reveal a vulnerability hidden since his teens. Another Aquarian man felt he was being pushed in a direction that did not fit in with his long-term ideals and simply refused to compromise or even talk things over with his partner. Admit that you have strong emotional feelings, and then search for the key to let them out. But don't follow the example of the brilliant Aquarian tennis star John McEnroe, who had given free rein to his emotions both on the tennis court and during his marriage to the Scorpio Tatum O'Neal!

Getting in touch with your feelings, especially if you've been blocking them for a long time, can be quite an awesome experience. I've noticed that Aquarians often find it difficult to cry. I'm not suggesting that you go and sit in a corner with a large box of tissues, but I do think you might try to examine your feelings after sitting through a few weepy romantic movies. I bet you would discover that you are not as unmoved by romance and melodrama as you pretend.

Possibly you consider yours to be an amazing social life, but you still feel alone inside. You don't have to continue to feel that way. One of your friends could turn out to be the soulmate you've always dreamed of but didn't know how to find. Open

yourself up to the possibilities around you and resolve not to
be quite so impersonal from now on.

How to Achieve Your Material Goals

A typical Aquarian's material goals usually involve expressing
your independence in every aspect of your life, answering to
almost no one else. To achieve this, you may temporarily
have to give up some of your independence and accept some
kind of structure and organization. This will actually improve
your motivation and thus your prospects of meeting your
goals, which often entail serving a higher cause as well as a
practical one.

Your ideas are often way ahead of their time, and because
you are a fixed Air sign you can be inordinately stubborn about
changing them. At times your views and beliefs are very
extreme, and you will go out on a limb to defend them. But
you can also be remarkably tolerant of other people, since you
understand that we are all different and have the right to be so.

The easiest way for you to achieve your material goals is to
keep in mind you do not need to sacrifice to them your principles or your sense of freedom. You are brilliant at analyzing
and rationalizing the reasons something should work, but
that comes from the head. Try to rely more on your heart for
direction, too. Once in a while you need to examine your
feelings a little more closely to be certain your actions are for
the best.

Because Aquarius is the sign of the humanitarian and truth
seeker, your material goals are often far-reaching and affect a
great number of people—including you. Creating positive
change is surely one of your most important ideals. Your open-
mindedness and compassion for the world lead you ever
forward and upward. Aquarian Oprah Winfrey seems to
demonstrate this with the format of her television shows, since

she is not afraid to talk about her own problems in addition to getting her audience to talk about theirs.

You have a strong social conscience, and this means that when you are materially secure you genuinely want to help people less fortunate than yourself.

However, sometimes your energy is too scattered, and you visualize success before it has a chance to materialize. This is why it is so important for you to organize your days well and be as pragmatic as possible in your approach to every situation. The drawback to your idealism is that sometimes you waste a great deal of time on impracticalities.

You are good at being "part of the crowd" and find it easy to work with other people as a team. Remember, though, that you are sometimes pretty difficult for others to read. Practice a little tact, tolerance, and diplomacy, to avoid upsetting those around you unwittingly.

There is really nothing you cannot do if you are truly determined, provided you concentrate as much on the present as you do on the future. You have a great advantage over many other signs, because your flashes of intuition are a wonderful asset, especially when it comes to planning the right moment to act in your best interests.

The Powerful Assets at Your Disposal to Become More Successful

The Power of Your Element . . . Air

Aquarius is the last of the Air signs, Gemini and Libra being the other two. In every way you are the most detached, intellectually oriented, and unemotional of the three Air signs. These traits can help to make you more successful, for they encourage you not to become panicky when problems arise. On the other hand, the Air element can also mean that you distance yourself too much from everyone and everything. Since understanding what people are all about is supposed to be your forte, this will often lead you down the wrong path.

As an Air sign ruled by Uranus, you look for truth in life and want to change the things you feel are wrong with the world. You are definitely a thinker, and often a smart one at that. Many important writers have been born under your sign, including Robert Burns, Lewis Carroll, Anton Chekhov, Colette, Charles Dickens, James Joyce, Norman Mailer, Somerset Maugham, Boris Pasternak, and Virginia Woolf.

Your Air qualities determine your idealistic, altruistic, and intellectual nature, but they can also send your mind floating away on a tangent, causing you to lose sight of your main objectives. Whereas the Earth signs—Taurus, Virgo, and Capricorn—may be too firmly rooted in the ground, you tend to have your head in the clouds, visualizing your utopian image but neglecting to work out just how you are going to achieve this vision.

You will benefit from talking through some of your ideas with people you consider more pragmatic than you. From them you will gain a more practical perspective on how to make your dreams realities, without having to compromise too much.

Maximize the potential of your Air element and you will also be able to rationalize your way out of any obstacle or setback that might arise in your daily life, and to climb higher up the ladder of success.

The Power of Your Ruling Planet . . . Uranus

Uranus is associated with invention, change, and independence, which are strongly related to your personality. This planet is the great awakener and has been called "the awakener of humanity to a new age." The power of Uranus is immense, for it endows you with your sense of initiative and originality, enabling you to stride ahead and achieve your ideals.

Take care, though, for Uranus is also responsible for your erratic, perverse, unpredictable, and unconventional approach to life and can also make you fanatical and anarchic in your aims and ambitions. Don't give way to the negative aspects of this planet. You must find ways to balance the negatives by ensuring that your nervous system remains in balance, for in the body Uranus relates to the nervous system and to the electrical force flowing through the nerve channels. Before Uranus was discovered, it was said that Saturn influenced your sign, and I've often thought that many of you could also benefit immensely from Saturn's restraining influence, because of your tendency to go to extremes.

With Uranus as your ruling planet, you are given carte blanche to be independent and original in your self-expression. This planet also encourages you to develop your creative talents, and your mind's abilities through inventive and sometimes unusual thought processes. Uranus also often inspires within you the urge to be a reformer or pioneer and to speak out against what you consider unfair or unjust.

In this technological age, you are fortunate to have Uranus as your ruler. This planet is connected with invention in general and with electricity, science, and electronics in particular. It was the Aquarian Thomas Edison who invented the light bulb! Many of you seem to have an inborn ability to be whiz kids with your computers, and the Internet could have been invented just for you.

To be ruled by inventive, inspirational and original Uranus, aided by the self-restraint of Saturn, means you have the ability to achieve success when you concentrate on turning your lofty ideals into reality.

The Power of Your Rising Sign

Your Ascendant, or rising sign, is the sign that was rising on the eastern horizon at the time of your birth. In many ways it is as

important as your Sun and Moon signs, for the way you live out your life is very much influenced by your rising sign.

You can determine your Ascendant using the tables on pages 278–79 The following are brief summaries of how different rising signs affect your personality; they help you to maximize your success potential.

AQUARIUS WITH ARIES RISING
You are more impulsive and definitely less detached emotionally than other Aquarians. You are also extremely enthusiastic about turning your idealistic visions into reality in the minimum amount of time. But don't be headstrong!

AQUARIUS WITH TAURUS RISING
A Taurus Ascendant gives you the determination to achieve your chosen goals in the most constructive way possible. But watch out that you aren't too stubborn and unyielding if other people don't always see eye to eye with you.

AQUARIUS WITH GEMINI RISING
You definitely are never boring. The only problem is trying to get you to sit still long enough to plan what you are going to do first. Variety definitely adds spice to our lives, but don't let your busy social life take up *all* your time.

AQUARIUS WITH CANCER RISING
You're an Aquarian with an openly sentimental streak. You find it much easier than most Aquarians to understand other people's feelings, and your own, too. Your domestic setup is extremely important and your Aquarian urge for freedom is muted.

AQUARIUS WITH LEO RISING
You are a real go-getter, but make sure your humanitarian goals don't get overshadowed by Leo's tendency to be wildly extravagant. You certainly think really big with this combination and you could end up a star!

AQUARIUS WITH VIRGO RISING

The Virgo Ascendant makes you very self-critical as well as hypercritical of others. This combination allows you to develop an analytical approach to everyday situations as you discover that you have quite a practical side to your personality.

AQUARIUS WITH LIBRA RISING

A double dose of Air gives you the ability to communicate on a myriad of intellectual and other subjects. You will be charming, sociable, and diplomatic and enjoy a wide circle of friends who love your company.

AQUARIUS WITH SCORPIO RISING

Intensity of passion and jealousy aren't usually found in your sign, but they definitely are present with Scorpio rising. Sometimes you may find it hard to know whether you want to be alone or enjoy a sizzling emotional life. Scorpio's influence causes you to work hard toward achieving your goals.

AQUARIUS WITH SAGITTARIUS RISING

You are free and easy in your lifestyle, with a real wanderlust to see more of the world. Confidence and optimism come to you easily. You inspire other people to share in your ideals, but don't take too many risks!

AQUARIUS WITH CAPRICORN RISING

Your Capricorn Ascendant gives you a more pragmatic yet original approach to life. You focus more easily on what is happening in the here and now instead of the future, and also are more disciplined in achieving your aims and ambitions than most Aquarians.

AQUARIUS WITH AQUARIUS RISING

Don't let yourself be too cool and emotionally detached from the rest of us. With this combination you could be a genius or an airhead and a loner. Talking about all your high-flying plans is one thing, just make sure you get on with them too.

AQUARIUS WITH PISCES RISING

You are one of the greatest visionaries of all time and produce wonderfully inventive schemes. But your impractical ways could mess things up unless you are prepared to take a responsible attitude toward financial and other material issues. You *are* wonderfully romantic!

How to Create Greater Success

Creating Greater Success . . . in Your Everyday Life

If you are a typical Aquarian, the very thought of having to create more structure and organization in your daily life will probably fill you with total horror. If you are completely honest with yourself you may well admit that you could become a whole lot more successful if you disciplined yourself. You often conceive wonderfully grandiose schemes, in which you visualize yourself as the star, but unfortunately you don't always go about realizing them in the right way. You tend to delay too long between the conception of an idea and putting it into action.

To be more successful, you must get a firm grip on reality and your feet on terra firma, and not live way up in the air! Invariably you are extremely intellectually innovative when you take the time and trouble to be so.

You are very open-minded, and you certainly don't mind experimenting with different methods of doing things; what's often missing in your life is motivation. At heart you are the most unpredictable and unconventional sign of the whole zodiac, which can be a drawback when you need to fit in. You often have a unique ability to "know" things way in advance of the rest of us, and I'm sure it must be frustrating when other people don't go along with your ideas. However, you also possess a clever way of putting your ideas across so that eventually their value is understood, even if it sometimes takes awhile.

If you are a typical Aquarius, you may feel that success is unimportant to you, as long as you're free to do your own thing. However, you might also feel that you would like greater success and that it eludes you through no fault of your own. The following checklist will give you some points on how you can create a better daily regime, without having to alter your Aquarian life *too* much.

DO . . .
- remain idealistic . . . but be realistic, too.
- stay original and inventive—but don't be too unpredictable.
- involve yourself with humanitarian causes, as long as you don't neglect the people closest to you.
- make sure you give your mind plenty of intellectual stimulation.
- continue to be curious about life, and especially the future.
- learn everything you can about technology—it's your forte.

DON'T . . .
- ever be a rebel without a cause.
- be stubborn if people don't want to accept your views.
- be a revolutionary just because you're an Aquarian.
- turn to anarchy—for the reason above!
- be afraid to let people understand how and what you feel.
- ever forget that friends are what makes your world go round.

Creating Greater Success . . . in Love

Before we can discover how an Aquarian can be most successful in finding true love, we need to define "love" carefully. You are invariably highly successful if we are to talk about universal love, selflessly giving everything you have for a higher cause. It's the one-on-one situation that tends to throw you.

You are not the most passionate of signs. In fact, you can come across as cold and unfeeling. Meanwhile you are perfectly brilliant at theorizing about love and passion in a general sense, and could probably discuss them both intellectually for hours and hours, which can be inordinately frustrating for anyone who might be in love with you.

To achieve successful, fulfilling love relationships, learn to let your feelings show a little more. Think of the warmth and coziness of a good emotional bond, and stop thinking of how it might cramp your freedom-loving way of life. You would probably find you wouldn't even miss your freedom if you were in a really good relationship.

If you want to be a loner, you will obviously stay set in your ways. But I'm sure there are many Aquarians out there who genuinely do want to feel closer to someone special. Learning from what your opposite sign, Leo, has to offer, you'll find a great deal of joy in giving and receiving love.

Try to show that special someone you care, rather than expect them to read your mind. Try to think of yourself as more than an interesting companion. You can be a wonderful lover, too, if you let yourself go a little more.

Creating Greater Success . . . in Dating

Since you are usually one of the friendliest souls, it should not be difficult for you to be successful in dating. But sometimes you seem to find safety in numbers, preferring a whole group of friends to a single person for companionship.

In looking for a partner, remember that you need to be mentally stimulated by anyone you date. A sexy body will not usually turn you on unless its owner has the brains to go with it. You may find a potential lover while volunteering for your favorite charity and that way you will meet people with the same kind of altruistic views as yours. They will also be able to see you at your best—in a group.

AQUARIUS DATING TIPS
- Show that you have a great sense of humor and that you can be warm and romantic, too.
- Make more of an effort to get to know someone you like on a deeper level so you understand their personality better.
- Don't get cold feet when you start to date someone who seems just right.

Creating Greater Success . . . in Family Ties

You are basically such a generous and friendly person that you are unlikely intentionally to let down anyone in your family. You *are* a loner, though, and you do not always keep in touch nearly enough with your relatives, whether they live near you or not. To sustain good family ties, you will need to make an effort to write, telephone, or visit more frequently.

If you're a typical Aquarian you hate to feel tied down in any way. However, there is also a side of you that doesn't always want to be alone and that definitely dislikes being forgotten. You probably know that your family members want to hear from you more often than they generally do. I have one Aquarian friend who has learned to keep in touch through the telephone with two of his aunts who live on the other side of the Atlantic, and they maintain a very close relationship. Another Aquarian friend is probably the best daughter that her elderly mother could ever have wished for, as she always makes sure to check in on her mother frequently, and even takes her off on holidays to France every year.

You are an extremely caring person by nature, and since Aquarius is the sign of tolerance, human brotherhood, and a sense of responsibility toward the world, include your family in your humanitarian feelings.

You always expect other people to accept your changes of mood, even when you know you are being perverse. You need to do the same for others.

As a parent, try a little harder to be more physically affectionate, since merely telling your children you love them doesn't mean as much as showing them. Hugs and kisses may not be easy for you to give, but they will often help you to achieve greater closeness to your children.

TIPS FOR SUCCESSFUL FAMILY TIES
- Be as good a friend to your family members as you are to everyone else.
- Try harder to express your emotions with a physical show of affection.
- Avoid being so unconventional and unpredictable that no one in your family can understand what you're all about.

Creating Greater Success . . . at Work

To be more successful at work, remember that deep down you hate routine. Unfortunately, it's not always possible for a person to control every aspect of his or her working life, but one way to maintain the maximum amount of freedom would be to seek out free-lance or consulting positions.

You are often extremely talented, but not always incredibly ambitious in the accepted sense of the word. You must be motivated by your own ideas or by a cause to which you are quite prepared to dedicate your whole self. Whatever you do, it has to be a little different from what everyone else is doing. Mental stimulation is incredibly important to you. If you're a typical Aquarian your mind seems to simply cut off after a while if you lose interest in what is going on. Aquarians can't do the same old thing again and again.

Because you are so innovative, original, and inventive, you definitely have what it takes to be successful. And of course it is a wonderful bonus to be technically inclined in this technological age.

The Aquarian talent is interesting, because just when we think we know you, you take off in a whole new direction, as demonstrated by the Aquarian John Travolta in his *Pulp Fiction* role. In the visual arts, there is no stereotypical Aquarian— Manet, Jackson Pollock, Norman Rockwell, and Francis Bacon were all born under your sign.

I have an Aquarian friend, Mark Hayles, who is one of the top make-up artists in America. His work has graced the covers of many glossy magazines the world over. He has made up many well-known faces, including Emma Thompson, Uma Thurman, Faye Dunaway, and Sarah Ferguson, adding to their looks his own unique vision, as Aquarians cannot do the same old make-over time and time again.

Believe wholeheartedly in your talents and abilities, Aquarius, even if you insist on hiding them away until their time has come. Try to conform a little more to the demands of your work situation, even if it doesn't satisfy you in every way.

The following do's and don'ts provide a guide for you to become more successful at work.

DO . . .
- try to work at something where you can use your imagination and flair for the unusual in a constructive way.
- remember that you are an idea person and need projects you can throw yourself into wholeheartedly.
- accept that you need constant stimulation and variety in your work.

DON'T . . .
- be so obviously different in your approach that you create a bad impression.

- refuse to listen to constructive advice because you think *you* know best!
- work at things that present no interesting prospects.

Creating Greater Success . . .
in Finding the Right Job

Look for a position that gives you the maximum potential to fulfill your need for self-expression and to achieve your goals. Your motivation comes from working on projects born of your particular vision, with an eye toward the future.

Because you are so original and inventive in virtually everything you do, it's hard for you to contemplate plodding away at a routine job with routine hours. Freedom is more valuable to you than a few extra dollars a week. You are a brilliant idea person, and when you are motivated and mentally inspired, you will cope with long hours and tricky deadlines.

Your humanitarian convictions would make you wonderful working for the United Nations or UNICEF, or for your own favorite cause. Ideal careers for the typical Aquarian include any profession that involves working with electricity, radio, TV, science, politics, astrology, astronomy, computers, archaeology, sociology, writing, and aviation. Work in the film industry may also prove rewarding, especially directing—John Schlesinger, Franco Zeffirelli, and Ken Russell are Aquarians who have made their special mark in this field, as was François Truffaut.

But whatever you choose to do, make sure your inventive flair has the chance to express itself fully so that greater success quite rightly comes your way.

Creating Greater Success . . .
in All Your Relationships

One of the most important factors in success is good relations with other people. Even though your Aquarian ability to communicate and make friends easily means you should be very successful at this, you may still benefit from a few tips on how to relate even better with those born under each sign.

AQUARIUS AND ARIES

Neither of you will ever get bored, and there could be fun times ahead. All that Arien energy could exhaust you after a while, and your unpredictability and friendly yet cool approach might easily infuriate the fiery and hot-blooded Ram.

AQUARIUS AND TAURUS

You are both fixed signs, and both can be pretty stubborn and determined when you want to be. The Bull's desire for security, stability, and lots of money might cramp your style if you value your freedom and hate the thought of being grounded, but it could do you good!

AQUARIUS AND GEMINI

Creatively you're on a perfect wavelength with your fellow Air sign, and there will be no lack of mental stimulation for both of you. But while you like to intellectualize on how to change the world, Gemini prefers to stick to the lighter side of life. Try to find some common ground.

AQUARIUS AND CANCER

You are more of a thinker than a feeler, and the Crab is the reverse. You want freedom; the Crab wants a cozy domestic nest. You're unconventional, while Cancer is moody. There is a great deal to learn and understand about each other here!

AQUARIUS AND LEO

You are both attention seekers in a big way, but Leo likes to call the tune, and you hate anyone telling you what to do! Although opposite signs attract, compromise on both sides is needed to make this work.

AQUARIUS AND VIRGO

Intellectual discussions will be no problem, but you will have to try to structure your life better if you don't want Virgo to constantly criticize you for your disorganized ways. Never accuse Virgo of being a hypochondriac, even if you do feel it's occasionally true!

AQUARIUS AND LIBRA

A perfect Air combination, since Libra can add balance, peace, and harmony to your unpredictable personality. You both enjoy being with people, but try to be a little more romantic when dealing with Librans. Also, keep in mind that Librans are indecisive.

AQUARIUS AND SCORPIO

You may be fascinated with each other at first, but don't forget that Scorpio is a passionately intense and jealous sign. Scorpio wants control, while you want freedom! Don't behave too unconventionally if you want to make this combination work.

AQUARIUS AND SAGITTARIUS

Good friendships usually result from this combination. You two share a good sense of humor, an optimistic disposition, and a free and easy approach to life. You make good traveling companions, too. But each of you thinks you know *all* the answers.

AQUARIUS AND CAPRICORN

Since both of you can be cool and emotionally remote, you will understand each other's ways. However, take heed of Capricorn's pragmatic approach to life, and try not to come across as too eccentric or unpredictable, as this sign is easily embarrassed.

AQUARIUS AND AQUARIUS

The mirror image you have in another Aquarius will show you how other people see *you*. At the least you should be good friends, depending on whether one is prepared to fit in with the other. Don't take anything for granted in this relationship.

AQUARIUS AND PISCES

Both visionaries in your own particular way, you both have enough intuition to know just how to make this relationship work. Be aware that Pisces is a very sensitive soul whose feelings can be wounded easily, so avoid sarcastic jibes.

Becoming a
More Successful
Pisces

PISCES

If you were born between February 19 and March 20, you were born under the sign of Pisces. It is the twelfth sign of the zodiac, a feminine, mutable, negative Water sign, ruled by Neptune, the planet of inspiration. Your planetary symbol is the Fish—actually, two fishes swimming in opposite directions! Known as the romantic dreamer of the zodiac, the Pisces personality sometimes seems to fit its symbol a little too well. If you are a typical Pisces, you often seem not to know whether you are coming or going. You also tend to view the world through rose-colored spectacles.

Many of you possess amazing creative ability, especially in the worlds of art and music. People born under your sign include the composers and performers Ravel, Vivaldi, Handel, Rossini, Rimsky-Korsakov, Glenn Miller, Nat King Cole, Quincy Jones, Nina Simone, Harry Belafonte, and Kiri Te Kanawa, as well as the painter Mondriaan.

Typically, those born under the sign of Pisces must try harder to become more practical in their day-to-day lives and live less in the world of their imagination to become more successful. All too often your dreaminess leads you into trouble, especially when it comes to dealing with financial and material issues. It is true that you are a gentle, romantic Water sign, but it is neither necessary nor wise for you to drift through life as if you were floating in the sea, taken wherever the currents might choose. Be emotional and creative without being careless. It is better for you to feel financially secure, rather than to worry continuously about your bank account.

Resolve to take off those rose-colored spectacles that create illusions. Perhaps life looks better with them on, but you cannot afford illusions if you truly want to be more successful. Try to sift the practical from the impractical and you will be surprised how much easier your life will become. Being the last sign of the zodiac certainly doesn't mean you have to come in last when they are handing out prizes for success.

Each sign of the zodiac relates to a different area of the body, starting with the head and ending with the feet, from Aries to Pisces. Pisces rules the feet and toes, which means you may suffer from gout, bunions, corns, and other foot problems. Because of the Piscean connection to the feet and toes, it comes as perhaps no surprise that the dancers Nureyev and Nijinsky were both born under your sign. Pisces also rules the lymphatic system, and it is said that if you hold back your emotions your lymph system can become congested, giving rise to swollen lymph glands and nodes.

You invariably "feel" things more than any other sign in the entire zodiac. However, trouble arises when you become too much of a chameleon, changing your ideas and your direction exactly like the two fish that represent your sign—one swimming upstream and the other down. To become more successful, try to find more of a balance between your inner and outer natures. Don't simply "go with the flow"!

The positive side of Pisces makes you one of the most tender, mystical, psychic, sympathetic, sensitive, idealistic, and compassionate people around. You also have a scintillating sense of humor when you want to use it. On the down side, you easily become melancholy, dishonest, unrealistic, cruel, and jealous.

You tend to be receptive to other people's influences, but don't be swayed by others unless you are absolutely certain they are interested in your own good. You possess an intuition bordering on the psychic, and you are able to sum up people extremely well.

I remember reading something by Oliver Wendell Holmes, that I feel applies particularly well to you: "A moment's insight is sometimes worth a life's experience." You must make use of that insight and not simply file it away in your scrapbook of dreams. I'm not telling you to stop being a dreamer, but rather to try and turn your dreams into reality, thus greater success.

Success means different things to different people. For Pisces it usually includes having the ability to feel secure within yourself, fearing neither rejection by nor criticism from other people. It means knowing exactly where you are going.

Defining Your Goals

Not every Pisces man or woman wants to be an artist, musician, or dancer. I'm sure there are some of you who would like to have a few more dollars, though you may not be interested in becoming millionaires. Pisceans are intuitive, possess great inspiration, and are blessed with an incredible imagination, and these traits should bestow upon you great success. However you must make sure that you use these talents to attain greater tangible success in your life.

How to Achieve Your Emotional Goals

To achieve your emotional goals in the easiest possible way, you must yet again take off the rose-colored spectacles to see people for who they are—warts and all.

Pisces is the most romantic and ultrasensitive sign of the zodiac, and you often think that if you are not anchored safely within a harmonious relationship you have no choice but to drift aimlessly through the sea of love, searching for a soulmate. When your idealistic vision does not materialize, you often see yourself as a victim. Furthermore, Pisceans sometimes make themselves martyrs and go from one difficult relationship to another. Don't make yourself a martyr to your emotions. I have known both friends and clients born under your sign who have insisted on repeating the pattern of a failed relationship, because they were too idealistic about relationships in the first place. Sometimes it's almost as though falling in love is for you a form of escape from yourself. In fact, you can function perfectly well and be extremely successful without someone to hold your hand.

These warnings shouldn't be taken to mean that Pisceans don't have long and successful relationships, for I have known many who do. The Piscean Joanne Woodward has been married successfully for more than twenty-five years to the Aquarian Paul Newman.

Neptune, your planetary ruler who provides you with inspiration, can also bring delusion your way if you don't listen to your inner psychic voice and take advantage of the knowledge your intuition provides. Pay more attention to the power of your intuition because it is one of your greatest assets. Draw on your inner strength to make you love yourself more, and you will be far less apt to fall for someone just because you think you need someone in your life.

It is an innate part of your personality to give to other people, and empathize with them on every level. However, you cannot be a shoulder to lean on for everyone who has a hard-luck story to tell. There is a wonderfully protective quality about you, but you must use it for yourself, too.

Pisces relates to the twelfth house of the zodiac, which is often known as the house of one's own undoing. This house harbors the secrets you like to keep hidden from the world. To achieve success, you need to come out from your private little world more often and be more positive about what you have to offer and what life has to offer you.

You are not only one of the most romantic signs around, but one of the most seductive, too. Be selective as to where you apply your seductive ways, though, and listen to your inner voice when it says no.

EMOTIONS AND THE PISCES WOMAN

If I were asked to give an example of the archetypal Pisces woman in the context of emotions, I think I would always put forward Elizabeth Taylor. For me, she embodies the true feminine Piscean attitude toward love and romance; she and Scorpio Richard Burton together created one of the great love stories of our time.

The typical Piscean is searching for a romantic fairy-tale ending to every love affair. Unfortunately, we don't have too many fairy-tale endings in real life! This is why it is so important for you to be realistic with your emotions, and to try not to throw yourself wholeheartedly and enthusiastically into something that doesn't really feel right. Don't you realize, Pisces, that you have an incredible advantage over many of us? Your powerful intuition definitely works when you decide to use it. The trouble is that many of you don't bother to maximize its potential, because those rose-colored spectacles obscure your view. You want to believe someone is perfect, and you talk yourself into seeing them that way. Try not to be so easily carried away and easily influenced. Sometimes you fall in love incredibly quickly, believing it will last forever, only to realize a few weeks later that you have locked yourself into a no-go situation from which you wonder how to escape.

Too often you fall in love with love, or with the idea of some mythical Prince Charming who is going to whisk you off on a white charger to a magical destination. Consequently, you may too easily fall under the spell of someone who has power and material resources.

If you are a typical Pisces woman who possesses strong emotions yearning to be fulfilled, don't let yourself fall for what seems to be a glamorous life because you chose not to listen to your intuition. Don't forget, you are changeable in your emotions, but your intuition springs from deeper sources. Your feelings flow this way and that. Sometimes you enjoy playing the helpless child, and then you switch to playing a cool yet sensual sex goddess, like Piscean Sharon Stone. Other times you make yourself suffer through a relationship, compromising yourself in the name of love. Don't let the ebb and flow of your emotions make you commit to a relationship you're not sure you really want.

Pisceans tend to devote their lives to helping other people, as you can see in the examples of the Pisceans Florence

Nightingale and the AIDS activist Elizabeth Taylor. To be most effective, many of you need to devote more time to understanding your own strengths and weaknesses to better deal with everyone else's. Tapping sources of emotional strength is never a mistake, and Piscean women don't have to fall to pieces when emotional traumas occur—as Pisces Cindy Crawford proved after the final split-up with Virgo Richard Gere. When you realize your strengths, you won't fall apart either. Some of the other women born under your sign include Ursula Andress, Glenn Close, Liza Minnelli, Drew Barrymore, Lynn Redgrave, and Gloria Vanderbilt.

EMOTIONS AND THE PISCES MAN

You are just as much of a romantic dreamer as your female counterpart and you sometimes find it hard to face the realities of life. Emotionally you are ultrasensitive and can be easily hurt. You are also inclined to run away from situations that you deem to be out of control. Your strong romantic desires and fantasies also make you feel let down far too easily when a relationship becomes mundane.

To have more successful relationships, it's important to let your head have a say in your emotional decisions. You are the charismatic poet and actor of the zodiac. You have the ability to express what you feel in the most wonderful ways, which is guaranteed to have admirers falling at your feet. Although you can fall in love as fast as any Aries, you can fall out of love equally fast. The symbol of two fishes swimming in opposite directions fits you only too well, as almost anyone who has thrown her hook in your direction will agree.

One of the most interesting things about a Pisces man is that you don't necessarily come across as the greatest seducer. We usually think of Scorpio in that role. But you are able to seduce someone in the most subtle ways. You aim not just for the heart, but for the very soul. This all sounds wonderful, and of course sometimes it is, but how many soulmates do you want on your journey through life? Some of you seem to be on an unending quest for an ideal partner. You even go as far as to indulge in romantic fantasies of this ideal person, who in reality exists only in your dreams.

Since you are an incurable romantic, you may invite unnecessary problems by falling for people you know deep inside are not right for you. As a typical Pisces, though, you often have a penchant for suffering, especially when it's in the cause of love.

Pisces is a feminine sign, which certainly doesn't mean your masculinity is in question but does make you more compassionate, sensitive, and imaginative than many other men. Often you are more vulnerable, too, and when your vulnerability is coupled with your inner fear of being trapped, it makes you very difficult to understand.

You need a relationship that offers you intellectual compatibility, sensuality, and lots of romance. Often you are happy to be the more passive partner in a relationship and seek a woman who is stronger and more dominant than you. You also dread the idea of boredom and too much routine in any emotional tie. When it comes right down to it, you want both security and freedom, combined with everlasting romantic love. If you do become dissatisfied with your life you are the sign most likely to turn to drugs and alcohol to forget your disappointment. This is why it is so important for you to balance your mind, body, and soul, so that you are capable of wholeheartedly loving someone with whom you truly feel compatible. Men born under your sign are very different, but they're all great romantics at heart! Just to name a few, we have Michael Caine, Billy Crystal, Roger Daltrey, Rob Lowe, Sidney Poitier, Kurt Russell, Bruce Willis, and Tom Wolfe.

How to Achieve Your Material Goals

If you are a typical Piscean, you may think of yourself as far too unworldly to possess material goals of any kind, and you are indeed one of the most impractical signs of the whole zodiac. You often appear to prefer floating through life hoping things will work out, without having to do too much to help them along. However, since Rupert Murdoch happens to be born under your sign and is constantly achieving his material goals, I wouldn't dream of saying *all* Pisceans fit this description.

Romance isn't the only concern in your life. Many of you are incredibly hard-working and determined to be recognized for your ability to mastermind big projects and become leaders in your chosen field. You're still a creative dreamer, but your dreams, rather than focusing on romance, become visions of the future in which you hope to participate. Sometimes you have big ideas about how to make money, but they aren't always very practical. You have a tendency to spend too much time dreaming wonderful dreams, and not enough time working out how you will turn them into reality. Often you are brilliant at theorizing (both Copernicus and Albert Einstein were born under your sign), but the practical side of life can often present insurmountable problems.

You need to immerse your whole being in something in order for it to be successful for you. Doing this also ensures that you don't simply drift with the tide, lacking a true direction. Make sure you do not end up as one of those Pisceans who prefer to live in a fantasy world and not confront the problems that unfortunately are an inevitable part of life.

If you have always found it difficult to achieve your material goals, ask yourself whether it could be partly your own fault. If you are a typical Piscean you are sometimes unable to make decisions, preferring to take a passive approach and wait for external factors to decide for you.

You are often amazingly intuitive, and sometimes you can even organize your life on the basis of your instincts. So don't ignore your intuition, but don't turn your back on realistic observations. You will achieve the best results when you balance analytical thought with intuition, and when you also become more positive and optimistic about your own particular talents and abilities.

Sometimes your sensitivity creates problems for you. You genuinely feel compassion for people who are worse off than you. Be careful you don't land yourself in projects or schemes where you really can't be effective. Astrologers tend to describe Pisceans as people who can never say no, but you had better make sure you learn to say no to projects and situations that go against your deepest instincts.

Once you have visualized your goals, the important part is making the vizualization work in the best possible way. By relating more positively toward yourself, and other people, too, you will find yourself moving onward and upward to greater success. You must stop drifting, whether it be up- or downstream; stop and establish a true vision of yourself in the place you want to be.

The Powerful Assets at Your Disposal to Become More Successful

The Power of Your Element . . . Water

Pisces is the last of the Water signs, Cancer and Scorpio being the other two. All three Water signs are strongly empowered to follow their feelings, instincts, and intuition. Somehow it is easier to sum up the behavior patterns of a Cancerian or Scorpion than of a Piscean. You seem to feel things at a much deeper level than others and to be more hypersensitive to a myriad of different sensations. Often you don't seem to know whether to swim with the tide or against it, and end up drifting in an uncertain direction. Perhaps your uncertainty comes from Neptune, your planetary ruler, a force that can make it hard to differentiate between reality and illusion. Whatever the reason for your confusion, never allow yourself to sink! Instead, maximize the potential of your intuition, and learn to flow with the right current so you come out where you want to be. As a Water sign you have a great advantage over many other people, for you are totally in touch with your feelings and your deepest emotions. You also believe something intangible, the power of the unconscious mind, can greatly influence your life. When you utilize this power in a positive way, you are able to soar to the heights of success. When you negate it, you become oversensitive to the slightest criticism or threat, and are also prone to irrational fears.

Because you are so sensitive, it is incredibly important not to let your emotions run away with you, but to channel your energies and your emotions into creating a more positive world for yourself and others. Never allow yourself to sink into a slough of despondency, for it is then that you are likely to resort to desperate attempts to protect yourself from being in touch with what you do not really want to see.

As a mutable Water sign, you will achieve the most success when you listen to your feelings at the deepest level and then start to channel them upward into your conscious mind. Think of those two fishes swimming in their opposite directions as being two options. Allow your intuition to lead you in the best direction.

The Power of Your Ruling Planet . . . Neptune

Neptune, the ancient god of the sea, is your planetary ruler. Neptune endows you with both your inspirational and your somewhat unworldly qualities. Neptune also makes you dissatisfied when things do not turn out as you had hoped. Neptune is associated with the psychic realm, imagination, intuition, and dreams, as well as illusions, obsessions, and hallucinations. This planet also rules alcohol and other drugs.

Neptune increases your creativity and idealism, your artistic sensitivity, and your romanticism. It often inspires you to embrace religious devotion or some kind of "universal love." You may even become fascinated by mysticism.

The negative side of Neptune can make you confused, self-deluded, gullible, obsessional, and prone to intangible fears and phobias, drug-addiction, vacillation, and emotional instability. It is said that there is only a thin line between genius and madness, so it is extremely important for you to maximize Neptune's potential in a positive way and allow yourself to be inspired to greater heights rather than dragged down in any way at all.

Neptune very often features prominently in the birth charts of actors, artists, musicians, composers, and poets. As your planetary ruler, Neptune will enable you to capitalize on your creative talents and abilities. Some creative souls ruled by Neptune include, in the movie world, David Puttnam and Bernardo Bertolucci, the poet Elizabeth Barrett Browning, the artists Michelangelo and Renoir, and the composers Ravel and Chopin. Another Piscean was the wonderful psychic healer Edgar Cayce, who helped so many people and was known as the "sleeping prophet of Virginia Beach."

Inspiration or illusion? The choice is up to you. With your highly attuned intuition, it should not be too difficult for you to avoid swimming in the wrong direction. Neptune will enable you to fulfill your dreams, but you are the one in charge of making sure your dreams are realistic. Vow that you will never lose yourself in fantasy or self-delusion, but that instead you will soar toward even greater heights by making the best possible use of your star sign with Neptune by your side. Neptune will enable you to attain your highest aspirations.

The Power of Your Rising Sign

Your Ascendant, or rising sign, is the sign that was rising on the eastern horizon at the time of your birth. In many ways it is as

important to the course of your life as your Sun and Moon signs.

To determine your Ascendant, consult the chart on pages 278–79. Here are a few short descriptions of how each Ascendant affects you as a Piscean.

PISCES WITH ARIES RISING

You are a romantic dreamer with an aggressive touch. You certainly know where you're going and the pace is fast. You fight to the end for what you believe in, but you'd better watch out for an extravagant streak where finances are involved.

PISCES WITH TAURUS RISING

Your inspirational visions combined with Taurean determination and common sense enable you to climb that ladder of success without falling off halfway up. You even find your bank balance looks fairly healthy, too.

PISCES WITH GEMINI RISING

A Gemini Ascendant makes you more detached emotionally than the archetypal Piscean romantic dreamer. But you still have flights of fantasy that need to be brought down to earth. You are definitely skillful at putting ideas across to others.

PISCES WITH CANCER RISING

Romantic, sensitive, intuitive, domestic, and sometimes moody. Watch out you don't hide yourself away when you should be out there making your mark on the world. Listen to your instincts and you'll soon know what needs to be done.

PISCES WITH LEO RISING

You may be a very extroverted Pisces with masses of self-confidence and optimism. This is a powerful combination, but you'd better have a good accountant to keep a careful check on your spending, which may well go over the top.

PISCES WITH VIRGO RISING

Having your opposite sign as your Ascendant enables you to be more disciplined and organized than a lot of other Pisceans. Don't give way to self-doubt, self-criticism, or just plain old worries if you can't always achieve as much as you'd like.

PISCES WITH LIBRA RISING

You are sweet, sensitive, diplomatic, and charming, but it may be hard to get you to make decisions. Make sure you don't vacillate so much that you miss the boat on great opportunities that come your way.

PISCES WITH SCORPIO RISING

Wow! This is a pretty intense combination. Your ability to psychically know everything that's going on makes you invincible in the power-playing stakes. Watch out that you don't get into some heavy emotional situations at the same time.

PISCES WITH SAGITTARIUS RISING

You are more fun-loving and energetic than the average Piscean and more free and easy when it comes to love relationships. Lots of extra confidence and the ability to sell yourself brilliantly help you to become more successful.

PISCES WITH CAPRICORN RISING

A truly practical Pisces! Your Capricorn rising sign might even make you into more of a workaholic than a dreamer, and you are very determined to achieve both financial and material security in abundance. But don't lose sight of your dreams!

PISCES WITH AQUARIUS RISING

With an Aquarius Ascendant, you could be the most unpredictable Pisces of all. Be careful that your visionary ideas aren't too off-the-wall and impractical. Try to have someone around who keeps your feet on the ground.

PISCES WITH PISCES RISING

Of course you're a romantic dreamer. How could you be anything else with a double dose of Pisces in your chart? You will be doubly intuitive, too. Use this to your benefit and don't let anyone take advantage of your sympathetic and compassionate ways.

How to Create Greater Success

Creating Greater Success . . . in Your Everyday Life

If you are a typical Piscean, you will admit that structure and organization are not things you think about very much. And self-discipline is not usually one of your greatest attributes.

However, if you want to be more successful in your day-to-day life, you must learn to equip yourself a little better to deal with practical issues and to differentiate between fantasy and reality. This means you simply cannot spend all your time dreaming in your make-believe little world.

Start to have more faith in yourself and in your ability to achieve your goals in the external world, and you will find it much easier to get on with life. Think what an advantage it is to feel instinctively what you should do, and resolve not to waste that advantage by drifting aimlessly because you fear making a decision. Make sure your goals are realistic, so you don't waste your time and energy.

If you have any doubts as to your ability to be an achiever, just think of Yuri Gagarin, who was the first man to orbit the earth, or of the great minds of Copernicus, Einstein, Victor Hugo, and the educator/philosopher Rudolph Steiner. To achieve greater success in your life you must stop undervaluing yourself and avoid being easily influenced by other people. You are amazingly creative in one form or another, and yet you sometimes are far too content to drift. You feel everything very deeply and are prone to self-pity when things go wrong. You have a good sense of humor, so why not start to take a more lighthearted look at yourself and realize how much you have to offer to a great many people, including yourself.

If you are a typical Pisces, you may feel you are worthy of greater success, and yet it eludes you through no fault of your own. In this event, the following checklist will give you some points on how you can create a better daily regime, without having to alter your Piscean life too much.

DO . . .
- listen to your intuition. It's *very* powerful!
- develop your creative talents to the fullest.
- involve yourself with people who have a positive outlook.
- handle your financial and business affairs in a practical manner and keep them under control.
- let your scintillating sense of humor shine through.
- make those realistic dreams come true—you can, you know.

DON'T . . .
- drift aimlessly through life without making the most of yourself.
- be an escapist—in any way at all!
- let yourself be influenced too much by others when you know the answers yourself.
- give way to negative thoughts and self-doubts.
- let your financial affairs get into a mess.
- try to drown your sorrows in drink; it doesn't agree with your system.

Creating Greater Success . . . in Love

For a typical Piscean to become more successful in love, you have to throw away those rose-colored spectacles—forever.

You cannot *always* be a romantic dreamer. Too many of those dreams seem to turn into nightmares where love is concerned. I've heard too many stories from Piscean friends and clients who fell hook, line, and sinker for someone who simply didn't live up to their expectations. You have to accept the blame when you delude yourself.

It is common for Pisces to fall for the *experience* of being in love. You want to escape from your daily life and feel something truly wonderful. You yearn to drown in a sea of emotions and forget about everything else. Unfortunately, you are often much more successful at achieving this kind of experience from a romantic movie rather than with another human being. This is because you are much too inclined to fantasize about love rather than to see it clearly, which is why you so often delude yourself.

Deep down you search for a soulmate—someone who can relate to you completely in mind, body, and spirit. So why don't you recognize this need, and stop getting yourself sidetracked along the way. Soulmates don't come along every day, but believing in your ability to attract the right person into your life will go a long way toward making it happen. Some of you may need to love and appreciate yourselves more before deciding on your soulmate, so your emotions become stronger and don't lead you astray. Listen to your head as well as your heart when you think romance is in the air, and don't make yourself a martyr to love.

Creating Greater Success . . . in Dating

Pisceans are often amazingly shy and timid, which means dating isn't always your favorite occupation. However, if you are on your own, either because you have never met Mr. or Ms. Right, or because of a death, divorce, or separation, dating is a necessary route to meeting someone new.

You are one of the most seductive signs around, in an amazingly subtle way. You are also wonderfully sympathetic and make a great listener, especially to a sob story. You invariably have a good sense of drama so you will be brilliant at attracting people to your side when that is what you want!

However, to be more successful in dating, it is also important for you to stop fantasizing about meeting your favorite movie star and to concentrate more on who is there for you in the here and now. Don't keep your head up in the clouds dreaming romantically of meeting someone wonderful who just happens to be sitting in the next seat on a plane trip. I'm not saying that couldn't happen, but you might also meet someone great by simply getting out there and socializing a whole lot more. Stop being one of those typical Pisceans who tend to brood about the past, fantasize about the future, and let the present drift on by.

PISCES DATING TIPS
- Develop your sense of humor.
- Demonstrate just how seductive and mysterious you can be.
- Listen to your intuition about people you meet.
- Don't fall for hard-luck stories or be a shoulder to lean on. You've probably done both too many times before!

Creating Greater Success . . . in Family Ties

Because you are a very adaptable sign, you get on well with most people and you definitely believe in the importance of close family ties. If you are living far away from the rest of your family you will usually manage to keep in touch one way or another. Since you *are* often financially impractical, watch out that you don't run up exorbitant telephone bills or take on too many financial responsibilities for family members that may leave you short of cash.

By nature you are one of the most caring people around. Being such a sensitive and compassionate person, you are always prepared to give a sympathetic ear to anyone else's problems, but be sure you don't take the problems of the whole world on your shoulders. Your tendency to strongly empathize with other people sometimes makes you become too personally affected by the emotional state of any of your relatives, and as a result, you tend to become extremely dejected if any members of your family or friends are having a rough time. This can throw you off balance. You need to keep your strength for yourself. You cannot be so self-sacrificing that you leave nothing for yourself, nor must you allow others to become so dependent on you that you begin to feel emotionally blackmailed.

If you are a parent, don't allow yourself to be put upon quite so much. Just because you hate to let your children down doesn't mean you have to indulge their every whim.

Because you are often hopelessly disorganized and tend to misplace things, you sometimes forget important dates like birthdays and anniversaries and end up feeling horribly guilty. Take care to be more responsible about such things, to avoid disappointing others—and yourself—in the future.

TIPS FOR SUCCESSFUL FAMILY TIES

- Do be sympathetic and understanding of everyone's moods or problems without exhausting yourself emotionally.
- Stay tuned in to your intuition, for then you will invariably know when someone needs you.
- Don't let anyone take advantage of you (especially financially), even if you hate arguments within the family.

Creating Greater Success . . . at Work

While most Pisceans will not be as ambitious as Rupert Murdoch, nor as successful, there is no earthly reason you cannot turn your own dreams of success at work into practical reality.

If you are a typical Pisces, one of the most important ways for you to create greater success at work is to be a whole lot more positive about your talents and abilities. You have something special to offer, and you are quite prepared to immerse yourself in it if you feel you have what it takes.

When you are truly positive about yourself (as you should be!), you will rise above any feelings of insecurity, inadequacy, and self-doubt, provided your goals do not belong in the realm of fantasy. Your instincts will help you to achieve greater success, but first you must find your chosen direction and stay on track.

Naturally, you will have to become more adept at making decisions, and you must definitely avoid getting yourself into a flap over every little mishap, turning minor problems into major crises. You will give your best performance when you are working in a harmonious atmosphere, but if it isn't exactly as you would like, you can and must overcome it.

Don't become discouraged by setbacks. Success requires putting in the necessary effort to achieve it. Most Pisceans have a deep need for recognition, and when you believe wholeheartedly in what you do you become positively inspired.

It is usually necessary for you to learn the value of structure and discipline in your working life, especially if you want to become successful. You must always maximize the potential of your creative and imaginative qualities for these assets will help to propel you to the top.

You are the last sign of the zodiac, but you are definitely not the least! Astrologically, it is always said that you have something of the other eleven signs within your personality, so why not take some of the Aries energy, the Taurus determination, the Gemini flexibility, and so on to reach your goals? Reading about the other signs will teach you something to become more successful in your working life.

The following do's and don'ts will also provide a guide for you to become even more successful at work.

DO . . .

- have faith in your creative talents and abilities, and listen to your sixth sense, too.
- make sure you do something that fulfills you and makes you happy.
- organize your days in a practical and methodical way.

DON'T . . .

- live in a fantasyland; turn those dreams into successful realities.
- turn to drink, even if the going does get tough and the pressure is hard to take.
- land yourself in chaos by forgetting to structure your days.

Creating Greater Success . . . in Finding the Right Job

You are more successful when you work at something in which you can lose yourself almost completely. It is therefore no wonder that so many Pisceans are drawn to art, music, theater, film, and writing. Could Victor Hugo and John Steinbeck be anything other than writers? Or Michelangelo anything other than the creator of the ceiling of the Sistine Chapel?

Naturally, not every Piscean will be involved in the arts, because your particular horoscope may lead you to follow other avenues. But you will all need to be fully involved in whatever you do choose, and to believe in your talents wholeheartedly. Often material security is not nearly as important for you as a desire for recognition, but since you are not always practical enough in your attitude to financial issues, it is important to take steps to earn sufficient money to meet your needs.

In addition to anything related to the arts, the careers associated with your sign include all the caring professions: healing, all forms of psychic work, nursing, social work, teaching, as well as sailing and photography. You are also extremely effective in any kind of community work.

Creating Greater Success . . .
in All Your Relationships

One of the most important factors in a successful life is relating well to others. Even with your ability to tune in intuitively to most people, you can probably still benefit from a few tips on how to relate even better with the other signs.

PISCES AND ARIES

Don't expect Aries to have much patience if you are hypersensitive and spend all your time dreaming of romance. Get your act together and show that you're not always indolent and indecisive, but that energy flows through your veins, too!

PISCES AND TAURUS

How wonderful to meet someone who keeps your feet on the ground and provides you with both moral and material support. Never push Bulls too far by accusing them of being too plodding in their everyday routines.

PISCES AND GEMINI

While you're still dreaming, Gemini is planning a thousand and one different schemes. Make sure you keep up to date with what is happening in the outside world. Be a good listener, and don't go on about romance too much or Gemini will soon get bored.

PISCES AND CANCER

There could be a mutual attraction between you two Water signs. You are both sentimental and romantic dreamers. Watch out that your sensitive emotions and moods don't get in the way of everything else. Ask Cancer to teach you how to be more practical!

PISCES AND LEO

Provided you give Leo plenty of praise and don't let the Lion dominate you too much, this can be a pretty nifty combination. Never let Leo feel left out of anything or too far away from center stage, especially when you're in a social setting.

PISCES AND VIRGO

You have lots to learn from your opposite sign—structure, organization, and being realistic and practical, just for starters. Virgo often feels just as insecure as you do, and hates to be criticized, too.

PISCES AND LIBRA

Both of you know instinctively how to relate to other people, but you're both incredibly indecisive, too. Libra likes to have a romantic soulmate as a partner. But don't frighten him or her away by being overly emotional. Librans are often more detached than you.

PISCES AND SCORPIO

Scorpio may be even more psychic than you and will see deep into your soul. Try to accept that Scorpio men and women are very private people who need their own space, even if they are possessive and jealous with everyone else.

PISCES AND SAGITTARIUS

You will benefit from some of Sagittarius's positive and happy-go-lucky approach to life. Don't appear to be too dreamy-eyed and clinging with this free and easy sign. Don't overreact if his or her honesty strikes you as downright tactless.

PISCES AND CAPRICORN

Work and material success are all-important to the Mountain Goats of the zodiac; try to learn something from their practical approach to life. Capricorns will help you to be more successful and to make more money, too. Just don't expect too much romance!

PISCES AND AQUARIUS

Intellectually you may decide you have lots to learn from Aquarius, but it may be hard to communicate about affairs of the heart, especially if you expect the Water Bearer to be as emotional as you. Try to appear cooler than usual for this to work well.

PISCES AND PISCES

Now *you* will see what it's like to be around someone who drifts in two different directions. You will see your best and your worst points when you relate to another Pisces. You can help each other by appreciating the good things and modifying the bad.

TABLE OF ASCENDANTS[1] FOR NORTH AMERICA

(Based on 40° North Latitude)

BIRTH DATE	ARIES	TAURUS	GEMINI	CANCER	LEO	VIRGO	LIBRA	SCORPIO	SAGITTARIUS	CAPRICORN	AQUARIUS	PISCES
1st Jan	11:30	12:45	14:15	16:15	18:30	21:00	23:30	02:00	04:45	07:00	09:00	10:30
10th Jan	11:00	12:15	13:45	15:30	18:00	20:30	23:00	01:30	04:00	06:30	08:15	09:45
20th Jan	10:15	11:30	13:00	15:00	17:15	19:45	22:15	01:00	03:30	05:45	07:45	09:15
1st Feb	09:30	10:45	12:15	14:15	16:30	19:00	21:30	00:00	02:30	05:00	07:00	08:30
10th Feb	09:00	10:15	11:45	13:30	15:45	18:30	21:00	23:30	02:00	04:30	06:15	07:45
20th Feb	08:15	09:30	11:00	12:45	15:15	17:45	20:15	22:45	01:15	03:45	05:30	07:00
1st Mar	07:45	09:00	10:15	12:15	14:45	17:15	19:45	22:15	00:45	03:15	05:00	06:30
10th Mar	07:15	08:30	09:45	11:45	14:00	16:30	19:00	21:30	00:15	02:30	04:30	06:00
20th Mar	06:30	08:00	09:15	11:00	13:30	16:00	18:30	21:00	23:30	02:00	03:45	05:15
1st Apr	05:45	07:00	08:15	10:15	12:45	15:15	17:45	20:15	22:45	01:15	03:00	04:30
10th Apr	05:00	06:15	07:45	09:45	12:00	14:30	17:00	19:30	22:00	00:30	02:30	04:00
20th Apr	04:30	05:45	07:00	09:00	11:15	13:45	16:15	19:00	21:30	23:45	01:45	03:15
1st May	03:45	05:00	06:15	08:15	10:45	13:15	15:45	18:15	20:45	23:00	01:00	02:30
10th May	03:15	04:15	05:45	07:45	10:00	12:30	15:00	17:30	20:15	22:30	00:30	02:00
20th May	02:30	03:45	05:15	07:00	09:30	12:00	14:30	17:00	19:30	21:45	23:45	01:15
1st Jun	01:45	03:00	04:15	06:15	08:30	11:15	13:45	16:15	18:45	21:00	23:00	00:30
10th Jun	01:00	02:15	03:45	05:45	08:00	10:30	13:00	15:30	18:00	20:30	22:30	23:45
20th Jun	00:30	01:45	03:00	05:00	07:30	10:00	12:30	15:00	17:30	19:45	21:45	23:15
1st Jul	23:45	01:00	02:15	04:15	06:45	09:15	11:45	14:15	16:45	19:00	21:00	22:30
10th Jul	23:00	00:15	01:45	03:45	06:00	08:30	11:00	13:30	16:00	18:30	20:30	22:00
20th Jul	22:30	23:45	01:15	03:15	05:30	08:00	10:30	13:00	15:30	17:45	19:45	21:15
1st Aug	21:15	22:45	00:15	02:15	04:45	07:15	09:45	12:15	14:45	17:00	19:00	20:30
10th Aug	21:00	22:15	23:45	01:45	04:00	06:30	09:00	11:30	14:00	16:30	18:30	19:45
20th Aug	20:15	21:30	23:00	01:00	03:15	06:00	08:30	11:00	13:30	15:45	17:45	19:15

1st Sep	19:30	20:45	22:15	00:15	02:30	05:15	07:45	10:15	12:45	15:00	17:00	18:30
10th Sep	19:00	20:15	21:45	23:30	02:00	04:30	07:00	09:30	12:00	14:30	16:15	17:45
20th Sep	18:15	19:30	21:00	23:00	01:15	03:45	06:15	08:45	11:30	13:45	15:45	17:15
1st Oct	17:45	18:45	20:15	22:15	00:30	03:15	05:45	08:15	10:45	13:00	15:00	16:30
10th Oct	17:00	18:15	19:45	21:45	00:00	02:30	05:00	07:30	10:00	12:30	14:30	15:45
20th Oct	16:30	17:30	19:00	21:00	23:15	02:00	04:30	07:00	09:30	11:45	13:45	15:15
1st Nov	15:45	16:45	18:15	20:15	22:30	01:15	03:45	06:15	08:45	11:00	13:00	14:30
10th Nov	15:00	16:15	17:45	19:30	22:00	00:30	03:00	05:30	08:00	10:30	12:15	13:45
20th Nov	14:15	15:30	17:00	19:00	21:15	23:45	02:15	04:45	07:30	09:45	11:45	13:15
1st Dec	13:30	14:45	16:15	18:15	20:30	23:00	01:45	04:15	06:45	09:00	11:00	12:30
10th Dec	13:00	14:15	15:45	17:30	20:00	22:30	01:00	03:30	06:00	08:30	10:30	11:45
20th Dec	12:15	13:30	15:00	17:00	19:15	21:45	00:30	03:00	05:30	07:45	09:45	11:15

The table shows the approximate times (to the nearest 15 minutes) when a new Ascendant sign starts to rise. To work out your Ascendant, or rising sign: Find the date on the left that is nearest to your date of birth. Then moving along the row, find the nearest time *before* your time of birth, not the nearest time. Finally, follow the column up to find your approximate rising sign.

¹Calculations are based at 40 degrees of latitude in the Northern Hemisphere. Although the table works best at 40° North, you can use it as a rough guide from 25° (northern Mexico) through 50° (southern Canada). All times are set for Standard Time: EST, CST, MST, PST, HST. Deduct one hour from the time for a summer birth if daylight saving time was in operation. For greater precision, check your workings with a consultant astrologer or a reputable astrology service.

The Ascendant table is an approximate guide. If your Ascendant appears to fall on the cusp of two signs, or you're unsure whether Daylight Saving Time or War Time instead of Standard Time was in effect when you were born, or your place of birth is in the far north or south, you may require more precise calculations. If you would like to have your Ascendant sign calculated by professional astrologers, invest $10 in having your Natal Wheel calculated by Equinox. They can provide an accurate birth chart showing your Ascendant to the exact degree, along with the planetary positions at the time of your birth.

USA: EQUINOX, 250 "H" Street #596, Blaine, WA 98231-8110 Telephone: 1-800-836-6966. Fax: 604 530-6790

Canada: EQUINOX, P.O. Box 61514, Brookswood, Langley, B.C., Canada V3A 8C8 Telephone: 604-530-6740.

Mexico: EQUINOX, Privada Rufino Tamayo no. 92, Col. Acapantzingo, Cuernavaca, Mexico 62440

Europe: EQUINOX, 78 Neal Street, Covent Garden, London WC2H 9PA, U.K. Telephone: 0171 497 1001.
Fax: 0171 497 0344 (From outside UK, country code: +44 171)

Australasia: EQUINOX, Level 1, Suite 1, 56 The Corso, Manly, N.S.W. 2095, Australia

Table prepared by EQUINOX, The Astrology Shop, 78 Neal Street, Covent Garden, London WC2H 9PA, U.K.